RITUAL AND DOMESTIC LIFE
IN PREHISTORIC EUROPE

Ritual is often invoked as a way of accounting for the apparently inexplicable, and is contrasted with the routines of daily life. This book contests that view.

Richard Bradley argues that for much of the prehistoric period, ritual was not a distinct sphere of activity. Rather, it was the way in which different features of the domestic world were played out with added emphasis until they took on some of the qualities of theatrical performance. Farming, craft production and the occupation of houses are all examples of this ritualising process.

Successive chapters discuss the ways in which ritual has been studied and presented, drawing on a series of examples ranging from Greece to Norway and from Romania to Portugal. They consider practices that extended from the Mesolithic period to the Early Middle Ages and offer a series of studies of the ways in which ritual and domestic life were intertwined. Richard Bradley's argument will be of importance to prehistorians and field archaeologists alike.

Richard Bradley is Professor of Archaeology at the University of Reading, and is the author of *The Significance of Monuments* (Routledge, 1998), *An Archaeology of Natural Places* (Routledge, 2000) and *The Past in Prehistoric Societies* (Routledge, 2002).

RITUAL AND DOMESTIC LIFE IN PREHISTORIC EUROPE

Richard Bradley

Routledge
Taylor & Francis Group

LONDON AND NEW YORK

First published 2005
by Routledge
2 Park Square, Milton Park, Abingdon, Oxon OX14 4RN

Simultaneously published in the USA and Canada
by Routledge
270 Madison Ave, New York, NY 10016

Routledge is an imprint of the Taylor & Francis Group

Typeset in Garamond 3
by Keystroke, Jacaranda Lodge, Wolverhampton
Printed and bound in Great Britain
by The Cromwell Press, Trowbridge, Wiltshire

British Library Cataloguing in Publication Data
A catalogue record for this book is available from the British Library

Library of Congress Cataloging in Publication Data
Bradley, Richard, 1946–
Ritual and domestic life in prehistoric Europe / Richard Bradley.
p. cm.
Includes bibliographical references and index.
1. Rites and ceremonies, Prehistoric—Europe. 2. Architecture,
Prehistoric—Europe. 3 Agriculture, Prehistoric—Europe.
4. Tools, Prehistoric—Europe. 5. Human remains (Archaeology)—Europe.
6. Antiquities, Prehistoric—Europe. I. Title.
GN803.B659 2005
936—dc22   2004019540

ISBN 0–415–34550–2 (hbk)
ISBN 0–415–34551–0 (pbk)

FOR COLIN RENFREW

CONTENTS

List of figures and tables ix
Preface xiii

PART I
The importance of ordinary things 1

1 Death and the harvest: how archaeologists have distinguished between ritual and domestic life 3

2 The consecration of the house: how domestic buildings took on special qualities 41

3 A duty of care: how everyday activities assumed a special significance 81

PART II
Where the stress falls 121

4 A house with a pool: rituals and the materials of farming 123

5 Multiplication and division: the problem of utilitarian bronze hoards 145

6 The rites of separation: domestic rituals and public ritual in the Iron Age 165

7 What remains to be seen: some implications of the argument 191

Bibliography 211
Index 231

FIGURES AND TABLES

Figures

1.1	The Galician hórreo and its decoration	4
1.2	Early drawing of a group of Inca qollqas	7
1.3	The areas of Europe considered in Chapter 1	10
1.4	Henge monument at Durrington Walls	11
1.5	Iron Age enclosure at Gussage All Saints	13
1.6	Burials in storage pits at Gussage All Saints	13
1.7	The siting of Viereckschanzen in Central Europe	17
1.8	The archaeological sequence at Holzhausen	18
1.9	Evidence of iron working at Mšecké Žehrovice in relation to the later Viereckschanze	22
1.10	Ard marks and a long house beneath a round barrow at Handewitt	25
1.11	Plough marks around the edge of a Bronze Age cairn at Diverhøj	27
1.12	The dates of publications relating to ritual in anthropology and archaeology	31
1.13	Two conceptions of ritual, and their areas of overlap	32
1.14	The areas of Europe considered in Chapter 2	36
1.15	The areas of Europe considered in Chapter 3	37
1.16	The areas of Europe considered in Chapters 4 to 6	38
2.1	Excavated post holes beneath the cathedral at Gamla Uppsala	42
2.2	Reconstructions of the pagan temple at Gamla Uppsala	43
2.3	Reconstruction of an Iron Age feasting hall	44
2.4	Elite dwellings at Tiryns and Thermon	45
2.5	Plans of a Maori marae and meeting house	49
2.6	Late Bronze Age/Early Iron Age house urns in Italy	51
2.7	Late Bronze Age houses and associated deposits at Pryssgården	54
2.8	Late Bronze Age and Iron Age round houses at Bancroft	55
2.9	House and associated enclosure buried beneath an Iron Age burial mound outside the Heuneburg	58

2.10 Timber long house buried beneath a Bronze Age round barrow
at Trappendal 61
2.11 Early Neolithic round and rectangular houses in Northern
and Western France 63
2.12 Neolithic long cairn and associated structure at Stengade 64
2.13 Large rectangular buildings at Balbridie, Antran, Acy-Romance
and Verberie 66
2.14 Copper Age palisaded enclosures and associated buildings at
Pléchâtel-La Hersonnais 68
2.15 Bronze Age cult houses at Sandergergård and Hågahögen 71
2.16 Bronze Age and Early Iron Age long-beds in Northern Europe 72
2.17 Late Neolithic timber buildings at Trelystan, Durrington
Walls and Woodcutts 74
2.18 Iron Age timber buildings at Navan Fort 77
2.19 Iron Age enclosure at Zeijen and a long house at Fochteloo 79
3.1 Human bodies in Northern Europe 82
3.2 Wooden ard from Vebbstrup 83
3.3 Carving of a ploughman at Litsleby 87
3.4 Raised storehouse in the Trobriand Islands 91
3.5 Carved bucrania at Escoural 94
3.6 Scenes of ploughing at Mont Bégo 96
3.7 Structures identified as houses at Valcamonica 97
3.8 Bronze Age house urns in Northern Europe 99
3.9 Decorated rotary quern from Ticooly-O'Kelly 101
3.10 Passage grave and Neolithic quarry at Beorgs of Ulyea 105
3.11 Stone setting beneath a Bronze Age burnt mound at
Rinkeby 106
3.12 Late Bronze Age well and associated deposits at
Frankfurt-Lossow 109
3.13 The contexts of Bronze Age metal finds in the Southern
Netherlands 110
3.14 The decorated cave sanctuary at El Pedroso 112
3.15 Copper Age and Bronze Age enclosure at Castelo Velho 114
3.16 The Neolithic enclosure at Sarup 115
3.17 Bronze Age enclosure at Odensala Prästgård 117
4.1 Locations of the Neolithic settlements at Skumparberget and
Skogsmossen 124
4.2 Plans of Neolithic houses at Skumparberget and Dagstorp 125
4.3 The Neolithic house and nearby pool at Skogsmossen 126
4.4 Neolithic houses, graves and pits at Tofta and Dagstorp 133
4.5 Pit houses in the Neolithic settlement at Åby 135
4.6 Deposits of burnt flint axes at Svartskylle 137
4.7 Neolithic palisaded enclosures at Rispebjerg 140
4.8 Plan of the Neolithic platform at Alvastra 141

5.1   Bronze Age sickles showing traces of use from Auvernier   149
5.2   Sickle fragments from the hoard at Uiorara de Sus   152
5.3   Axe fragments from the hoard at Uiorara de Sus   153
5.4   Sword fragments from the hoard at Szentgáloskér   154
5.5   Principal sources of the artefacts in the hoard at Le Petit
       Vilatte   156
5.6   Principal sources of the artefacts in the hoard at Venat   157
5.7   Location of the metal finds from the Ría de Huelva   158
5.8   Complete and broken weapons from the Ría de Huelva   160
6.1   The siting of the successive shrines in the hill fort at Danebury   166
6.2   The distributions of house urns and storage pit burials in
       North and North-West Europe   171
6.3   The contexts of iron sickles in the Roman Iron Age   173
6.4   The contexts of iron sickles in the Migration Period   174
6.5   Burials in Iron Age storage pits in Northern France   176
6.6   The Iron Age sanctuary and associated buildings at
       Acy-Romance   178
6.7   The Iron Age settlement and sanctuary at Montmartin   181
6.8   The evolution of the Iron Age temple at Hayling   183
6.9   Plan of the first Iron Age settlement at Gallows Hill,
       Thetford   185
6.10   The first sanctuary and associated structures at Gallows Hill,
       Thetford   186
6.11   Plan of the latest sanctuary at Gallows Hill, Thetford   187
6.12   Plan of the shrine and other timber buildings at South
       Cadbury   189
7.1   A scheme for comparing excavated assemblages   201
7.2   The scheme in Figure 7.1 applied to four key sites   202

Tables

2.1   The structure, development and associations of houses in
       Northern Europe, compared with the evidence from Britain
       and Ireland   57
5.1   The treatment of the main types of bronze artefacts from the
       Ría de Huelva   160

PREFACE

This book has a simple premise. Archaeologists have been writing about ritual for many years, but their discussion has often reached an impasse. Nowhere is this more obvious than in accounts of prehistoric Europe.

There are two main reasons for this situation, and each results from a different source of confusion. Some writers have been influenced by studies of state religion, but these have little relevance for the simpler societies that characterise the prehistory of Northern and Western Europe. At the same time, archaeologists working in these areas have made much of the distinction between rituals and practical affairs. Human behaviour seems be governed by pragmatic concerns, whilst ritual follows a logic of its own. It stands out through its difference from the norm. This has led to the disagreements I discuss in Chapter 1.

My book takes a different approach. In these studies ritual is viewed as a specialised form of behaviour which emphasises some of the concerns of daily life through a kind of performance. It is not opposed to domesticity, and often it grows out of it. Successive chapters discuss some of the areas in which this happened. I consider such basic activities as food production, the building and occupation of houses or the making of artefacts. How were these such tasks ritualised during prehistory, and how can they be studied in the present?

This book has two main sources. It is one of a number of works which attempt to devise a framework with which to interpret the prehistoric archaeology of Europe. In that sense it is a sequel to *The Significance of Monuments: An Archaeology of Natural Places* and *The Past in Prehistoric Societies*. At the same time, it has developed out of a single lecture I delivered in Cambridge in November 2002. This was concerned with 'The ritualisation of domestic life in later prehistoric Europe'. Although that paper was published not long afterwards, it kept growing in my mind until it assumed the proportions of a book.

The final version is in two parts. The first introduces the problems that have arisen in studying this subject and illustrates the ways in which everyday activities were ritualised in prehistoric Europe. The second supports that argument with case studies taken from Neolithic, Bronze Age and Iron Age societies, before discussing the wider implications of this research. The title of Chapter 3 – 'A duty of care' – recalls my days as a law student. 'Where the stress falls' – the title of Part 2 – refers to a book by Susan Sontag.

I have many people to thank for their assistance. I am grateful to Chris Scarre, the editor of the *Cambridge Archaeological Journal*, for encouraging me to elaborate the original lecture and for allowing me to reuse short extracts from it here. I am grateful to the McDonald Institute for Archaeological Research for inviting me to talk about this subject and, in particular, to Anthony Snodgrass who introduced me to work of Mazarakis-Ainian discussed in Chapter 2. I must thank all those who commented on the original lecture or who have discussed my work at later presentations in Amsterdam, Kalmar, Leiden, Porto and Stockholm. I am grateful to Martin Henig and Tim Phillips who suggested improvements to the text and to Heinrich Härke and Eva Theate for help with the bibliography. Aaron Watson prepared the illustrations with his usual flair and attention to detail.

Wherever possible, I prefer to discuss places that I have visited, and here again I have many people to thank. I am grateful to my colleagues on the excavation of El Pedroso, Rámon Fábregas and Germán Delibes, and to Stefan Brink, Per Karsten, Kirsten Lidén, Lars Larsson, Mats Larsson and Michael Olausson for showing me sites in Sweden. I am also indebted to Susana and Vitor Oliveira Jorge for a memorable excursion to Castelo Velho, to Maria de Jesus Sanches for showing me Crasto de Palheiros, and to Lara Bacelar Alves for arranging a visit to Escoural.

If this project has grown out of a lecture given in Cambridge, it has also been influenced by a seminar at the McDonald Institute of which Colin Renfrew was one of the organisers. His name appears frequently in the text. His contribution is apparent to every student of the period, but many of my generation owe him a special debt for his personal interest and encouragement, extending over many years. Because this is less tangible, it is less often acknowledged. Ritual is one of the fields that he has studied in detail, and no doubt he would have written about it in a different way. But I doubt whether I would have embarked on this book without his example to follow. For all these reasons it is dedicated to him.

Part I

THE IMPORTANCE OF
ORDINARY THINGS

1

DEATH AND THE HARVEST

How archaeologists have distinguished between ritual and domestic life

Introduction: granaries and shrines

Rituals and symbols permeate everyday life, but all too often they escape the attention of archaeologists. The agricultural history of Spain provides a good example of how this happens.

For many years the rural economy of Galicia has been a source of inspiration for prehistorians working in other parts of Europe. It is the raised storehouses or hórreos that have attracted most attention (Figure 1.1; Frankowski 1918; Martínez 1975), for they are often quoted as parallels for small timber buildings discovered in the excavation of Bronze Age and Iron Age settlements in Britain, Germany, the Netherlands and France (Fowler 1983: 183; Gransar 2000). The prehistoric buildings are most often represented by four large post holes and are conventionally referred to in English as 'four posters' or in German as 'Speicher' (granaries). That may not be their only interpretation, but it finds some support on sites where wooden structures of this kind had been burnt, as they are sometimes associated with carbonised grain.

The existence of the Galician hórreos provides a structural parallel that is very helpful, as are similar comparisons with farm buildings in Central Europe, but the archaeological analysis of four post structures has extended much more widely, so that in some respects it typifies one type of economic archaeology. The distribution of these buildings, like that of storage pits, is used to map the extent of a distinctive economy (Gent 1983; Gransar 2000). Their locations are interesting, too. Four post granaries can be found in several different settings within open settlements, enclosures and hill forts. They may be attached to individual houses, they can be grouped in distinctive zones within the settlement area, and occasionally ditched or palisaded enclosures contain these buildings to the exclusion of other kinds of structures, suggesting that they played a part in the large-scale mobilisation of grain (Müller-Wille 1966; Schindler 1977; Gent 1983).

One reason why the Galician parallel has been so popular is because this area is linked to North-West Europe by sea (Cunliffe 2001: chapter 8), and it is only too easy to suppose that here farming methods survive unchanged from

Figure 1.1 The Galician hórreo and its characteristic decoration. Information from
Frankowski (1918).

later prehistory. Hórreos are one example, the use of ards is another, whilst the
third is provided by the existence of 'Celtic' fields in the modern landscape
(Leser 1931; Fowler 1983: 95–119). That wholly inappropriate term reveals
the hidden assumptions, for these comparisons assume that the agriculture of
North-West Spain preserves the working practices of the Bronze and Iron Ages
(P. Reynolds 1981).

Such similarities can be exaggerated. Ards are certainly used for cultivation,
but the 'Celtic' fields in Galicia are farmed by slash and burn techniques and
are sown once every twelve years (Felipe Criado pers. comm.). Similar systems

4

do not seem to be associated with prehistoric sites, and in any case the comparison is anachronistic. The traditional Galician landscape has a quite specific history, and it is a history that has little to do with Iron Age Celts. In fact many of these developments date from the post-medieval period, for it was with the introduction of maize from the New World that the economy seems to have changed. The hórreos probably developed to store the new crop.

This might seem to dispose of the problem, but in fact it suggests a another way of viewing this comparison. One of the weaknesses of modern field archaeology is its obsession with adaptation, but another is the emphasis on what survives below ground. The stone pillars that support the hórreo are the structural equivalent of the post holes found in excavation, but few prehistorians are interested in the rest of the building. They have given too little thought to the visual impact of such structures and need to consider their place in the local topography and their impact on the people living among them. Archaeologists have preferred to treat such buildings as an index of one kind of agricultural regime.

The architecture of the Galician hórreos has certain distinctive features (Frankowski 1918; Martínez 1975). These buildings are made of granite and often they are massive constructions. They may also occupy conspicuous positions in the farms and villages so that they overshadow both the houses and the church. They may be placed on higher ground than those buildings or they are attached to prominent outcrops. Some of the granaries are balanced precariously on top of the walls surrounding farms and gardens, and they gain still more height in this way. In other cases they are placed beside roads so that they catch the eye of the passing traveller. They are not just agricultural buildings; they are also monuments.

Their sheer size can be important and individual buildings may be far longer than the norm. Alternatively, they can be grouped in clusters which dominate the local terrain. Galician rural architecture may be divided into a number of regional styles, some of which mirror the abrupt changes of climate in different parts of the country, but there are other breaks in the distribution of hórreos which seem to be independent of ecological considerations (Martínez 1975). These regional groups are often quite small and their boundaries are as tightly defined as those of any style of prehistoric pottery. Their distribution does not cover the entire country, yet there are no fewer than ten regional groups among the supports on which these buildings were based, and eighteen among their superstructure. On one level people obviously saw these buildings as an expression of local identities. Their siting ensures that strangers would be immediately aware of these distinctions. This is a classic example of the way in which material culture is used to communicate information.

One feature is all-important. These distinctions concern the above-ground structure of the hórreo; apart from differences of size, their foundations would have remained more or less the same. That has obvious implications for those archaeologists who wish to use them as parallels for prehistoric buildings. The easiest way of recognising regional differences among the hórreos is to consider the details of their architecture. They are of two different kinds. There are parts of the buildings that highlight these local differences and there are purely symbolic features of the design.

The supports consist of granite pillars. Usually, these are plain, but occasionally they are decorated, in which case the embellishment includes the kinds of baroque moulding that are found on churches and houses. The walls may be either of stone or of wood and the roofs are built of granite, tiles or thatch. The stonework can be either roughly or finely finished and may also be used to decorative effect. The height of the hórreos varies. Sometimes the superstructure is tall and narrow, and in other cases the floor is raised further above the ground. Some of the more impressive hórreos are approached by a flight of stone steps. The gable ends of certain of the buildings are decorated, and this makes them look more like houses and churches. The roof may be enhanced by pinnacles, of no functional significance whatsoever. Again some of these features echo the decoration associated with other kinds of architecture.

The symbolism of these structures can be rather more explicit. Sometimes the granary is surmounted by a simple cross. As a result, foreign visitors can easily mistake these buildings for shrines. The significance of the cross is hardly given a second thought, but that is only because it is still possible to interpret that symbol. It speaks about very basic notions of death and regeneration, scarcity and abundance, which are entirely appropriate to a building that is constructed to store crops. Farming provides a whole series of metaphors in the Christian religion, from the parable of the sower to the Harvest Festival, and similar equations have been formed in many other parts of the world. Having said that, it is important to remember how rare it is to have an insider's view of symbolic systems in the past. Rituals and symbols will always be easier to recognise than they are to interpret.

The Galician hórreo, perched on a farmyard wall, resembles another kind of structure in the countryside. This is the stone-built cemetery where individual tombs are displayed in a strikingly similar manner. That is supposed to happen because the dead are buried in a confined space – it is not possible for some of these cemeteries to increase their area – and yet this may be a rationalisation of a still more basic relationship. The visual resemblance between granaries and tombs is so striking that it cannot have gone unremarked, even if it was not originally intended. The presence of these constructions in the landscape helps to establish a parallel symbolism to the Christian cross on the roof of the hórreo, for here again the imagination equates the cycle of death and rebirth with the fertility of the land. Symbolic systems of this kind are found in many different cultures, and such notions are nicely captured in the title of Bloch's and Parry's edited volume *Death and the Regeneration of Life* (Bloch and Parry 1982). The sowing and harvesting of crops form an unbroken sequence that goes on from one generation to the next. The appearance of these buildings tells the faithful that similar processes extend to human society.

If the hórreo developed in order to store crops that were first introduced from the New World, it is hardly surprising that a similar symbolic system should have existed in the archaeology of South America, although there is no suggestion of a direct link between these two phenomena (Sillar 1996). One of the most striking features of the Inca state was the creation of raised storehouses or qollqas (Figure 1.2). These are stone structures that were designed to hold foodstuffs such as potatoes and maize, as well as a variety of other goods. They seem to have been constructed by the state in order to feed and equip large numbers of people who were working on specific projects. The principle was a simple one. The structures were erected on raised ground where air could circulate freely so that their contents would be kept both dry and cool. The use of these buildings seems to have played an important role in the Inca political economy.

Figure 1.2　An interpretation of a contemporary drawing showing two figures amidst a group of Inca qollqas. Information from Moseley (2001).

Sillar has compared these distinctive buildings with another kind of structure. These are the chullpahs which take the form of stone towers. Again they were built on hills or on other raised ground, but in this case they were used to store the remains of the dead. These worked in much the same manner as the qollqas, for they made use of the way in which air circulated through the structure. But in this case the effect was very different, for where the qollqas had been used to keep foodstuffs, the chullpahs were where human bodies were dried. The two buildings seem to be mirror images of one another. As Sillar says, they 'share a common technical function to store and preserve their contents' (1996: 282), but what is the relationship between death and the harvest?

In South America there seems to have been a cosmological link between human remains and the storage of grain. This continues to the present day with the festival of the dead when ancestral skulls are provided with drink and decorated with flowers. Before the chullpahs were erected, it was evidenced by the burial of bodies in disused storage pits, a practice that also occurs in prehistoric Europe. Indeed, Sillar suggests that the mummified corpses may have been removed from the chullpahs and moved around the landscape during the period whilst the crops were growing, in the same way as Christian crosses are taken from the churches to shrines among the fields. He suggests that Inca storehouses developed because similar buildings were already used to preserve the dead:

> If my understanding is correct, the technological innovation of qollqa storage was inspired by the experience of chullpahs, but this is not just the transfer of a technique between two entirely separate spheres of activity. The pre-existing link between the dead and storage would have made the transfer of the technique conceptually possible and, in making the link, the qollqas would have acquired some of the meanings of regeneration and reciprocity with the ancestors that chullpahs expressed. Both the qollqas and chullpahs represent a bond between the people and the land, a continuing commitment to plough, to sow, to fertilise and to offer some of the harvest in sacrifice.
>
> (Sillar 1996: 282)

If we accept his interpretation, people on both sides of the Atlantic may have devised a similar conceptual system.

What can we learn from this example? Archaeology is impoverished unless it sheds its fixation with food production. Agriculture was crucially important to ancient societies, but it was not unproblematical, and even such simple features as farm buildings may have borne many layers of meaning which prehistorians ignore at their peril. The Incas exploited the existing symbolism of the chullpah in creating a network of raised storehouses as part of the economic infrastructure of the state. In Spain, on the other hand, the form of the raised granary has been used to signal regional differences between the separate communities in Galicia. In that case its architecture seems to have stressed the spiritual links between food production and the resurrection of life promised by the Christian church. Despite their apparent simplicity, the stone storehouses built in both these areas played many different roles.

This leads to a second observation. It is because modern visitors to Galicia are able to observe the uses and settings of hórreos that they are able to identify so many layers of significance. That is only possible since the history of these buildings is well documented. Were they to be deprived of these sources of information, there would be more scope for misunderstanding. They might work out the connection between hórreos and the storage of grain, and this would help them to reconstruct the workings of the subsistence economy. Alternatively, they might focus on the structure and settings of these buildings, in which case they could easily mistake them for shrines. What they might not perceive is that these are farm buildings whose design and operation have been ritualised by their use of Christian imagery.

The same kind of confusion has caused problems in South American archae-ology, for it has not always been easy to distinguish between the buildings used to keep foodstuffs and those associated with the dead. That is because their forms and operation had so much in common. As Sillar says, 'if the Inca qollqas are an elaboration of a previously existing domestic form of storage, it is . . . only when they are built in a regimented form and are located outside contemporary settlements that we can be certain of identifying them'. Because these structures have been abandoned and often looted, their significance is more difficult to understand than that of the hórreos.

The seventeenth-century statesman and philosopher Francis Bacon once wrote that 'truth comes out of error more readily than out of confusion', a sentiment that David Clarke echoed when he quoted these words in his book *Analytical Archaeology* (1978: 487). They apply to two aspects of the study of prehistory. Errors are likely to arise in the analysis of particular kinds of data, whilst the sources of confusion may go further back. They reflect the ideas behind the practice of archaeology itself.

To treat the techniques of Galician agriculture as survivals of an Iron Age way of life is an error, for it depends on a misunderstanding of history. To consider the raised granaries as religious buildings is also incorrect but in this case it results from a kind of confusion that is deeply rooted in archaeological thought. It involves our understanding of the relationship between the ritual and the practical, the sacred and the mundane. The confusion arises because they are not related to one another in a coherent manner. The same uncertainty affects the investigation of societies in other parts of Europe. The Galician example makes this point especially clearly, but such problems of interpretation are especially prevalent in prehistoric archaeology, where any studies must be based on material remains. I shall illustrate this point with three examples taken from different periods. I begin with a Neolithic henge monument. The

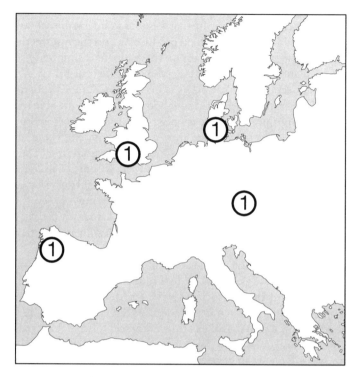

Figure 1.3 The areas of Europe considered in Chapter 1.

Bronze Age is represented by accounts of 'ritual ploughing', whilst Iron Age Viereckschanzen supply the third example. They will be considered again in later chapters (Figure 1.3).

The sources of confusion

Sacred sites and settlements: the case of Durrington Walls

This site is a large henge monument in Southern England, part of which was excavated in the late 1960s before a new road was built. It consists of an enormous circular earthwork, defined by an external bank and an internal ditch, enclosing the head of a dry valley <u>above the River Avon</u> (Wainwright and Longworth 1971). It may originally have had several entrances, and geophysical survey suggests that a small circular earthwork had been built just inside one of them (Figure 1.4). A similar feature on the higher ground overlooking Durrington Walls contained six concentric rings of posts. It is why that monument has become known as Woodhenge (Cunnington 1929).

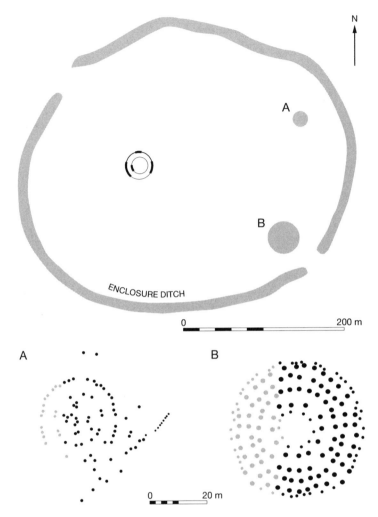

Figure 1.4 Plan of the henge monument at Durrington Walls, Southern England, together with details of the excavated timber circles. There was probably a third example inside the north-western entrance to the enclosure. Information from Wainwright and Longworth (1971).

The excavation of Durrington Walls found at least two similar constructions. The Southern Circle was located on the axis of one of the entrances. Beside it there had been a rubble platform. The other excavated timber setting, the Northern Circle, was approached by an 'avenue' of paired posts which passed through a screen in front of the building. Neither of these structures was replaced by a setting of stones, although this happened at comparable sites in Southern England. All these features can be dated to the <u>later third millennium</u> BC.

Apart from these structures, the excavation produced an enormous number of artefacts and large quantities of animal bones. The artefacts were dominated by the variety of decorated pottery known as Grooved Ware, although sherds of Beaker ceramics were associated with later phases. Flint artefacts were also common on the site and included some pieces of exceptional quality, especially arrowheads. Finds of faunal remains were abundant and they were dominated by pig bones, as they usually are at sites of this kind (Albarella and Serjeantson 2002). Certain items were also rare or absent. Flint and stone axes appeared in unexpectedly low numbers and there were few wild animal bones.

The excavation report (Wainwright and Longworth 1971) focused on several important aspects of the site. The henge had been built on a massive scale and the construction of the perimeter earthwork may have taken half a million worker hours. It was located in a landscape with other exceptional monuments. Woodhenge was built next to Durrington Walls, and Stonehenge is little more than three kilometres away. At the same time, the timber structures inside the excavated area were unusually large and the authors of the excavation report provided a careful discussion of whether it would have been possible to roof them. Moreover the rich assemblage of artefacts and food remains drew attention to a further feature of this site. It seemed possible that feasts had taken place within the earthwork (Albarella and Serjeantson 2002). Like the other activities happening inside the enclosure, these may not have been open to everyone, and the characteristic structure of the henge might have meant that more people could gather on the bank and observe what was happening in the interior. They would have been cut off from those activities by an enormous ditch. Still more could have seen into the arena from the high ground outside the monument.

Taking these elements together, it seemed legitimate to suggest that Durrington Walls had played a specialised role. It was most probably a ceremonial centre and it was interpreted in this way in the final publication of the project. Only four years later the excavator offered a new interpretation and suggested that the enclosure had actually been a major settlement (Wainwright 1975). What accounts for this change?

Not long after the excavation of Durrington Walls, Wainwright investigated an Iron Age enclosure at Gussage All Saints, in Southern England (Figure 1.5). This was almost two millennia later in date than the henge monument but in his view it had some of the same characteristics (Wainwright 1979). Like that site, it had an earthwork boundary, inside which there were timber structures, although it differed from the other site as it also included numerous storage pits. Wainwright's excavation identified many finds of artefacts and food remains. Like the henge monument, some of those pits contained unusual deposits within their filling, but in this case they included human and animal burials (Figure 1.6). This is particularly striking in the light of the South American evidence considered earlier.

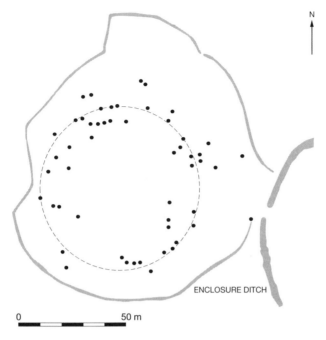

Figure 1.5 Plan of the Iron Age enclosure at Gussage All Saints, Southern England, showing the positions of the storage pits containing deposits of specialised artefacts. Note how they are ranged around the perimeter of a circular space which does not reflect the course of the perimeter ditch. Information from Wainwright (1979) and Hill (1995).

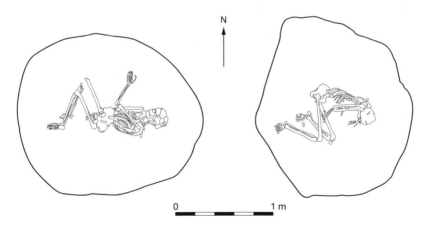

Figure 1.6 Burials in Iron Age storage pits at Gussage All Saints, Southern England. Information from Wainwright (1979).

These pits are of particular interest as many of them share a common form, with a narrow mouth and a deep bell profile. It has been shown by experiment that features of this type are ideally suited to keeping seed corn during the winter, and this interpretation is confirmed by deposits of carbonised grain which were left behind when pits were cleaned before reuse (Fowler 1983: 180–5). Human and animal remains were placed inside them once the primary use of these containers was over. Similar deposits are not unusual in the Iron Age storage pits of Central Southern England and seem to have conformed to a few fairly well-defined conventions, although some of these may have been specific to individual sites. Certain combinations of animal bones or bird bones are often found in these deposits; there are recurrent associations between different kinds of artefacts; the human burials normally shared a common orientation; and different types of material might be associated with different stages in the filling of the pits (Whimster 1981: 5–15; Cunliffe 1992; Hill 1995). Many of these patterns have been observed in the excavated material from Gussage All Saints, and further conventions seem to have governed the deposition of artefacts and bones in the ditch that enclosed the site. It even seems possible that much of the material initially interpreted as occupation debris had been carefully selected for deposition in the ground. An unknown proportion of the waste generated during the use of this site may have been removed and spread on cultivated land.

As I have suggested, the assemblage from Durrington Walls is exceptional, and the same applies to the configuration of the site itself. That is not true of Gussage All Saints, for the distinctive deposits that have been found here have their counterparts at most Iron Age settlements in Wessex. Moreover, there is clear archaeological evidence that this particular site played an important part in the production of food and not just in its consumption. There are grain storage pits, but there are also what may have been raised granaries of the kind that have been compared with the hórreos of Galicia. The evidence for domestic buildings at Gussage All Saints is much more limited, but this can be explained as a result of later damage to the features inside the enclosure.

In fact the comparison between the relatively modest enclosures at Gussage and Iron Age sites elsewhere in Wessex has an added dimension as it has played a significant part in recent discussions of the roles of hill forts in Southern England. For a long time it appeared likely that these would have been high-status settlements and it even seemed as if it was from such places that food production was managed by a social elite (Cunliffe 1991: chapter 14). One mechanism might have been redistribution, which is one of the classic attributes of 'chiefdoms'. But recent work has questioned all these assumptions by showing that there were very few differences between the archaeological evidence from the excavation of hill forts and that from less elaborate enclosures or open settlements. The artefact assemblages were much the same, but three features did help to distinguish Iron Age hill forts from other locations. They were defined by more elaborate earthworks; they contained a higher density of storage structures than the other sites; and they seemed to provide significantly more evidence of 'ritual' (Hill 1996). The latter point is especially important here, for not only were the defended sites associated with the kinds of special-ised deposit recorded at Gussage All Saints, there were occasional buildings inside them that could be identified as shrines. These places may have had more in common with henges than had originally seemed possible.

Such changes in the interpretation of Iron Age hill forts were influenced by developments in Neolithic studies. There is a certain irony here. Wainwright reinterpreted the henge monument that he had excavated in the light of his later work at Gussage All Saints. Might Iron Age hill forts have been used like ceremonial centres because they share so many features with henge monuments?

An important influence on this debate was a new analysis of the excavated material from Durrington Walls (Richards and Thomas 1984). This considered the organisation of material culture across the site. It had two main elements. First, it investigated the ways in which different assemblages had entered the archaeological record, placing a special emphasis on what has become known as 'structured deposition'. Thus Richards and Thomas argued that certain items had been carefully placed at the foot of individual posts in the timber circles. Again the accumulation of what Wainwright had called a 'midden' beside the Southern Circle had been carefully controlled. They also argued that there were specific patterns of association or avoidance between the contents of differ-ent components of the site. For example, in that same timber setting pieces of pottery were deposited separately from flint artefacts, and across the excavated area as a whole sherds with more complex decoration had different associations from those with simpler designs. They made similar claims concerning the distribution of animal bones, but it now seems as if this part of the study may have been biased by the ways in which that material had been stored after the completion of the original project (Albarella and Serjeantson 2002). Even so, they provided sufficient evidence to suggest that the placing of cultural material within the henge was governed by a number of conventions. That suggests a certain degree of formality, and Richards and Thomas argue that this is an important characteristic of ritual:

> Our analyses were designed to show whether the finds from Durrington Walls exhibit the clear-cut spatial patterning that might be expected in a ritual context. The results of this investigation do suggest that this is the case.
>
> (1984: 215)

That was not the end of this particular debate. Fourteen years after he had published his reinterpretation of Durrington Walls the excavator returned to the subject as part of a more general account of henge monuments (Wainwright 1989: 50–62). By now he had returned to his original view that they were

15

ceremonial centres. He quoted the paper by Richards and Thomas, but this does not seem to have been a decisive influence on his thinking. As we shall see, the problem may not be resolved by the fine details of the field record. It needs to be thought about in a different way.

It is instructive to compare this discussion with the interpretation of Galician hórreos. In that case it was possible to show how one kind of farm building could fulfil practical and symbolic roles at the same time. The granaries played an important part in the workings of the subsistence economy, but they also provided a medium for social display. More than that, their distinctive architecture made an explicit reference to the structure of local churches and to the dominant symbol of the cross. As a result, the creation and operation of the granary was also related to the metaphors of death and regeneration that are at the heart of Christian doctrine. There was no choice to be made between functional and symbolic interpretations of these buildings, for they reinforced one another so completely that it is misleading to pull them apart. Yet this is exactly what studies of henge monuments have tried to do. They have been structured around a false distinction between daily practice and ritual action, so the discussion has shifted between two extremes. On the one hand, the scale and formality of henge monuments have encouraged the idea that these were ceremonial centres, a view which might be supported by the rules that obviously prevailed governing the deposition of cultural material inside them. On the other hand, there seems little doubt that similar conventions were obeyed at Gussage All Saints, an occupation site that was actively engaged in food production. Wainwright was obviously influenced by the similarities between what he found in both excavations, but is it necessary for interpretations to oscillate between these two extremes? I shall consider the same problems in the examples that follow.

Sacred sites, settlements and craft production: the case of Viereckschanzen

Viereckschanze is an unsatisfactory term since the word merely describes the form of a rectangular enclosure. But in practice its application has been restricted to a distinctive group of earthworks of the La Tène Iron Age in Central Europe and, in some accounts, to rather similar monuments in France, Belgium, the Netherlands and the British Isles. It is with the sites in Southern Germany and Bohemia that this account is concerned (Buchsenschutz *et al.* 1989; Bittel *et al.* 1990; Bittel 1998; Wieland 1999).

Here the enclosures tend to be up to a hectare in extent, with just one entrance which is usually to the south, east or west but never to the north. The earthworks are slight and on some sites their place was taken by a palisade. These features can never have been defences and the sites rarely occupy particularly conspicuous positions. In Bavaria they are often located on poor soils, but there are other cases in which they can be associated with large Iron Age

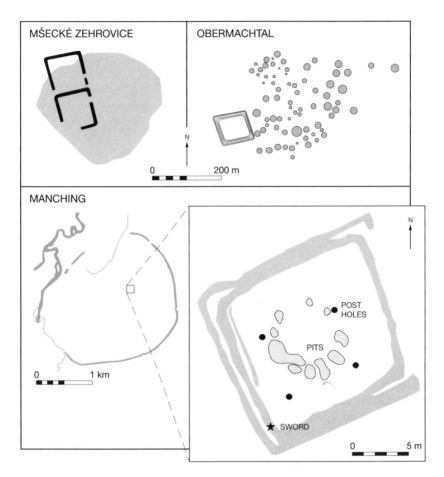

Figure 1.7 The siting of Viereckschanzen in Central Europe. Mšecké Zehrovice was built over the site of an open settlement, indicated by light tone; Obermachtal was located on the edge of a barrow cemetery; and the example at Manching was situated within the oppidum and associated with an Iron Age sword. Information from Waldhauser (1989) and Sievers (1991).

settlements. Viereckschanzen may be found in isolation or can occur close together in small groups. A number of sites are also found with cemeteries of burial mounds (Figure 1.7). There are variations in the number of associated artefacts but only rarely do they occur with any quantity of finds.

Their significance has always been debated. The initial interpretation of these enclosures was as specialised ritual monuments or shrines. As so often in archaeology, this view was strongly influenced by the results of the first large-scale excavation of one of these earthworks. This was at Holzhausen in Bavaria,

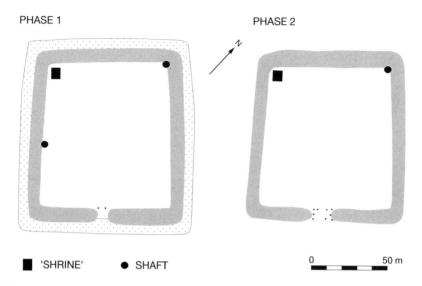

Figure 1.8 The archaeological sequence at Holzhausen, Bavaria. Information from Schwartz (1962 and 1975).

where the work revealed a timber building and two deep shafts or wells, one of which contained an upright post towards its base (Figure 1.8). It was thought to preserve traces of blood, and so it seemed logical to suppose that this feature had been used for offerings. The building was exceptional too, and had an unusual ground plan which could be compared with that of temples in the Classical world (Schwartz 1962 and 1975). Even so, there are problems. The finds from the excavation have not been fully published and the chronological relationship between the timber building and the enclosure is not entirely clear.

Later fieldwork modified this simple outline. It soon became apparent that some Viereckschanzen did not include any wells or shafts and that other kinds of building could be found which were of similar character to those recorded from settlements in the same regions. Not only was there an overlap between the structures within these enclosures and what were interpreted as domestic buildings, parallels to the specialised 'shrine' identified at Holzhausen were discovered on occupation sites (Venclová 1993 and 1997; Murray 1995). How far was it appropriate to distinguish between this group of earthworks and other components of the Iron Age landscape?

For a while it seemed as if a clearer distinction might be made on the basis of the excavated material, but it was limited in quantity and in many cases its stratigraphic context was not clearly defined. For example, a number of Viereckschanzen were built over the remains of open settlements and part of the artefact assemblage may predate these earthworks altogether. In certain cases this applies to the structural evidence too, and at Dornstadt-Tomerdingen it is clear that the excavated shaft was there before the enclosure bank (Zürn and Fischer 1991). In other cases, a site may have remained in use as a settlement after its specialised functions were over. Viereckschanzen also contain quantities of burnt bone, but there is little to show that these were different from the finds at occupation sites. In the same way, Murray (1995) suggested that the ceramic assemblages from Viereckschanzen had an unusual composition and might provide oblique evidence of feasting, but a more recent study has cast doubt on even this claim (Venclová 1997). Other distinctive finds are rare. There are very few human remains and the occasional hoards of iron artefacts are no different from those associated with the settlements of the same period.

Several authors have contrasted this evidence with what is known about the La Tène sanctuaries of Northern Gaul, certain of which are also associated with rectangular enclosures, although in fact the two groups of monuments are so far apart that there may have been little connection between them (Brunaux 1986; Buchsenschutz et al. 1989). Here very large numbers of artefacts have been discovered in excavation, including deposits of damaged weapons, coins and human bones. Some of these sites were the direct precursors of Roman temples. The contrast between such places and their counterparts in Central Europe has led some scholars to question whether the Viereckschanzen of Southern Germany and Bohemia had a specialised character. It seemed just as likely that they were settlements or parts of settlements.

Over the years the interpretation of Viereckschanzen has become more contentious, perhaps because the evidence from Holzhausen has so rarely been repeated. In 1993, Venclová suggested four possible interpretations for these sites. They may have been where ceremonial activity took place. This is very much the traditional interpretation of such monuments. Alternatively, they might have been used for food storage and redistribution. This idea is based on the presence of a few four- and six-post granaries at these sites, but it also bears the influence of work on the hill forts of the British Iron Age. Another possibility is that Viereckschanzen were simply small farms, which archaeologists had treated in isolation by paying too much attention to the shape of the perimeter earthwork. Again there was scope for more than one opinion, as these farms might have been of higher status than the open sites of the same period.

Some of the difficulty arises, as it did in my English example, because prehistorians have been looking for an absolute separation between sacred sites and the settlements of the same period and have failed to find one. This is particularly true in the case of Viereckschanzen. I have already mentioned that there is a certain overlap between the buildings inside these enclosures and those on other sites. There are a number of instances in which such earthworks contain houses and what may have been raised granaries that are of the same types as those found in open settlements. Even the specialised 'shrines' are not peculiar to these monuments. Moreover, there are other cases in which Viereckschanzen were located within a larger area of domestic activity so that the distribution of timber buildings extends well outside the confines of the enclosure itself. A related monument, with part of an Iron Age sword in its ditch, was found within the famous oppidum at Manching (Gerdsen 1982; Sievers 1991), whilst Waldhauser (1989) has shown that four of the Bohemian Viereckschanzen were placed towards the outer edges of more extensive settlements (Figure 1.7).

On an empirical level it is certainly possible to qualify the sharp distinction between the ritual and everyday uses of such sites, but any attempt to rationalise all the features of Viereckschanzen seems to go too far. It is possible that the shafts were really wells, but that hardly explains why the excavated examples on a single site like Holzhausen were dug to such different depths. Nor does it account for the upright posts in the fillings of such features. In the same way, this class of earthwork enclosure may have played a variety of different roles but this does not explain the strict conventions in the placing of their entrances, some of which were unusually elaborate structures. At different sites they were aligned on three of the cardinal points, but they avoided any orientation towards the north.

Venclová (1993) has suggested strict criteria for distinguishing the sacred significance of Viereckschanzen from the characteristics of ordinary settlements in Central Europe. These are very revealing, not least because they depend to a large extent on comparisons with sites in France and England which may represent a different phenomenon. According to her account, shrines should occupy prominent positions apart from any domestic structures. They should contain what she calls 'votive objects', and domestic artefacts should not occur. Similarly, the buildings associated with sacred places should be quite different from those found on occupation sites. In her study she also identified Iron Age shrines through their similarity to Classical architecture. She concluded that:

> There are no reliable explicit criteria for the identification of Celtic sacred structures where they are not accompanied by votive objects and are not situated at sites with continuous ritual activity.
>
> (1993: 64)

This is an unnecessarily restrictive scheme, for it is a product of modern Western assumptions about the past, in which ritual and belief are largely separated from the everyday. As my Galician example shows, that need not be the case. In fact there is no reason to accept Venclová's first criterion. It is unnecessary to insist that shrines should be set apart from domestic buildings and quite arbitrary to suppose that they should have been located at conspicuous points in the landscape.

Her second criterion raises even more difficulties, for it is not entirely clear how we are to identify 'votive objects' as a class of artefact, nor how they are to be distinguished from those employed in daily life. Archaeologists can only work with those elements of material culture that have survived to the present day, and it seems clear that this often happened because they had been deposited intentionally and with some formality. If we follow that line of argument, virtually any kind of object could have been used as a votive offering (Bradley 1998a). There is no sound basis for inferring that exceptional pieces like a flesh hook from Holzhausen belonged to a special class of votive objects, whilst apparently mundane artefacts like metalworking tools and axes were somehow different in kind. To do so simply imposes contemporary values on the past.

Lastly, it may be correct to isolate certain types of timber building as being different from those ordinarily found in settlements and even to compare them with well-documented temples in the Classical world, but that is no reason to suppose that other kinds of structure might not have been imbued with a particular significance as well. The case of the Galician hórreo shows quite explicitly how domestic buildings may also have had special connotations. To suppose otherwise is to prejudge the issue. We should accept that there was a certain overlap between the contents of Viereckschanzen and those of domestic sites and must study that relationship in its own terms.

Since her 1993 paper it seems that Venclová's position has become less dogmatic. Writing five years later, she favoured a more nuanced interpretation:

> Summarising what we know about the function of the rectangular walled enclosures in Central Europe, it should be admitted that there are a number of possible interpretations. Their ritual signifi-cance remains one of the alternatives, it is not, however, the only solution. The possibility cannot be excluded that ritual activities might have been performed simultaneously with the secular activity or that only some enclosures served religious purposes . . . It is probable . . . that the ritual and private spheres had been strongly interlinked in the La Tène period. *Their artificial separation would, therefore, be most unnatural.*
>
> (1998: 220–1; my emphasis)

That seems a more convincing interpretation.

Venclová herself has excavated one of the most important Viereckschanzen in Bohemia, Mšecké Zehrovice. This sheds light on yet another aspect of the problem. Her work shows that rectangular earthwork enclosures were not used throughout the history of this site. The one convincing shrine was confined to a single phase (Venclová 1998).

Mšecké Zehrovice began as a large open settlement and was associated with houses, pits and industrial activity (Figure 1.9). It appears to have been located in relation to two important resources: iron, and a form of black coal known as sapropelite which was used for making personal ornaments. These items may have possessed a special significance. Sapropelite shares the unusual physical properties of jet, and the rings that were made out of it were often deposited in graves. These were produced in enormous numbers. Each would have taken about eight hours to complete, and even quite small-scale excavation provided evidence for the production of nearly 1,300 of these artefacts.

Ironworking also took place on a large scale, and finds of bloomery slag extend over an area of about three and a half square kilometres. The metal must have been exported from the site in the form of artefacts, as regular ingots are not known in Iron Age Bohemia. Clearly the inhabitants of Mšecké

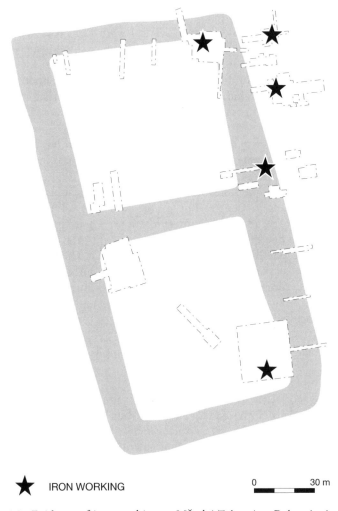

★ IRON WORKING   0 ___ 30 m

Figure 1.9 Evidence of iron working at Mšecké Zehrovice, Bohemia, in relation to the excavated areas of the later Viereckschanze. Information from Venclová (1998).

Zehrovice enjoyed a wide range of contacts with other areas and this may explain why the settlement seems to have been unusually prosperous. But could it also explain why it developed into a sanctuary?

The ethnography of metalworking has been reviewed in a number of publications and one point is clear (Herbert 1984 and 1993; Reid and Maclean 1995; Budd and Taylor 1995; Barndon 1996 and 2004; Hingley 1997; Haaland 2004). Metallurgy is not always regarded as an industrial process in the terms that are familiar today. It is a way of transforming raw materials that is attended by danger and magic, and the entire process is bound by social conventions. It involves restricted, even secret knowledge and has to be accomplished with the aid of specialised rituals. There may be prohibitions on who is permitted to view the work and on where it can take place. It owes some of its power to the transformation of an exotic substance and to the significance of the objects that are made. To consider this process as an everyday occurrence could be entirely misleading. In the past, the making of personal ornaments that were buried with the dead might have been just as problematical, and again it could have been carefully controlled. If so, then the building of an enclosure and a shrine may simply have formalised the established importance of the site. In Venclová's interpretation its construction brought the operation of the 'industrial settlement' to an end, but its very creation may be linked to the ways in which craft production was associated with ritual in ancient society. The sequence at Mšecké Zehrovice could have been more complicated than it seems.

Farming and the <u>treatment of the dead</u>:
the case of 'ritual ploughing'

Just as archaeologists have found it hard to distinguish between settlements and sacred sites, there are processes in the past which have been surprisingly difficult to understand. As we have seen, one example is provided by metalworking; another consists of the evidence for ploughing found under burial mounds in Northern Europe. Here again opinion is polarised between the claim that these features are related to one another in a significant way and a purely pragmatic explanation of the same phenomenon (Rowley-Conwy 1987; Kristiansen 1990; Tarlow 1994).

The evidence is clearly defined. The furrows left by primitive ploughs or ards are frequently preserved in the buried soils sealed beneath later monuments, just as they are often recognised in the excavation of field systems. The earliest evidence comes from about 3300 BC and is found with long mounds and passage graves (Thrane 1989; Tegtmeier 1993). It is more often associated with round barrows and is especially abundant in the Early Bronze Age when many of these monuments were built. Although this phenomenon is found widely in Northern and Western Europe, it has been studied in most detail in Denmark, and it is here that it has raised most problems of interpretation.

Little is known about the arable economy of the Neolithic and Early Bronze Age periods in Northern Europe, because the creation of formal field systems appears to be a later development. Although individual plots may have been defined by fences (Theunisson 1999), that process probably started in earnest during the first millennium BC and reached a peak in the Pre-Roman Iron Age (Nielsen 1984). Until then, the clearest evidence comes from land surfaces that have been protected from later disturbance. Most of these have been found during the excavation of round barrows. Such evidence is widespread, but before its full extent was apparent it seemed to have an exceptional character. This led to the first suggestions that specific sites had been prepared for their use as mortuary monuments by a process of 'ritual ploughing'. It represented the initial stage in the organisation of a funeral.

This was not an implausible hypothesis, for similar practices are documented in the Vedic hymns and also in the writings of Homer (Pätzold 1960), but it is an idea whose initial impetus has been weakened by the discoveries of recent years. Several objections have been raised to the idea as it was originally formulated. The preserved land surfaces beneath barrows are among the very few locations in which plough furrows could have been preserved, so that the close relationship between these two phenomena might be fortuitous. With more detailed excavation, it has become clear that on certain sites there is evidence for several successive phases of cultivation before the mound was built. Only the last of these could possibly have been linked with the con- struction of the barrow. In some cases the plough marks may be confined to the area occupied by the mound simply because they would not have survived beyond its limits (Thrane 1989; Kristiansen 1990). At others, the plough marks surrounded the original mound or cairn and were clearly a secondary feature, although they remained intact because they were covered by later extensions to these monuments. In any case there was little doubt that barrows had been built within the settled landscape as there were other examples in Northern Europe which overlay boundary fences or the remains of older houses (Theunisson 1999). In every case the idea that ploughing was imbued with a special significance was countered by practical arguments.

In the end those objections probably went too far. Kristiansen, for example, suggested that much of the settled area of Denmark had been cultivated during the Early Bronze Age (1984: 92), and yet the juxtaposition of round barrows and plough marks remains the exception rather than the rule; on plenty of well-excavated sites such evidence is lacking. There were a small number of cases in which the cultivation had been confined to the position occupied by the later earthwork, and there were even cases where the floor of a burial chamber seems to have been ploughed after building had commenced (Tarlow 1994). There were also sites at which the position of the kerb had been indicated by a ring or rings of plough marks before the stones were erected. All of these were considered to be exceptional cases.

That is not necessarily true. Rowley-Conwy (1987) has drawn attention to experimental evidence that ard furrows may not survive unless they are protected soon after they form, and once it is conceded that the circular spaces enclosed by ploughing might have had a special significance there is no reason in principle why all the other examples of cultivation marks must be explained in practical terms.

It is just as important to consider the broader setting of this evidence. Although the main critic of the idea of 'ritual ploughing', Kristiansen (1990), considers that the relationship between barrows and plough marks is coincidental, few scholars take the same attitude to the remains of houses that may also be preserved beneath these mounds. As we shall see in Chapter 2, this can apply to individual buildings or even to whole groups of domestic structures. In such cases the monument acknowledges the positions of these dwellings, and this seems to have been a major influence on the siting of the graves. At Handewitt the relationship goes even further (Aner and Kersten 1978: 39). Here the long house itself overlay an area of cross-ploughing and its walls had been carefully aligned with the orientation of the furrows (Figure 1.10)

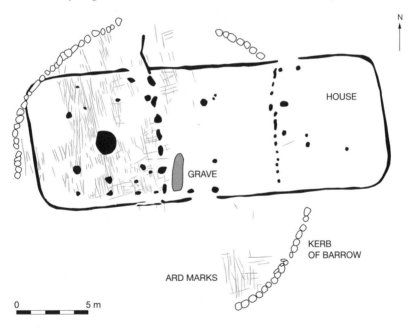

Figure 1.10 Ard marks and the remains of a long house buried beneath a round barrow at Handewitt, Denmark. The kerb of the barrow respects the western end of the house and the position of an internal partition, whilst the associated grave was close to the entrance of the older building. The house walls and the grave follow the same axes as the plough furrows. Information from Aner and Kersten (1978).

Kristiansen has written about the lavish expenditure of turf in the construction of Bronze Age barrows and has interpreted this process in terms of the conspicuous consumption of pasture (1984: 94). This is surely an analogous position to the one that he is questioning, for by placing barrows or groups of barrows over recently cultivated ground people were voluntarily giving up areas of arable land. Rather than assuming that the relationship between barrow building and cultivated areas was fortuitous, we might consider why it happened at all. This is especially important if Rowley-Conwy (1987) is right in suggesting that the plough furrows would only have survived intact for a short period after they were made. Some of this land had recently been tilled.

In fact there is convincing evidence that these furrows were still visible when many of the mounds were built. Just as the house at Handewitt was exactly aligned with the earlier plough furrows on that site, the same applies to a high proportion of the graves in Denmark. This relationship was first observed by Randsborg and Nybo (1984) in their study of the round barrows of Period 2 of the Nordic Bronze Age, in which the graves are often aligned east–west, but in fact it is much more common than their account might suggest. In those cases in which adequate records are available, there is a consistent relationship between the alignment of the grave and the orientations of the plough furrows (these might have more than one orientation because of the practice of cross-ploughing). There are sites with a limited number of graves where all of them are aligned with plough furrows, but even where such graves are more frequent the coincidence accounts for more than half the burials. This is not because both had been aligned on the same features. Although Randsborg and Nybo stress the importance of the sunrise and sunset during Period 2, the plough marks recorded beneath round barrows adopt every possible orientation. The same was true of the burials, and the corollary is clear: the configuration of the cultivated surface must still have been apparent when these monuments were built. That weakens the argument that such barrows were linked with cultivated areas by chance.

There are individual sites where this is especially apparent. For example, at Harrislee three graves beneath a round barrow were carefully located in the unploughed area defined by arcs of concentric plough furrows. It almost seems as if these had originally been intended to define two circular enclosures, but in the event it was the area where they converged that provided the site for the burials (Aner and Kersten 1978: Abb. 44). Something similar may have happened at a further site at Harrislee where the graves were laid out along one edge of a cultivated plot preserved beneath the middle of a later mound (ibid.: Abb. 52). At another site, on the island of Bornholm, the position of a small round barrow was left intact but a square annexe containing additional burials was defined by several rows of furrows (ibid.: Abb. 70). None of these relationships seems to have been fortuitous.

In its extreme form the pragmatic argument loses some of its force. Not only was the organisation of burial mounds closely related to the configuration of earlier houses and fields, the later development of certain sites was influenced by similar concerns. Thrane (1989) and Kristiansen (1990) have argued that the rings of plough marks just outside the kerbs of several round barrows were secondary to the construction of those monuments. These furrows had survived because their remains were protected when the earthworks were enlarged. This kind of sequence happens at several different sites and it is wrong to take it for granted. The ard furrows are most densely distributed against the base of the mound or cairn (Figure 1.11). In fact these furrows come so close to the kerb that this manoeuvre would have been difficult to execute. Experimental archaeology shows how hard it is to control a plough team when it is working in a restricted space, and the excavation of Celtic fields certainly suggests that it would have been no easy matter to cultivate so close to a solid barrier. In any case this task is more likely to have been performed with spades or hoes (Fowler 1983: chapter 2). We must ask why it was necessary to plough right up to the edges of recent burial mounds, when it was clearly the custom to extend them during later phases. It seems logical to suppose that these different activities

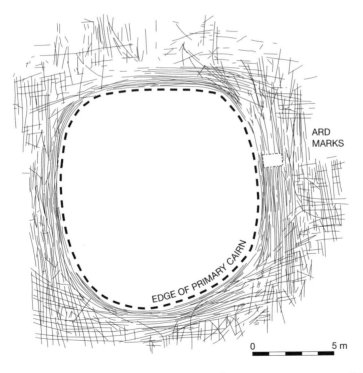

Figure 1.11 Plough marks around the edge of a Bronze Age cairn at Diverhøj, Denmark. Information from Asingh (1987).

were linked to one another and that the people who ploughed around the edges of these mounds did so in anticipation of later developments at the monuments. Once again it is unsatisfactory to explain this sequence in terms of prehistoric economics, especially when many other barrows were built on undisturbed ground.

These problems arise for familiar reasons. As we saw in the cases of henges and Viereckschanzen, prehistorians have found it difficult to escape from a simple distinction between the sacred and the secular. If fields were cultivated to grow crops – and no one denies that – then it has seemed unthinkable that ground might also have been cultivated immediately before the construction of barrows. In the same way it has been hard to accept that the alignment of graves could ever have been influenced by the direction of ploughing, for farming is a practical activity whilst funerals are occasions for ritual. In fact, the question to ask is how practical and cosmological concerns were related to one another in antiquity, and that will not become clear until prehistorians are more sensitive to the detailed patterning that can be identified in their source material. Again it is obvious that the distinction between the ritual and the everyday has done little to advance our understanding of Early Bronze Age Denmark. Archaeologists seem to have become the prisoners of their own assumptions.

Those same assumptions run through all the examples that I have considered here. They have led to considerable confusion in the interpretation of Neolithic henges, Iron Age settlements and hill forts in prehistoric Britain. They underlie the sharp disagreements that characterise current thinking on the Viereckschanzen of Central Europe, and there are very similar divisions in the interpretation of craft production. That was suggested by the sequence at Mšecké Žehrovice. A similar distinction may account for the lack of unanimity concerning the identification of 'ritual ploughing' beneath the Bronze Age burial mounds of Scandinavia. Is there any way of resolving these problems?

Cause and effect

Oddly enough, very few of the writers quoted so far explain what they mean by ritual. Their definitions remain implicit and have to be inferred. So far these cases have been organised according to their subject matter. Thus they consider the relationships between settlements and ritual monuments, domestic activity and craft production, farming and funeral rites. They have also been selected to cover a wide chronological range, extending from the Neolithic of Southern England to the Late Iron Age of Bohemia. But they could be grouped according to the assumptions on which they depend. There are two main themes which run through all these examples.

The first assumption is that ritual activity is directly opposed to domesticity. Venclová's account is particularly explicit in this respect (Venclová 1993). Her

28

position is clear from her discussion of Iron Age shrines. These ought to be set apart from domestic structures. They should adopt a distinctive architectural style and they must be associated with specialised artefacts, rather than those found on occupation sites. It is because these different elements are so clearly kept apart that she finds it hard to interpret the subtleties of the archaeological sequence at Mšecké Zehrovice, where an industrial settlement with a wide range of long-distance contacts seems to have been transformed into a ceremonial site. Kristiansen (1990) takes very much the same line, although his argument is less explicit. He finds it hard to contemplate a direct relationship between the act of cultivation, which belongs to the domestic domain, and the construction of mounds which were to be used in mortuary ritual. Because such a development juxtaposes two different domains, he treats the relationship as coincidental and looks for practical arguments to support that view. Much the same applies to Wainwright's discussion of Durrington Walls (1975). So long as it seemed to possess a distinctive character he was quite content to interpret it as a ceremonial centre. Once rather similar practices were evidenced in a settlement, albeit one of Iron Age date, he had no alternative but to reject his original position. That was because ritual activity and domestic life seemed to be mutually exclusive, and for that reason they could not have been combined in the same setting. Richards and Thomas (1984), who revisited the same evidence, took a rather similar line. They supported Wainwright's original idea that Durrington Walls had been a ceremonial centre, but they did so by studying the processes by which artefacts and animal bones had been deposited there. They emphasised the degree of formality that this showed and argued that it was a defining characteristic of ritual. It was quite distinct from normal practice within settlements. In every case, then, ritual was identified as something set apart from daily life. It happened at different places and times and may even have involved particular kinds of artefacts and architecture.

Second, it seemed as if rituals employed a different kind of logic from the processes in which people engaged on a regular basis. This is particularly clear where questions of technology are involved, but the point has a wider application. There seems to be an implicit assumption that where people used specialised knowledge to transform the physical properties of raw materials they were engaging in a purely instrumental process: they were making something happen by using their practical skills. By contrast, rituals seem to have involved supernatural agency and so they worked through some kind of magic. For that reason they could not be implicated in purely technical procedures. This is clear from the attitude of some of the writers quoted earlier. Ritual involved a different relationship between cause and effect from many of the skills employed by prehistoric people. If certain processes could be explained in physical terms, there was no need to complicate the argument. Thus ironworking was considered as a completely straightforward activity, for it depended on the properties of the metal and the ways in which it was worked by human agency. The same would surely apply to the production of personal ornaments. According to the same logic, it seemed to be a valid objection to the idea of 'ritual ploughing' to show how the same evidence could be explained in more mundane terms.

In a recent paper Brück suggests that these approaches result from a set of ideas that are widely shared in the West today. She takes the view that 'the identification and isolation of ritual is based on models of human practice and ways of knowing that are peculiar to contemporary society' (1999a: 314).

She places the main emphasis on different kinds of rationality. She considers Western thought since the Enlightenment to be permeated by a mechanical, scientific model of causality based on the premises of modern science:

> Direct action on a material object (that is, acts in which there is a mechanical link between means and end) became the primary means of intervening in the world and processes such as experimentation and exploration became central to the acquisition of knowledge. . . . It is easy to see how the objective functionality espoused by post-Enlightenment science came to be contrasted with ritual practice in which no intrinsic means–end relationship can be recognised. Because it does not meet modern Western criteria for practicality, ritual is frequently described as non-functional, irrational action.
>
> (Ibid.: 318)

Brück argues that this kind of rationality is not found in all societies, and for that reason many communities lack any conception of ritual as a distinct kind of activity. In her terms, they have 'a "monist" rather than a "dualist" mode of thought' (ibid.: 319). She suggests that archaeologists and anthropologists have sometimes imposed contemporary models of causation on societies in which these would have lacked any meaning. Moreover, because certain activities seemed to them to be irrational, it has been assumed that they had another role:

> As ritual acts do not appear to *do* anything, anthropologists have concluded that they must *stand* for something else: in other words ritual action is symbolic.
>
> (Ibid.: 318; emphasis in the original)

The migration of ideas

Theories often migrate from one discipline to another. In an unpublished lecture given at the end of his life David Clarke described his 'waterfall model' of archaeology. Academic subjects could be compared with a series of rapids. Ideas emerged at a high level, but, as they gained in influence, they overflowed and passed down from one cataract to another. For instance, research in human

30

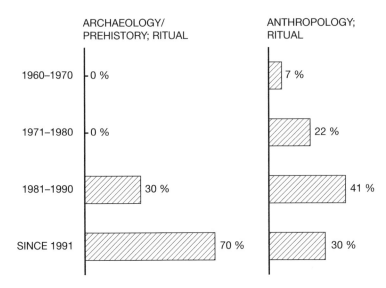

ARCHAEOLOGY/
PREHISTORY; RITUAL

ANTHROPOLOGY;
RITUAL

	ARCHAEOLOGY/PREHISTORY; RITUAL	ANTHROPOLOGY; RITUAL
1960–1970	0 %	7 %
1971–1980	0 %	22 %
1981–1990	30 %	41 %
SINCE 1991	70 %	30 %

Figure 1.12 The dates of publications since 1960 relating to ritual in anthropology and in archaeology or prehistory, based on the keywords recorded in the catalogue of the Bodleian Library, Oxford.

geography was located far upstream, whilst prehistory was towards the lower end of the system. This meant that it received many ideas from other fields, but, by then, some of them were already discredited. For Clarke, archaeological theory mixed a number of elements that had already been developed – and even abandoned – by other researchers. One example was social anthropology.

That pattern is clearly illustrated by studies of ritual. In this case it is interesting how archaeologists followed the course charted for them by anthropologists without realising how far ideas in that discipline had developed. This is clear from the published output of both subjects. The catalogue of the Bodleian Library in Oxford shows that books with the keywords 'ritual' and 'anthropology' were published in growing numbers between the 1960s and 1980s, before decreasing in frequency after 1990. Books with the keywords 'archaeology' and 'ritual' hardly feature before the 1980s, suggesting that this topic played a more prominent role in that discipline as the interests of social anthropologists were changing (Figure 1.12). The same is clear from a number of recent books. In the *Dictionary of Anthropology* edited by Barfield 'ritual' occupies little over two pages (T. Barfield 1997) and in the *Encyclopaedia of Social and Cultural Anthropology* edited by Barnard and Spencer (1996) it takes just four. That same applies to two accounts of anthropological theory. There are just three references to ritual in the index of *History and Theory in Anthropology* (Barnard 2000) and none at all in *An Introduction to Theory in Anthropology* (Layton 1997).

31

Books on
RITUAL

Perhaps that is because the term has become too general and all-embracing. There are a number of elements that archaeologists have associated with ritual which are considered separately in these books. Barnard's and Spencer's *Encyclopaedia* has sections on 'belief', 'magic', 'oratory', 'pilgrimage' and 'sacrifice', as well as 'rites of passage', whilst Barfield's contributors add 'cults', 'death ritual', 'fertility rites', 'religion' and 'rites of intensification'. Something similar happens in the *Companion Encyclopaedia of Anthropology* edited by Ingold (1994). There are separate chapters on a number of themes that might once have been considered as integral parts of ritual – symbolism, magic, music and dance – but there is only one entry on ritual itself, and this considers it together with performance. As we shall see, that is very revealing.

In fact there seem to be two strands among modern conceptions of ritual. These are illustrated in Figure 1.13.

One strand reflects the idea that rituals express fundamental propositions about the world and that they are strongly associated with religious beliefs (Rappaport 1999). For that reason they are often addressed to the supernatural. The other strand considers the outward characteristics of rituals and emphasises that these are really performances carried out according to certain conventions (Turner 1969). Here the emphasis is as much on the formality of the procedure as the message it conveys.

Although this diagram portrays these elements as if they had equal weight, not all of them need be found together and each of these strands could be

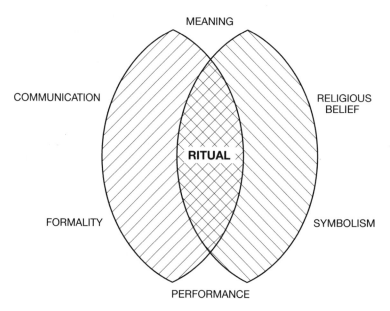

Figure 1.13 Two conceptions of ritual, and their areas of overlap.

studied separately. In one case the emphasis might be on the content of a particular transaction:

Performance – Symbolism – Religious belief – Meaning

In another, it might be on its form:

Performance – Formality – Communication – Meaning

It is the latter approach that is currently in the ascendant.

The theatre of the everyday

Social anthropologists are far from unanimous in their attitudes to ritual. For some, it is a universal characteristic of human societies: so much so, in fact, that it has lost any value as an analytical category (Goody 1977). For others, it is a specialised method of communication, shielded from critical appraisal by its own conventions (Bloch 1989). This may be true in certain cases, but rituals do not necessarily refer to deeply held or widely shared beliefs, and they are more easily identified as actions of a specialised kind than they are as propositions about the world (Bell 1992; Humphrey and Laidlaw 1994).

In any case it is not true that all rituals are connected with religious beliefs or, indeed, with relations to the supernatural. For some time it has been accepted that there are secular rituals as well and that the two really merge into one another. Nor are the procedures of ritual as formal as they may appear, for there are often important divergences in the ways in which they are conducted. What matters is not to adhere to a strict set of procedures but that they should 'work' (Humphrey and Laidlaw 1994). This may override the need to believe in the message of a specific ritual. It is participation and commitment that count far more.

Once it is accepted that ritual is a kind of practice – a performance which is defined by its own conventions – it becomes easier to understand how it can occur in so many settings and why it may be attached to so many different concerns. Once we reject the idea that the only function of ritual is to communicate religious beliefs, it becomes unnecessary to separate this kind of activity from the patterns of daily life. In fact, rituals extend from the local, informal and ephemeral to the public and highly organised, and their social contexts vary accordingly.

That is why some anthropologists have begun to place less emphasis on ritual as a thing in itself and more on the practice of *ritualisation* (Bell 1992; Humphrey and Laidlaw 1994). This is an important development for it acknowledges the range of behaviour that is actually observed. Once ritual is seen as a form of action rather than a specialised kind of communication, it becomes easier to understand how it operates, for it is a social strategy of a distinctive kind. That makes it possible to consider the contexts in which rituals were created and performed in the past, and the consequences of such actions, whether they had been intended or not. In short, it allows archaeologists to consider the development of specific rituals over time and to trace their social and political histories.

Ritualisation is both a way of acting which reveals some of the dominant concerns of society, and a process by which certain parts of life are selected and provided with an added emphasis. Again that process is essentially historical, for it is unlikely to develop instantaneously. In principle, that means that it can be traced over time and studied in its wider setting. By following the development of rituals in this way it should be possible to identify a few of the ideas that they were meant to express.

Ritualisation has another significance as well. It is really a process by which certain actions gain an added emphasis through particular kinds of performance. That means that at any one time the investment of ritual in specific arenas will be largely a matter of degree: certain transactions may be attended by greater formality than others. For that reason rituals can extend from the private to the public domains and from the local, even personal, to those which involve large numbers of people.

As a result of such processes, rituals form a continuum: they are not set apart from other areas of life, as prehistorians have often supposed. But that statement introduces problems of its own. How far will it be possible to trace such practices back to their points of origin? Do rituals need to follow clear conventions before their very existence can be recognised by archaeologists? It may be that certain practices became established more rapidly than others. This is particularly true in the state where changes could be executed through an administrative infrastructure.

At the same time, it is important to distinguish between rituals that depend on successful performance, with all the scope which that allows for innovation, and those that follow a prescribed liturgy where there will be less room for manoeuvre (Humphrey and Laidlaw 1994: chapter 7). Much depends on the ways in which rituals are transmitted (Connerton 1989; Bradley 2002a). In traditional societies this process may well depend on the operation of social memory, but they can also be governed by written texts. Although the interpretation of those writings may change from one period to another, they provide an added constraint on the directions in which such practices can develop. Christianity is a 'religion of the book' and I suspect that this feature has coloured modern Western perceptions of the nature of ritual in the past. In later prehistoric Europe – and especially in the regions that I have discussed so far – there is probably more evidence for rituals based on performance than those constrained by a liturgy (Humphrey and Laidlaw: chapter 7).

How do archaeologists distinguish between ritual and the everyday? In Europe I suggest that they have done so on a largely intuitive basis, influenced by their experience in an increasingly secular world. It is a world in which ritual and religious belief have been pushed to the margins. That has had two consequences, neither of which has been good for the discipline. They have seen ritual as something that happens beyond the limits of everyday life: an activity that involves special people, special places and a distinctive range of material culture. They have also assumed that ritual was quite separate from the concerns of daily life. In fact it may not have been the case, and this book will contest that view.

I have attempted to illustrate the difficulties that archaeologists make for themselves by considering their treatment of ritual in three short studies of different contexts in prehistoric Europe. I have also presented an ethnographic case study which illustrates the interplay between religion and practical concerns in contemporary Spanish agriculture and compares it with practice in the Inca state. What do these different examples have in common?

In each case the problems of interpretation are particularly severe because there seems to be so much overlap between the contents of prehistoric rituals and those of domestic life. Thus rather similar deposits can be identified in henges and in the settlements and hill forts of the British Iron Age. In the same way, there is a considerable overlap between the archaeological evidence from open settlements in Central Europe and that from the enclosed sites known as Viereckschanzen. In each case it may be possible to recognise the extreme forms taken by those monuments – enormous timber circles inside henges, the deep shafts within the Viereckschanzen – but there is also a middle ground where there is greater ambiguity. The same applies to the other examples considered in this chapter. There seems little doubt that in Bronze Age Denmark there was a significant relationship between cultivation and the treatment of the dead. Sometimes the perimeter of a burial mound had been marked out by ploughing, but there is more uncertainty in those cases where individual graves seem to have been aligned with earlier furrows. The uncertainty is greater still where the perimeters of existing mounds appear to have been tilled before those monuments were extended. In the same way, it is relatively uncontroversial to suggest that certain kinds of metalwork may have played a specialised role in society. They could have been associated with particular people or particular activities, and when these artefacts finally went out of use they may have been deposited with some formality, in rivers, graves or in settlement sites. On the other hand, it is not so obvious whether the production of these objects was attended by a similar degree of formality, as I suggested may have happened for the production of iron and personal ornaments at Mšecké Zehrovice. In every case there was surely an overlap between domestic and ritual practices.

That brings me to a second point. Even the contexts that do provide evidence of specialised activity contain the kinds of artefacts associated with daily life. By depositing them with such formality people imbued them with a greater significance. I am not suggesting that every component of prehistoric ritual referred, even obliquely, to the domestic sphere, for that would not be true, but this relationship is so widespread and so persistent that it must not be ignored. In this book I wish to claim that these areas of overlap should not be regarded as problems but as vital clues to the origin and nature of many of the rituals undertaken in prehistoric society. They played an important role in the communities concerned. Rather than presenting an insoluble problem for archaeologists, they offer an opportunity of composing a more rounded version of prehistory.

The organisation of the argument

In the pages that follow I shall explore the nature and extent of this relationship between ritual and domestic life, as evidenced in the prehistory of Northern and Western Europe. The account begins with houses and settlement sites and considers the range of evidence for rituals that were associated with these domains (Figure 1.14). I shall discuss the ways in which houses were built, inhabited and abandoned and the manner in which those structures could assume a special role in the commemoration of the dead. These buildings might be imitated by burial mounds or even buried underneath them. I shall also discuss the ways in which ordinary domestic dwellings might provide the

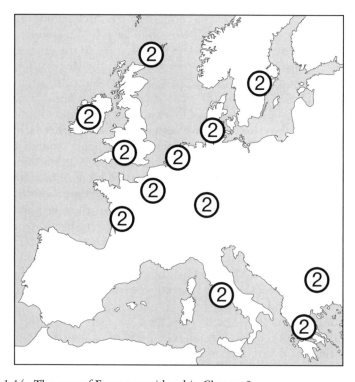

Figure 1.14 The areas of Europe considered in Chapter 2.

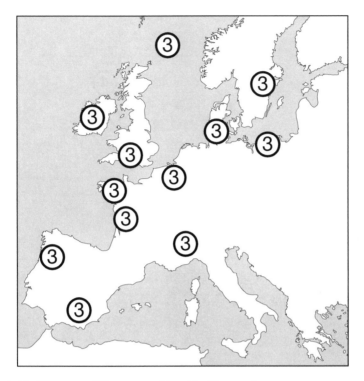

Figure 1.15   The areas of Europe considered in Chapter 3.

prototypes for enormous public monuments, like the feasting halls of Iron Age Scandinavia or the temples of Classical Greece. Then, in Chapter 3, I shall take the same approach to a series of activities that contribute to the domestic economy (Figure 1.15). In each case I shall return to some of the specific examples introduced in earlier sections of this chapter, but I shall also discuss the ways in which practical activities concerned with food production and the making of artefacts were ritualised in prehistoric societies. As a counter-point to that discussion, I shall consider Malinowski's account of the role of rituals in subsistence farming, *Coral Gardens and their Magic* (Malinowski 1935).

   There follow three detailed studies, taken from successive periods of European prehistory (Figure 1.16). The first is concerned with the Neolithic and revisits some of the problems already considered in my short account of henges. It discusses the way in which specialised deposits have been interpreted in relation to early agricultural societies in Northern Europe. In particular, it comments on the complicated relationship that developed between monu-ments, votive sites and the places where people lived. The second case study is an account of the hoards of Bronze Age metalwork and emphasises the

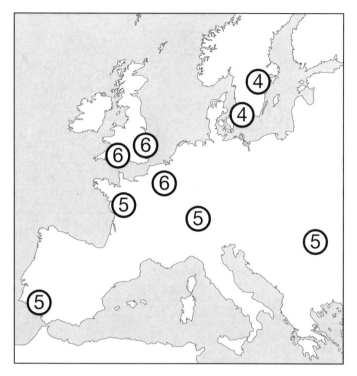

Figure 1.16 The areas of Europe considered in Chapters 4 to 6. The numbers relate
to those of the individual chapters.

problems created by the circulation of incomplete objects and their representation in different collections of artefacts. In doing so, it re-examines current
interpretations of scrap hoards and suggests a rather different approach to
the study of ancient metallurgy. The final study investigates the contents of
occupation sites and shrines in the Iron Age of France and England. It studies
some of the deposits of artefacts associated with daily life and compares them
with the kinds of material that were sacrificed at sanctuaries. Although this
discussion is concerned with Western rather than Central Europe, it returns to
the ideas explored in my earlier account of settlements and Viereckschanzen
and locates them in a wider context.

Finally, Chapter 7 considers the wider significance of this enquiry. Why
should domestic life have been ritualised during prehistory, and how far was
this development related to the workings of the political economy? What
were the limits of these practices? Did they maintain their significance in
more complex societies, and to what extent did rituals and everyday activities
draw apart with time? That raises the question whether it is possible to separate
functional and symbolic concerns in the ancient world. If the processes of daily

life were played out with the added emphasis that this book suggests, what are the implications for field archaeology, and what are the lessons for archaeological theory? In this case it is the very character of the discipline that is at stake.

Let me conclude by emphasising the scope of this enquiry. The obvious starting point is provided by its title. This is an account of *ritual and domestic life*, and it is restricted to the archaeological evidence *from prehistoric Europe*.

Both these elements are important. This is not an enquiry into the nature of ritual as a universal feature of human experience (Rappaport 1999). I shall pay little attention to the archaeology of the ancient mind (Mithen 1998), nor am I concerned with conceptions of the supernatural and the reasons why they developed (Boyer 1994). The book offers no advice on the archaeological identification of cult from one society to another (Renfrew 1995), and for the most part it analyses local developments at the expense of more general trends. All these are important issues, but they are subjects that have been well researched already. In contrast to those studies, I shall investigate just one topic: the problematical relationship between ritual and domestic life. Although this is an important theoretical issue, its significance is just as central to archaeological fieldwork.

This is also a study of prehistoric Europe, and the distinctive character of the evidence from this region needs to be acknowledged. In contrast to many other parts of the world, much of the archaeological evidence concerns small-scale societies rather than states or empires. That is to say, the book will be concerned mainly with communities which lacked an elaborate administrative superstructure. That is not to deny that such groups formed parts of larger social networks or that they were influenced by the growth of stratified societies at a distance, but simply to make the point that the studies of state religion which have been so important in other continents should not concern us here. In fact this account will make little reference to the Classical world, and only three examples – Greek temples, Late Iron Age sanctuaries and Early Medieval feasting halls – will come from what have been described as complex chiefdoms or states.

This is not intended to be a comprehensive account of the roles played by ritual in ancient Europe. Rather, the book has two distinct aims. First, it seeks to trace one specific theme among the many manifestations of ritual and ritualisation in this part of the world and to investigate the ways in which it has been understood – and misunderstood – by prehistorians. In doing so, this account may have a contribution to make not only to theoretical enquiry but also to the practice of archaeology.

Lastly, this book is an attempt to indicate how it might be possible to write a more integrated prehistory, free of the arbitrary thematic divisions that make this subject so difficult to understand. There has been little contact between those who study social archaeology and those who investigate the domestic economy, and this division is now so well established that it no longer seems possible for the same people to discuss symbolism and food production, ritual and everyday life. That is an unfortunate and quite unnecessary schism that the present account may do something to ameliorate. It is my contention that archaeology will only achieve some measure of intellectual maturity when such positions are seen for what they are: temporary stages in a long-running debate that has yet to reach a conclusion.

THE CONSECRATION
OF THE HOUSE

How domestic buildings took on
special qualities

Introduction: the public house

One of the most influential texts in the archaeology of South Scandinavia was written by Adam of Bremen in 1076. This describes the monuments of Gamla Uppsala and the rituals that took place there. Its reliability has been questioned for it is clear that he depended on informants rather than his own observations, but nevertheless his account refers to three important elements. There was a kind of theatre at the site, from which an audience might watch human and animal sacrifices taking place, and there was also a pagan temple:

> In this temple, which is decorated entirely with gold, people worship images of three gods. The mightiest of them, Thor, has his throne in the middle of the room, with Odin and Frey sitting on either side of him. They are said to have the following meanings. Thor, people say, rules the air and commands thunder and lightning, wind and rain, sunshine and crops. Odin, meaning fury, governs war and gives man the strength to fight his enemies. The third, Frey, gives peace and enjoyment to mortals . . . They also worship men raised to the gods and granted immortality by reason of great deeds.
>
> (Littmark 2002: 14)

This text was well known in later centuries and because the ceremonial centre was eventually replaced by the medieval city of Uppsala it played an important part in the history of Sweden. By the sixteenth century these discussions had gone so far that architectural reconstructions of the temple were being published (Olsen 1965). It may be no accident that the first of these resembles a Renaissance cathedral, whilst a version issued in the following century looks more like a Baroque church.

Fieldwork began in 1846. By then the burial mounds on the site had a special significance for Swedish national identity, but it was not until the 1920s

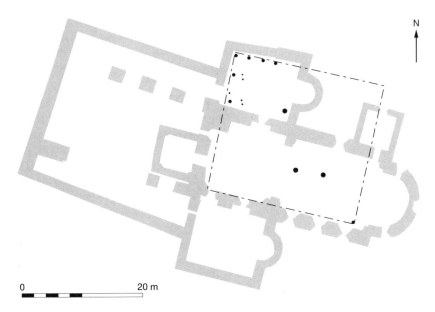

Figure 2.1 Outline plan of the cathedral at Gamla Uppsala, Sweden, showing the extent of the excavated area and the distribution of post holes. Information from Olsen (1965) and Nordahl (1996).

that a concerted effort was made to locate the remains of the temple. The most likely site seemed to be the medieval cathedral that had been built there before the present city of Uppsala was established. Beneath the remains of that early cathedral Lindqvist found a number of post holes (Figure 2.1; Lindqvist 1923, 1929 and 1936).

He identified just eleven of these, four running in a straight line, and two others offset from them at right angles. Two further rows, running parallel to one another, were suggested by excavation. These features were scattered over a considerable area, but that did not deter him from producing detailed architectural drawings of the temple. Indeed, over the years he offered more than one version, and other scholars followed his lead. Their interpretations range from a relatively modest rectangular building, set within a fenced enclosure, to grandiose multi-storey structures that seem to combine the attributes of stave churches with those of a pagoda. In the end these versions were as extravagant as any produced before the fieldwork took place (Figure 2.2). It was not until 1965 that Olsen returned to the excavated evidence from Gamla Uppsala and concluded that there was no support for any of these interpretations. Indeed, it seemed just as likely that the post holes observed by Lindqvist were those of a wooden church which predated the stone structure that occupies the site today (Nordahl 1996).

Figure 2.2 A selection of hypothetical reconstructions of the pagan temple at Gamla Uppsala, Sweden, based on the post holes found in excavation beneath the cathedral. Information from Olsen (1965).

Since Olsen's study was published there has been further fieldwork at Gamla Uppsala (Duczko 1993 and 1997). Now it is clear that the burial mounds were accompanied by a major settlement, so it seems even less obvious that the post holes beneath the cathedral belonged to the temple mentioned by Adam of Bremen. More important, an artificial terrace located not far from the surviving church has proved to be the site of an enormous hall. It was similar to other examples discovered at high-status sites of the Late Iron Age.

Price summarises the current state of knowledge:

> New studies of sources for the Gamla Uppsala 'temple' have suggested that it may have been a very large feasting hall in which pagan festivals took place at certain times, rather than a dedicated religious building in its own right . . . Cultic rituals were held . . . in the homes of the leading families – or in the royal hall in the case of Gamla Uppsala. The notion of prominent buildings taking on a temporary role as 'temples' for . . . ceremonies or other ritual is now generally accepted.
>
> (2002: 61)

In fact it is possible to see these halls as forming part of an even wider symbolic system. Their basic ground plan does not differ materially from the larger dwellings found in settlements of the same period (Herschend 1993; Dillmann 1997; Løken 2001). Both are long and rectangular, and some of them have bowed side walls that bear some resemblance to a ship (Figure 2.3). The main difference between the feasting halls and the other structures concerns the earlier buildings of this kind. Although the situation changed in the later first millennium AD, long houses originally contained a number of distinct compartments, separating the living and working areas from a byre, whilst the earliest halls spanned a larger space and lacked those subdivisions. The significance of this layout may have extended into other domains. Herschend has recently suggested that the objects deposited in ship burials were organised as if they had been displayed in such a hall (2001: 69–91). Thus the buildings could have doubled as temples, and some of the most elaborate funerals may also have referred to this archetype.

This is not an isolated instance. Very similar relationships can be identified in Classical archaeology and in the ethnographic record.

The Classical example is neatly summed up in the title of Mazarakis-Ainian's monograph *From Rulers' Dwellings to Temples* (1997). The thesis is a deceptively simple one. Between the Mycenaean Age and the development of the Greek polis, there is little evidence for formal religious buildings of any size, nor is it clear how archaeologists are to distinguish between the residences of a social elite and the locations where public rituals took place. Between the eleventh and eighth centuries BC, in the Protogeometric and Geometric periods, it seems as if cult buildings and high-status houses may have overlapped (Figure 2.4).

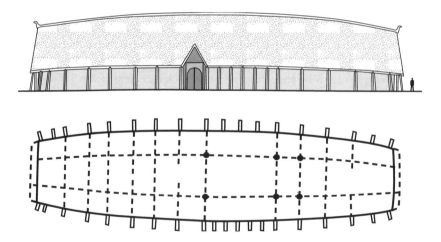

Figure 2.3 Reconstruction of an Iron Age feasting hall, based on the example at Lejre, Denmark. Information from Herschend (2001).

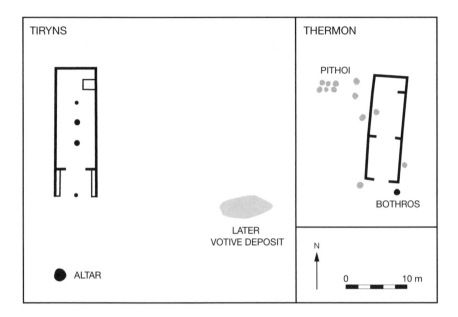

Figure 2.4 Elite dwellings at Tiryns and Thermon, showing the positions of an altar, a votive deposit, a pit (*bothros*) and storage jars (*pithoi*). Information from Mazarakis-Ainian (1997).

Several criteria have been suggested for identifying the dwellings of an elite, but few are sufficiently diagnostic. These buildings may share architectural features with other houses on the same sites or in the same cultural context and often they occupy prominent positions within the settlement, but neither criterion is convincing in itself. Their interior fittings can supply additional clues, and the same may be true of the nature and distribution of the artefacts associated with them. For example, they may include numerous storage vessels, as well as loom weights and spindle whorls, suggesting that day-to-day activities were important there.

On the other hand, later cult buildings may have rather similar features. Like domestic houses, they can contain foundation sacrifices, and certain rectangular or apsidal structures may be of exceptional length. Like elite dwellings, they can be distanced from other buildings or found in close proximity to tombs. They can also be sited in especially prominent locations, but the only features that allow them to be identified with any confidence seem to be the following: the presence of altars; the remains of sacrificed animals; or deposits of cult objects. Even these attributes present problems. Altars can be difficult to identify, and it is hard to distinguish formal deposits of food remains from those associated with domestic occupation. In the same way, there are few reliable methods of identifying cult objects, although the presence of large

45

numbers of artefacts of the same type may provide one clue. Otherwise the most reliable way of defining early temples could be through the lack of internal subdivisions within these buildings. It is interesting that exactly the same feature distinguishes the Scandinavian feasting halls from other structures of the same period.

In fact, the features of Greek cult buildings and elite residences overlap to such an extent that it may be wrong to think of them as mutually exclusive categories. One reason for taking this view is their chronological distribution. Mazarakis-Ainian (1997) observes that very few formal temples have been identified before about 750 BC, although other kinds of Early Iron Age cult site are commonplace. At the same time, the first appearance of 'urban temples' coincides with the abandonment of many of the elite dwellings built during earlier phases. That happened at a time when the nature of political power was changing, and there are certain cases in which elite buildings were obviously converted into temples.

There is some evidence that the social elite may have played an important role in public ritual. This is apparent from the writings of Homer and is supported by other, purely archaeological evidence. Like the halls at Gamla Uppsala, some of the rulers' dwellings provide abundant evidence for feasting, and literary evidence suggests that this may have included sacrifices and ritual meals. There are large deposits of meat bones on some of these sites, as well as vessels for serving food and drink. These buildings may contain internal hearths where such meals could be prepared and they include benches that could have accommodated large numbers of participants.

Of course these two examples are very different from one another, both in their architecture and in their institutional setting. In the Scandinavian example, the feasting halls represented merely the upper level in a hierarchy of timber structures associated with major settlements. There was a certain continuity between the dwellings found on these sites and more specialised buildings where large numbers of people could congregate. Such constructions were clearly associated with a restricted section of society and were used for a variety of transactions. Their main function was for communal consumption, but on occasion they assumed additional roles in public ritual, and that is why Adam of Bremen could mistake one of these structures for a temple. He was projecting his own experience of Christian Europe on to a society that had different conventions.

Perhaps the study of Iron Age Greece has suffered from similar preconceptions. Because the Classical polis contained a series of formal temples, it has seemed natural to look for similar buildings in earlier periods, but few, if any, have been identified. At the same time, the architectural prototypes for the urban temples do not appear to have been specialised cult buildings but the houses of a restricted group who exercised power over the rest of the community. The activities that took place in these dwellings have a number of features in common with those at later temples, and yet they may have played a less specialised role. This is not to argue that public rituals had lapsed between the eleventh and eighth centuries BC, but that they took place within the domestic domain. Like the Scandinavian halls, such buildings might assume more specialised roles on certain occasions, but it was not until about 750 BC that a distinct class of temple can be identified in Greece. Before that time there was no clear division between ritual activity and domestic life, and both occurred in the same architectural setting.

A similar overlap can be observed in the ethnographic record. In this case there has been an unusual convergence between the writings of archaeologists and those of social anthropologists. Although there was already a substantial literature concerned with the social and symbolic significance of houses, the 1990s saw a significant increase in the number of publications in this field and, in particular, in the production of edited volumes dedicated to this theme. Archaeological sources included *Domestic Architecture and the Use of Space* (Kent 1990), *The Social Archaeology of House* (Samson 1990), *Abandonment of Settlements and Regions* (Cameron and Tomka 1993) and *Architecture and Order* (Parker Pearson and Richards 1994). Among the major contributions from social anthropologists were *Inside Austronesian Houses: Perspectives on Domestic Designs for Living* (Fox 1993), *About the House: Lévi-Strauss and Beyond* (Carsten and Hugh-Jones 1995) and *House Life: Space, Place and Family in Europe* (Birdwell-Pheasant and Lawrence-Zuñiga 1999). Several of these volumes included contributions from both disciplines and the collections edited by Fox (1993) and by Carsten and Hugh-Jones (1995), whilst directed mainly to anthropologists, both made use of archaeological evidence. Similarly, Blanton's ambitious study *Houses and Households: A Comparative Analysis* used ethnography to expand the range of hypotheses available to prehistorians (Blanton 1997). At the same time, certain of these volumes ally themselves with different traditions in archaeology itself. Thus Blanton's book and the collection edited by Cameron and Tomka looked for general patterns in the manner of processual archaeology, whilst *Domestic Architecture and the Use of Space* was equally concerned with the functions and meanings of settlement sites.

Taken together, these collections did much to undermine the belief that human dwellings could be interpreted in simple functional terms. Rather they emphasised

> the value of seeing houses together with the people who inhabit them as mutually implicated in the process of living. Houses have many aspects . . . They are born, live, grow old, die and decay . . . On the one hand, people and groups are objectified in buildings; on the other hand, houses as buildings are personified and animated both in thought and in life. At one extreme are the lifeless ancestral houses . . . or tombs, frozen in time but vividly permanent; at the other extreme are those highly animated houses, in a constant state

of changing but ultimately ephemeral. But all of these, container and contained, are related as parts of a continuous process of living.

(Carsten and Hugh-Jones 1995: 46)

One example, taken from the collection edited by Fox, provides a bridge with the archaeological cases considered so far and emphasises the impossibility of separating the ritual importance of such buildings from their sources in daily life. This is an account of the Maori meeting house or whare-runanga (van Meijl 1993). It is important because it brings together so many different sources: ethnographic studies of how these buildings are used today, architectural accounts of the ways in which those structures have developed, and archaeological evidence for the character of their original prototypes. Taken together, these provide an insight into the relations of domestic and public life over a lengthy period of time.

It seems unlikely that meeting houses existed as a specialised category of building until after the first contacts with Europeans, but their architectural sources are older and are probably related to the dwellings of chiefs and the buildings in which their followers slept. The meeting houses may have developed for several reasons: as locations where guests could be accommodated and where public business could be transacted; as symbols of local identities in the colonial world; and as explicit statements of ancestry and descent (Metge 1976: chapter 15). As each of these features gained in importance, the buildings came to bear a greater weight of symbolism, and some of them were decorated with elaborate wood carvings.

Today the meeting houses rarely exist in complete isolation, for they are associated with an open plaza (the marae) and sometimes with ancillary structures (Figure 2.5). Their character varies according to the occasions on which they are used, so that they can be considered as council houses or houses for the ancestors, and they play their part not only in the affairs of the living but also in the commemoration of the dead. They are where their bodies are displayed in open coffins and where their images will be shown once the rites of passage are complete. Meeting houses are status symbols and the scale on which they are built is also a source of prestige. Another is provided by the complexity of their external decoration.

The Maori meeting house is considered in terms of the human body. In that sense it is a living organism and takes the form of an ancestor. The junction of the eaves and the veranda represents his face, and the porch represents his brain. The interior of the building is the chest and the ridge pole stands for the spine. In keeping with this scheme, the separate rafters symbolise the ribs. At the same time, the ridge pole also expresses the succession from the founding ancestor, and the sequence of rafters indicates the separate lines of descent from that point of origin. Thus the building describes the bodily form of an ancestor and the genealogy of those descended from him. In some cases the same basic scheme extends to the decorated surfaces. Carved panels mark the slabs where

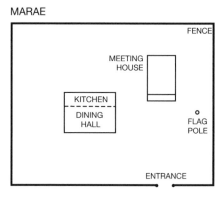

MARAE

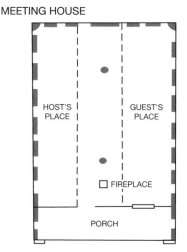

MEETING HOUSE

Figure 2.5 Outline plans of a Maori marae and meeting house. Information from Firth
(1929) and Metge (1976).

individual rafters end. These images explain the origins of different groups
within the community. The veranda may also be elaborately decorated, but
this displays the external face of the building to the wider world.

It would be wrong to treat all the parts of these structures in the same ways.
Although the meeting house is regarded as sacred in relation to the world
outside, not all its components share the same significance. Thus it has a special
character that does not extend to the dining room and kitchen. The central
part of the whare-runanga is the most powerful of all, for it is where visitors
are welcomed and where orators perform. In the same way, the two sides of
the structure have a different significance from one another. Such differences
are mirrored in the use of some of those buildings, and formerly they could
even determine the places where the leaders or their guests would sleep and

49

where the coffins of the dead could be displayed. Some of these distinctions also relate to the Maori sense of time, so that the front of the building might be associated with the past and the far end with the future. In that way movement through the house takes on a historical dimension. It links the fortunes of the living, from birth to death, with the genesis of the society of which they form a part.

In all these cases there is an important overlap between the sacred and secular functions of domestic buildings. Indeed, they are so completely integrated with one another that such a distinction becomes meaningless. The feasting halls of Iron Age Scandinavia seem to have played many roles, from the residences of local leaders to ceremonial centres. In the same way, Greek temples appear to have developed out of the dwellings of a social elite, and yet it is clear that both these different structures were employed in similar ways. Only in the eighth century BC were some of the specialised functions of these houses transferred to urban temples. A similar sequence took place in New Zealand, where the Maori whare-runanga appear to have developed out of the houses of local leaders. As we have seen, even in its developed form it continued to play many different roles, some of which it would be easy to characterise as 'domestic' and others as 'ceremonial'. Every component, from its porch to the individual rafters, carries such a weight of meaning that it is difficult to remember that it is a standing building.

Many of the same elements pervade the archaeology of prehistoric Europe and in the following sections I shall indicate a number of the ways in which the house and its occupation were ritualised in the societies of the past.

The living house

One of the clearest indications that such buildings had a special significance is the fact that in many different cultures they are represented by stone or ceramic models. In the Viking Age, for instance, the characteristic features of long houses could be copied in the form of tombstones (Lang 1984), just as there are models of both houses and granaries in Classical Greece (Mazarakis-Ainian 1997). But this practice extends far beyond the examples that have been quoted so far. Among the wide variety of ceramics found in Neolithic or Copper Age settlements there are many models of houses, some of which depict the contents of these buildings in detail. These come from Israel, Anatolia, Bulgaria, Romania, former Yugoslavia, Hungary, Greece and the Ukraine (Müller-Karpe 1968). They take on an added significance once it is accepted that they could be deposited with some formality.

The same applies to the 'house urns' of the Late Bronze and Early Iron Age. These are found in two quite different areas of Europe, although it seems likely that the people who made and used them were in contact with one another (Behn 1924; Bradley 2002b). Those in Central Italy are clearly copies of the timber dwellings of the same period and share their characteristic distribution

Figure 2.6 Late Bronze Age/Early Iron Age house urns from Central Italy. Information
from Bartolini *et al*. (1987).

(Figure 2.6; Bartolini, Bartolini *et al*. 1987). In this case their special significance is demonstrated by the fact that they occur in cemeteries. In the light
of this evidence it seems hardly surprising that the tombs of the Etruscan period
should present the dead in a domestic setting (Barker and Rasmussen 1998:
chapter 7).

Perhaps that provides one indication of the wider significance of prehistoric
houses, but the excavated structures have revealed many other kinds of evidence. It may be useful to recall two of the distinctive features of the Maori
meeting house. It was simultaneously regarded as a living being and as a way
of representing the passage of time. Thus many of the architectural features
stood for parts of the body of an ancestor, whilst movement along the axis
of the building involved a progression from the past to the future. Both ideas
can be combined, for if the house is considered as a living being it can be born,
grow old and die. In that way its biography is linked directly to conceptions
of time.

I have already mentioned the foundation deposits which seem to be shared
between elite dwellings and urban temples in Iron Age Greece. Such deposits
occur in many different parts of prehistoric Europe, but some of the clearest

instances come from the Neolithic and Copper Age periods in the Balkans, where they include human bones. Here it is clear that houses could be built and used in a specific cycle, in which abandoned buildings were burnt down before they were replaced in the same positions (Stepanovic 1997). That sequence was monumentalised through the accumulation of tells. The levels of burnt material often contain burials, suggesting that the stages in this sequence were punctuated by the provision of human remains. In this way the buildings themselves were given life (Chapman 1999).

A similar process may have happened in other areas. In the Greek Neolithic, for instance, houses were associated with the bones of children, but adult remains were found in other contexts (Perlès 2001: chapter 13). Towards the opposite end of Neolithic Europe, in the Paris Basin, child burials are found in the borrow pits that flank the houses of the Linearbandkeramik (Veit 1996). Nor was this practice limited to early farmers. Many centuries later, something similar may have happened in the Iron Age of Southern England where the bones of young people, including neonates, are associated with the interior of settlements and sometimes with individual houses, whilst adult burials are more common around the edges of the occupied area (Hill 1995: chapter 9). At Danebury, for example, the bones of neonates were nearly all found in the parts of the site containing rows of houses, whilst those of adults had a different distribution (Cunliffe and Poole 1991b: chapter 8). Another example of this pattern occurs at the Glastonbury 'lake village' where the remains of children were associated mainly with the dwellings and clay platforms. One focus for such deposits was the hearth. Most of the skulls of adults were placed around the limits of the settlement (Coles and Minnit 1995: fig. 8.10).

At other sites the deposits associated with the creation of the house might include food remains as well as human bones, but in each case the basic principle seems to have been the same. The newly built house was animated by offerings of living matter. The positions of these deposits were carefully chosen (Carlie 2004). They might be associated with the entrance, the roof supports, the fireplace or major thresholds within the building. Frequently deposits of this kind were made before the first posts were set in place. Although many of these were not sacrifices in the strict sense of the term, it is a process that links the temples of the Classical world with settlements in other parts of Europe.

Rather different deposits seem to have formed during the use of the house and, particularly, on its abandonment. These take many forms. The English evidence is particularly revealing here. The sites of disused buildings can include the burials of people and animals beneath the floors, metal artefacts that were put there when these structures were no longer occupied, and deposits of foodstuffs, pottery and agricultural tools. So much material accumulated on the abandonment of one Middle Bronze Age site that the position of a house was indicated by a low mound like a barrow (Barrett et al. 1991: 183). At Callestick in South-West England, where the house floor had been dug down into the subsoil, the resulting hollow was filled in and the outline of the demolished building was marked by a setting of quartz (Jones 1999).

Other practices left an equally obvious trace. In Northern Britain a series of stone-walled houses dating from the Later Bronze Age were closed down and again their positions were marked. At Gardom's Edge the first stage in this process was to block the doorway by placing a quern across the threshold. Subsequent activity resulted in the accumulation of large amounts of rubble across its entrance and along the course of the outer wall (Barnatt *et al.* 2002). This practice has been identified at a number of recently excavated sites, and seems to have involved the transformation of a ruined dwelling into a field monument similar in appearance to the ring cairns associated with the dead.

In some cases parts of the abandoned building were carefully retrieved for use in the structure that replaced it, but in others its remains were simply left to decay. In Neolithic Orkney, for instance, it seems as if the stone-lined hearths which were such a feature of the buildings at Barnhouse were recovered to be used again, as if to emphasise the continuity between each building and its successor (Richards 2004). In the Netherlands the waterlogged Iron Age settlements of the Assendelver Polders could have seen a similar process and in this case some of the structural timbers were recycled from one house to another. This process was so carefully controlled that it may have little to do with the parsimonious use of raw materials (Therkorn 1987a; Therkorn and Abbink 1987). It must have been important to maintain the links between the inhabitants of one building and those of the dwelling that took its place. That is also true in the Balkans where burnt daub from levelled Neolithic and Copper Age houses was carefully incorporated into the fabric of their successors (Chapman 1999).

There are also cases in which it is possible to compare the deposits created when a house was built with those associated with its use and abandonment. This line of enquiry has been pursued in South Scandinavia and can be illustrated by the Late Bronze Age settlement at Pryssgården in Eastern Sweden (Stålbom 1997; Borna-Ahlvist *et al.* 1998; Borna-Ahlvist 2002). It introduces another issue raised by my description of the Maori meeting house: the different conceptions of time embodied in these buildings.

At Pryssgården we may be able to distinguish between those deposits made on the construction of individual buildings and those created during, or even after, their period of use (Figure 2.7). This is made easier by the fact that each house was replaced in a different location. Foundation deposits are indicated by the material that had been set in post holes when the buildings were erected. The later deposits come from pits in their interior which would either have impeded circulation around the house or even removed the sockets for individual roof supports.

Four main categories of material were deposited in components of these houses: axes, querns, pottery and animal bones, although a figurine that is so

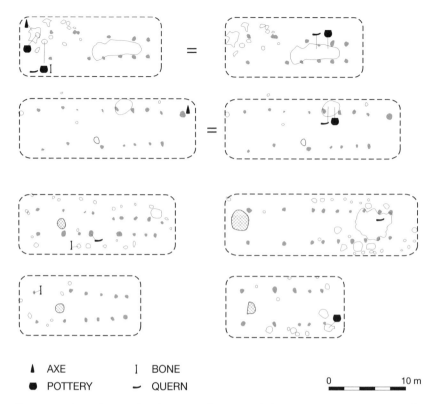

▲ AXE   I BONE

● POTTERY   ⌣ QUERN

0   10 m

Figure 2.7   Late Bronze Age houses and associated deposits at Pryssgården, Sweden. The post holes are shown in black, with the hearths hatched and the likely positions of the outer walls suggested by a dashed line. Internal pits are depicted in outline. The plans in the left-hand half of the figure show the positions of deposits associated with creation of the buildings and those on the right indicate deposits associated with their use or abandonment. The first two drawings show successive deposits within the same structures. Information from Borna-Ahlvist *et al.* (1998) and Borna-Ahlvist (2002).

far the only one of its kind in Sweden was also found in a pit. Although the sample is limited, it seems as if there were few distinctions between the kinds of material deposited towards either end of the use-life of these buildings. Ceramics were common to both these episodes, but axes tended to be connected with the genesis of the house. In my interpretation, quernstones were associated with both the creation and abandonment of these dwellings.

Despite the large scale of excavation, the sample is quite small but there seems to have been a contrast between the positions in which these separate deposits were made. All the houses were rectangular and were probably entered by doors located in the side walls. The buildings were generally aligned from south-east to north-west, but for the most part it was the north-western half of the dwellings that was associated with foundation deposits and the south-eastern section that contained the other groups of material. The different sections of the building may have been used in different ways and the closer spacing of the post holes towards one end suggests that this may have marked the position of a byre. The sequence of deposits also suggests that these parts of the house had different symbolic associations. As in the Maori meeting house, one area may have been associated with the future (the inception of the building) and the other with the past (its abandonment). It may be no accident that the deposits connected with the creation of the house were often close to the hearth.

I also mentioned the houses of the same period in Britain. The comparison between these groups of buildings is most revealing. With only a few exceptions, the insular structures were round rather than rectangular, and, after the Middle Bronze Age, there is little to suggest that they changed location in the same manner as their counterparts at Pryssgården. Rather, the positions of successive houses overlapped or were superimposed (Figure 2.8; Brück 1999b). The majority of these buildings were entered through a door on the south-east, which is the direction of the rising sun, although that axis may have been defined more exactly during the Iron Age (Oswald 1997). The passage of

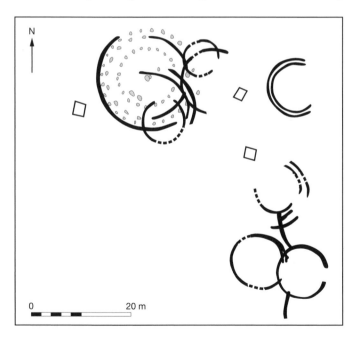

Figure 2.8 Outline plans of overlapping Late Bronze Age and Iron Age round houses at Bancroft, Southern England. The open squares represent the positions of wooden granaries. Information from Williams and Zeepfat (1994).

sunlight through the doorway divided the internal space in half, and this feature may be emphasised by the layout of the roof supports which often include an upright post directly opposite the centre of the porch. In the Iron Age there are some indications that the main density of internal deposits was in the left-hand half of these buildings and that the other segment was largely empty. Fitzpatrick (1997) has claimed that this distinctive arrangement matches the movement of the sun around the outer wall of the house: the southern half was associated with daylight, whilst the other part was where people slept at night. There is some merit in this argument, for many of the monuments of the same period, from simple enclosures to hill forts, conformed to a similar layout.

Although structured deposits have been identified inside Bronze and Iron Age round houses in Britain they do not show much variety. Again they consist mainly of pottery and animal bones, although human remains and items of metalwork are occasionally found. What seems more striking is that, after the Middle Bronze Age, it is difficult to distinguish between the material introduced when individual houses were built and that associated with their closure and abandonment. This contrasts with a clearer pattern in the Middle Bronze Age when houses in Southern England were usually replaced in a different position (Brück 1999b).

Perhaps these observations can be combined. If one of the roles of the round house was to emphasise the annual cycle of the seasons, it seems less surprising that these buildings should have been replaced in the same positions. Indeed, whether or not successive buildings were exactly superimposed, their sites seem to have overlapped. The associated deposits are connected with the spatial organisation of the building rather than its development over time. That is to say, they mark significant parts of the structure, such as the doorway or the hearth, but put less emphasis on the moments at which these houses were built or abandoned. Perhaps that is because their very organisation places so much emphasis on continuity from one year to the next. It seems as if that cyclical conception of time extended across the generations.

Regional differences were extremely important. As we have seen, a very different situation is found in Northern Europe, where distinctive offerings were associated with the creation and abandonment of Late Bronze Age and Early Iron Age houses. That is particularly striking as these buildings were rarely replaced in the same positions (Gerritsen 1999 and 2000). In this case it seems important that particular dwellings should have been abandoned whilst some of them were structurally sound, and that this event was marked by the provision of special deposits (Carlie 2004). They might be in a different location from the offerings associated with the creation of the building. If the round houses of Late Bronze Age and Iron Age Britain expressed a cyclical notion of time, their rectangular equivalents in Northern Europe suggest that human experience was punctuated by the creation and dissolution of the household. The contrasts are summed up in Table 2.1.

Table 2.1 The structure, development and associations of houses in Northern
Europe, compared with the evidence from Britain and Ireland

	Northern Europe	*Britain and Ireland*
Prevailing architectural style	Rectangular houses	Round houses
House offerings	Distinct deposits associated with the creation and abandonment of the houses	Uniform range of deposits associated with thresholds throughout the history of the house
Sequence over time	Successive houses in different locations	Successive houses often superimposed or overlapping
Prevailing conception of time	Linear, punctuated, generational?	Cyclical?

The dead house

That account might give the impression that individual houses were either
abandoned or were replaced in the same positions. In fact there are other
possibilities to consider.

Studies of European prehistory have often gone through two phases. For
understandable reasons, the investigation of artefacts had priority over that of
settlement sites, for until radiocarbon dating was well established it was
through typological studies that any chronology could be formed. Closed
groups of objects such as those found in graves or hoards were vital for this
purpose. It meant that the investigation of burial mounds often took place
before the exploration of the houses of the same period. That process has had
an unfortunate consequence, for it meant that some of the best preserved
domestic buildings were discovered during the excavation of barrows.

For example, one of the first high-status dwellings to be excavated in the
Hallstatt Iron Age of Southern Germany was found by chance beneath a round
barrow outside the Heuneburg (Schiek 1959). It seemed to have been closely
associated with the mound that occupied the same site. It was located directly
beneath the centre of that barrow and the later burial chamber was located over
the position of its principal room. The house had been enclosed by a rectangular
palisade, the corners of which were respected by the barrow ditch (Figure 2.9).
Moreover it had clearly been burnt down before the mound was built. There
is little likelihood that the juxtaposition of the two structures was coincidental.

What happens when the same kind of relationship occurs more widely?
Some of the first Early Bronze Age dwellings to be identified in South

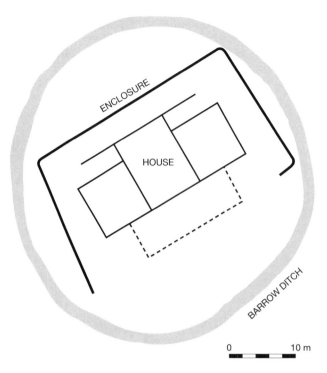

Figure 2.9 Rectangular house and associated enclosure buried beneath an Iron Age
burial mound outside the Heuneburg, South Germany. Note how the
barrow ditch respects the limits of the earlier enclosure. Information from
Schiek (1959).

Scandinavia were also discovered during barrow excavations. Only more
recently have similar structures been found in any number at other sites
(Rasmussen 1993). This has led to confusion. As long as burial mounds and
houses occurred together, it seemed quite likely that their creation was related
in a systematic manner: a house went out of use, perhaps because the occupants
had died, and then they would be commemorated by an earthen mound.
The case was harder to substantiate when domestic buildings were found
elsewhere.

In many ways the problem is similar to the discovery of plough marks underneath these monuments, and it raises the same questions. Was the relationship
entirely coincidental? Was it simply an artefact of preservation, or should it
be taken more seriously? Rasmussen (1993) has estimated that in Denmark
almost half the well-recorded burial mounds of the Early Bronze Age were
built within the settled landscape, so that the juxtaposition of domestic and
funerary remains is not enough to suggest a significant relationship between
them. Something more is required.

In my discussion of 'ritual ploughing' I argued that several additional factors had to be taken into account. In a few instances, the plough marks were confined to the precise area where the mound was to be built. There were other cases in which ploughing extended to the limits of an existing monument before it was enlarged, even though this would have been difficult to achieve. Still more important, there were many instances in which the graves underneath those mounds followed the same alignment as the plough furrows. Is it possible to take a similar approach to the remains of houses?

One point is worth making at the outset. The buildings preserved beneath older round barrows are not quite like those excavated in other contexts, but this is where the evidence may be influenced by differential preservation. The posts of the outer wall may not have been set as deeply in the ground as those supporting the roof, and the same may apply to some of the internal subdivisions. It is hardly surprising that such details are less often represented in the houses found at other sites. Similarly, there are cases in which the buildings themselves had been built in conformity with areas of cultivated land, so that the long axes of these structures may follow the same orientation as the plough marks. Alternatively, the positions of abandoned buildings might have been cultivated but may well have constrained the direction of the furrows.

Considerations of size and orientation are important too. Were individual houses the same size as the barrows that were built on top of them, so that the long axis of the building established the diameter of the mound? Were the positions of the graves influenced by the organisation of the older building, and did their axis follow the same alignment as the house? It seems possible that other features may have influenced the configuration of the later monument. For instance, were the positions of the burials related to the entrance of an older dwelling? Only if a number of relationships of this kind can be demonstrated is it reasonable to envisage a significant relationship between the successive structures.

It follows that the construction of barrows on the sites of domestic buildings may not have been significant in itself. The relationship has to be investigated one example at a time. For example, in one case the remains of a series of Late Neolithic houses were preserved beneath a round barrow dating from the Early Bronze Age (Asingh 1987). The layout of these buildings did not conform particularly closely to that of the burial mound which also overlay a series of ard marks. On closer examination, those furrows cut across the remains of the buildings but took no account of their orientation. Thus a substantial period of time may have elapsed between the two sets of structures, and in the circumstances the relationship between the houses and the barrow could have been fortuitous.

Another interesting case was at Hyllerup where a multi-period mound was built over the site of another domestic building (Pedersen 1986). Again their positions did not quite coincide, with the result that the grave beneath the

59

centre of the barrow was rather awkwardly placed in relation to the older house. But this example is more ambiguous. Again the position of the dwelling had been ploughed before the barrow was built, and the sequence is confirmed because the spoil excavated from the central grave buried a post hole of the building. On the other hand, the plough furrows followed the long axis of the abandoned house. Its porch was laid out at a slight angle to the side wall. As a result, its entrance was actually aligned on the place where the grave would be located. Still more important, that building had been destroyed by fire.

In this case the evidence is less clear-cut. In two other instances, it is hard to avoid the conclusion that the juxtaposition of a round barrow and a house was carefully contrived. One of these sites has already featured in the discussion of 'ritual ploughing' in Chapter 1.

At Handwitt, the position of the house was beneath the centre of the later barrow but extended beyond its limits on one side (Figure 1.10; Aner and Kersten 1978: 34). The layout of the mound seems to indicate an awareness of its existence. One edge of the barrow followed the end wall of the long house, whilst on the other side its perimeter followed the course of a partition within the older building. Radiocarbon dates associated with the house and the central grave suggest that the entire sequence took place over a short period of time. There are two additional clues to the significance of this relationship. The burial was laid out at right angles to the long axis of the house and, like those at other sites, it followed the same alignment as a series of plough furrows. Still more important, it was located beside the south door of the building and its long axis reflected that of the entrance.

A single instance is rarely convincing in itself. For that reason it is useful that a very similar sequence has been observed at another Bronze Age round barrow, Trappendal. In this case the barrow selected the entire extent of an earlier long house, but that did not happen at once, for the mound was enlarged on three separate occasions (Boysen and Andersen 1983). The perimeter of the completed monument coincided almost exactly with the end walls of the building (Figure 2.10). In this case the central grave beneath the barrow was located in the middle of the house and followed its long axis. Two other graves adopted the same alignment as its end wall, and one of these was positioned within the limits of the structure. Again the principal burial was just inside the southern entrance to the house. There may be some evidence of an even closer relationship between these successive structures, for the building had contained a large pit, possibly some kind of cellar. This was sealed by charcoal when the structure was burnt down, and was recut on exactly the same axis by the principal grave. Again the relationship between these different elements seems so close that it is likely to have been significant.

To sum up, these relationships concern a number of different elements but the connections between them amount to more than the sum of the separate parts. The size and location of some of these barrows may have been influenced by the positions of older buildings, and the same applies to the locations and

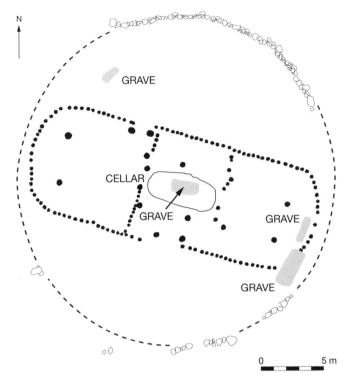

Figure 2.10 Timber long house buried beneath a Bronze Age round barrow at Trappendal, Denmark. Note how the perimeter of the barrow respects both ends of the building and how two of the graves are aligned with its east wall. A third is placed inside the main doorway and cuts into the remains of an earlier cellar. Information from Boysen and Andersen (1983).

orientations of the graves. These may either have been influenced by the layout of the building or by the axis of the plough furrows that were still visible in the surface. Even where the site of a levelled building was ploughed, a memory may have survived of its original configuration. The location of a grave may also be related to the orientation of the doorway in the south wall of the building. It may be more than a coincidence that two of these houses had burnt down, for this is not a common feature on other excavated sites.

Of course it is possible to raise objections to most of these arguments, but to do so overlooks an important point. There is no reason why burial mounds should have been built on the sites of older settlements, whether these are represented by ard marks, house foundations or by scatters of artefacts. Their juxtaposition did not come about by chance. However we interpret some of these specific relationships, there was obviously an interplay between daily life and mound building that was important in Bronze Age society. Again it would be quite wrong to make a dogmatic distinction between the beliefs of pre-historic peoples and their occupation of the land. As Rasmussen says in her discussion of the Danish evidence, 'the erection of barrows must be considered without the traditional distinction between ritual and subsistence activities' (1993: 171).

In those examples rectangular buildings were replaced by circular mounds. There are other cases in which the very form of the house was perpetuated by the monument that took its place. It is a familiar argument that the Linear-bandkeramik long house provided the source of inspiration for long barrows and long cairns (Bradley 2001a), but recent work in Northern and Western France suggests that a similar relationship once existed between round houses and some of the megalithic monuments known as passage graves (Laporte *et al.* 2004). This is not a new idea, but it is only recently that much field evidence has come to light. In fact it seems as if a tradition of circular domes-tic buildings may have existed along the Atlantic coastline during the Late Mesolithic period. It probably extended into the Iberian Peninsula. It seems as if the same kinds of building were constructed during the Early Neolithic, especially at settlements containing pottery with links to the West Mediterranean. At the same time, long houses were constructed on sites with a stronger connection to the Linearbandkeramik. For a while these two kinds of buildings seem to have co-existed, just as the first monuments to the dead show a mixture of rectangular and circular forms (Figure 2.11).

There are still stronger links between houses and mortuary monuments in Neolithic Denmark, but these have not been easy to interpret, for the long barrows and long cairns seem to be based on a domestic prototype that was no longer built. The houses that were occupied during the same period were less substantial structures, and this has led to confusion. The situation is illustrated by two excavated monuments at Stengade (Skaarup 1975).

These were investigated at a time when it was widely accepted that Neolithic settlements in South Scandinavia contained enormous long houses, not unlike those of the Linearbandkeramik many years before. The obvious examples of this type were two remarkable structures at Barkaer (Liversage 1992). The site at Stengade was rather similar. Again it contained a pair of elongated buildings, but there was a megalithic tomb nearby. Each of the principal monuments was interpreted as the remains of a long house, and this idea was supported by an extensive domestic assemblage, including the remains of cereals.

More recent work has questioned the excavator's interpretation, suggesting instead that these were the sites of two long barrows. The same interpretation has been applied to Barkaer. This revision raises problems. If such structures really were mortuary monuments, it seems likely that their characteristic form referred to the dwellings of an earlier time. Instead of being the remains of an actual settlement, Stengade would have to be interpreted as a more specialised site in which a series of mortuary monuments recalled the dwellings of the

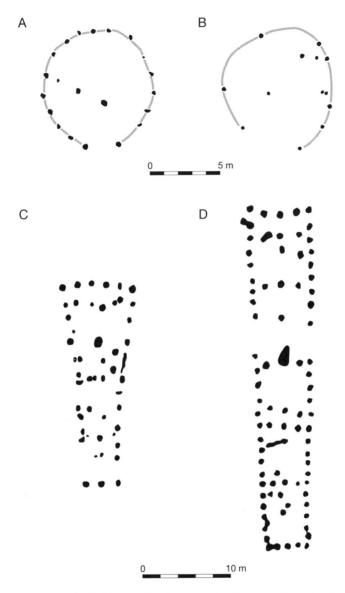

Figure 2.11 Early Neolithic round and rectangular houses at four sites in Northern and Western France. A: Herblay; B: Les Ouchettes; C: Le Haut-Mée; D: Poses. Information from Laporte *et al.* (2004).

past. They were not the homes of the living, as the excavator had claimed, but the houses of the dead. That view has been promoted by Madsen (1979) who has excavated a series of long mounds in Denmark.

Although Madsen has rejected Skaarup's interpretation of Stengade as a settlement, the new orthodoxy can hardly explain why the site contained an extensive collection of domestic artefacts. The excavation report suggests another possibility. Although there may once have been burials there, a number of the features associated with one and possibly both of the long mounds seem to define smaller oval or rectangular structures (Figure 2.12). These would not have made much sense at the time of excavation, but more recent work in Denmark and Sweden suggests that they represent the ground plans of wooden buildings. They are not the massive long houses that had once been postulated, but much simpler structures of a kind which has been excavated in growing numbers during recent years. Similar features were recognised underneath the long barrow studied by Madsen (1979) at Bigholm, but at first they seemed more likely to be specialised constructions connected with the burials on the site, for one of them enclosed a grave. Now it appears that these were domestic dwellings.

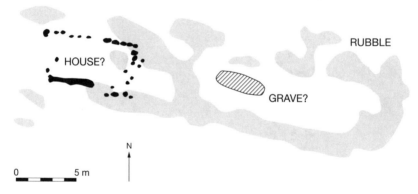

Figure 2.12　Outline plan of a Neolithic long cairn at Stengade, Denmark, high-lighting the possible positions of a grave and an earlier house. Information from Skaarup (1975).

If this interpretation is correct, Stengade can be reinstated as a settlement with houses – but houses very different from those originally postulated by the excavator. Moreover, these structures seem to have been replaced by two long barrows that are among the first monuments in Scandinavia. The implication is that such tombs may have reproduced the features of domestic dwellings on a massive scale. Some of the early long mounds in Denmark overlie older settlements and could even have been built on the sites of domestic buildings, but they present a distorted image of the everyday world because they are so large. How can this be explained?

The big house

DeBoer (1997) has studied a series of prehistoric ceremonial centres in the New World, whose locations extend from South America to the United States. They are also distributed across a considerable period of time, from prehistory to the present day. The common element, he suggests, is that all of them can be characterised as 'big houses'. They are massively enlarged versions of domestic prototypes that could be found within the same regions. Rather than the homes occupied by particular groups of people, they are conceived in metaphorical terms as those of entire communities.

There are two ways in which that might happen. The first is where particular buildings were constructed on a massive scale but maintained the same organisation of space as the structures on which they were modelled. The feasting halls at Gamla Uppsala might be an example of this process. The second is the situation described in the Neolithic period where the form of a domestic building provides the inspiration for a larger field monument. This increases its dimensions, but its proportions remain close enough to those of the original for the relationship to be understood. Even so, it was enlarged to such an extent that it is different in kind from its prototype. An earthwork mound cannot perform the same functions as a roofed building. My discussion will consider each of these models.

One of the curious features of the timber buildings in this group is how closely they resemble one another, even though they were constructed in different parts of Europe and at different times. It is worth comparing four of these structures directly (Figure 2.13): Balbridie in North-East Scotland (Fairweather and Ralston 1993), Antran in Poitou (Pautreau 1988 and 1994), Verberie in the Aisne Valley (Blanchet et al. 1983) and Acy-Romance in the Ardennes (Lambot 1989). Their ages vary considerably. Balbridie dates from the Neolithic period and Antran from the Copper Age, the building at Acy-Romance is Late Bronze Age, whilst that at Verberie was built during the Iron Age.

This was not apparent from the outset. Balbridie, for example, was originally excavated on the premise that it dated from the later first millennium AD. This hypothesis was based on its resemblance to the structures found on high-status settlements of that date (N. Reynolds 1978). The great timber building at Antran was found on a site with a considerable range of burials dating from the Later Bronze and Iron Ages and so it was initially thought to belong to the same period as those graves (Pautreau 1994). Like Balbridie, its origin was first established by radiocarbon. Until then it had been compared with the excavated structure at Acy-Romance.

Structural comparisons were important, too. When the great Iron Age building at Verberie was first identified it was difficult to work out how it might have been built and so the excavators compared it directly with the site at Balbridie. In the same way, Antran was originally assigned to the late

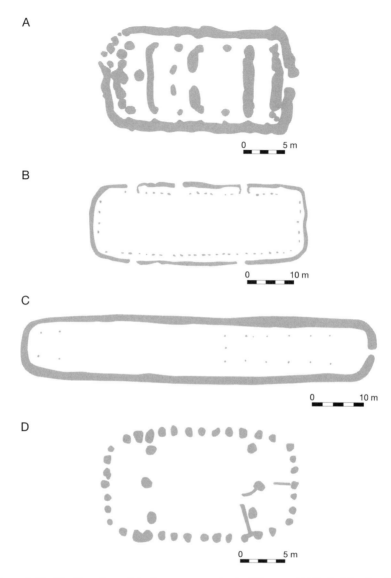

Figure 2.13 Outline plans of the large rectangular buildings at (A) Balbridie, Scotland, (B) Antran, Western France, (C) Acy-Romance, Northern France and (D) Verberie, Northern France. These structures range in date from the Neolithic to the Iron Age. Information from Fairweather and Ralston (1993), Pautreau (1988 and 1994), Lambot (1989) and Blanchet *et al.* (1983).

prehistoric period because it seemed to share the architectural features of the largest building at Acy-Romance. The early date of Balbridie was regarded as a problem because the structure was so similar to the timber hall at Doon Hill, Dunbar, which was ascribed to the Early Medieval period (N. Reynolds 1978). There were even suggestions that the latter site might really be of prehistoric origin.

These buildings extend widely across time and space, but they do have certain features in common: features that can also be identified at other prehistoric sites. All four are rectangular or sub-oval structures that were built on such a large scale that it may have been difficult to roof them. That accounts for the comparisons that were made between Verberie and Balbridie, both of which would have involved sophisticated building techniques if such large spaces were to be spanned. With the exception of Balbridie, they lack internal subdivisions, so that the interior may have been one continuous expanse. At the same time, some of these buildings appear in comparative isolation. Balbridie is apparently some distance away from any features of the same date, and the same may be true of Verberie. The other two sites are associated with mortuary monuments, but they are of various ages and need not be contemporary with these buildings.

It would be wrong to suppose that all 'big houses' would have been used in the same ways. The building at Verberie was found together with a series of Late Iron Age pits containing the residues of food consumption, and the timber structure at Balbridie was also associated with fine pottery and with an unusual amount of burnt grain. The great timber enclosure at Acy-Romance is interpreted as a cult building rather than a mortuary monument, yet a recently discovered building in North-West France may have a different interpretation.

At Pléchâtel-La Hersonnais excavation has revealed four enormous rectangular timber buildings, the biggest of which was 102 metres long (Figure 2.14; Tinevez 2002). These seem to have been built in succession, and three of them were enclosed by palisades. They date from between 2800 and 2500 BC. Where enough evidence survived, they seem to have had two entrances: one at the eastern end and the other providing access through the side wall towards the opposite limit of the structure. The door through the end of the building was sometimes emphasised by a porch. In two instances the area in between the enclosure and the main entrance was bounded by a fence which created a kind of forecourt.

The buildings were not symmetrically disposed within these enclosures. Rather, the boundary adopted a D-shaped ground plan, with its straight section following the long axis of the principal structure, which was between twelve and fifteen metres away. On the opposite side of the enclosure the distance could increase to between thirty and fifty metres. The side entrances provided access into the larger internal space.

The three well-preserved buildings had all been divided into a series of separate rooms. As we have seen, the main entrance was at one end, but there

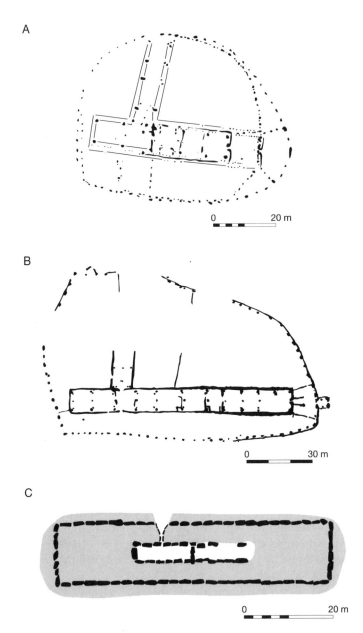

Figure 2.14 A and B: Two Copper Age palisaded enclosures and associated buildings at Pléchâtel-La Hersonnais, North-West France, compared with the plan of a megalithic tomb (C) at Kerlescan. Information from Tinevez (2002) and L'Helgouac'h (1965).

was a second doorway through the side wall towards its opposite extremity. The longest and best-preserved structure contained eleven compartments. A second, smaller example had about eight but had been built in stages. In each case a separate 'wing' led from the main range at right angles and communicated with an entrance in the palisaded enclosure. There is nothing to indicate that this wing had been subdivided and it may have provided access to the main part of the building. In one case it could be shown that it was a secondary addition.

The structures at Pléchâtel-La Hersonnais are very much larger than the houses known from the settlements of the same period, although other exceptionally large timber buildings are found in the Copper Age in Western France, including the example already discussed at Antran. The excavator of Pléchâtel-La Hersonnais interprets the site entirely in functional terms:

> Domestic use of these buildings may be suggested by certain criteria: the internal organisation of [the two largest] buildings, the peripheral enclosures and their internal subdivisions suitable for various activities such as stock breeding and agriculture. [Inside these buildings were] large storage vessels side by side with smaller ones. . . . The size and imposing architecture of these structures points to ostentation, the sign of a social structure developed by a large population well-adapted to its environment.
>
> (Tinevez 2002: 49)

That does not account for other features. Tinevez refers to the pottery associated with those buildings, but elsewhere he notes that flint tools were exceptionally uncommon in the excavation. Virtually all the lithic artefacts had been used to excavate the bedding trenches for the buildings and enclosures and had been recycled as packing stones. He also notes that the largest of these buildings had been burnt down: a feature which seems to characterise an exceptionally high proportion of the structures considered in this chapter.

He comments that 'this type of monumental architecture is unusual in the region. It contrasts strongly with our knowledge of the settlements of this period, which usually consist of smaller structures' (Tinevez 2002: 49), but perhaps this site seems so exceptional because he fails to make a more revealing comparison. Surely the closest analogy to the enclosures and buildings at Pléchâtel-La Hersonnais does not come from settlement sites at all, but from the megalithic tombs that were being built during the same period. The long rectangular buildings with an entrance at one end and a sequence of small compartments are of rather the same form as the stone structures known as *allées couvertes* (L'Helgouac'h 1965: chapters 12 and 13). These are recorded in some numbers in Brittany, although no examples are known close to this particular site. In the same way, at least two of the buildings at Pléchâtel-La Hersonnais were entered by a corridor at right angles to the main range of rooms. This led directly to an entrance in the outer palisade. Surely this is the same idea as the passage which communicates with the burial chamber of a number of megalithic tombs in Western France, and again they resemble one another in chronology and ground plan. The comparison even extends to the way in which the wings leading into these timber buildings were displaced towards one end of the side wall. Moreover the sub-oval palisades enclosing three of the four successive 'houses' on this site also have much the same outline as the mounds or cairns that cover similar features. If that is right, then, far from being an ordinary settlement site, this was a series of specialised structures rendered above ground in timber where they might otherwise be built out of stone and concealed beneath an earthwork.

In fact Pléchâtel-La Hersonnais presents some of the same problems as the Danish site at Stengade which I considered earlier in this chapter. Were the Breton tombs with which it compares in plan a rendering in stone of a domestic building, of which this is clearest example? Or were these timber constructions a form of ceremonial architecture, which could be represented in either material according to local circumstances? In that case it becomes all the more important to discover whether they might represent enlarged versions of a simpler prototype found at domestic sites. That was one possibility in South Scandinavia, but in the French example there is not enough evidence to take this argument further. Perhaps more information will come to light as other 'great houses' of this date are excavated in Atlantic France.

Some of the same issues arise with the Bronze Age 'cult houses' of Scandinavia (Victor 2002). These raise several problems, for individual examples can be associated with settlements or burial sites. At the same time, the smaller buildings are of approximately the same size as the domestic dwellings of the same period and adopt a similar ground plan, so not all of these can be described as 'big houses'. They were often built in a distinctive manner. Their walls were of stone rather than timber and the foundations of these structures were particularly massive (Figure 2.15). They incorporated large quantities of burnt material and yet food remains are largely absent. Some structures lacked an obvious entrance and again it is not clear whether they had been roofed.

Certain sites do stand out because of their unusual length and the proximity of major burial monuments: a well-known example is found close to the rich burial at Kivik in Southern Sweden (L. Larsson 1993). Otherwise the argument that they were specialised developments of a domestic prototype must be based on different features. Victor (2002) has recently pointed out that 'cult houses' may resemble ordinary dwellings in plan but they adopt a quite different orientation. She suggests that they may have acted as mortuary houses, for their distinctive layout echoes that of domestic buildings but they were built of stone like burial cairns.

Excavation supplies further details of these structures. They do not seem to be associated with the range of artefacts associated with ordinary houses;

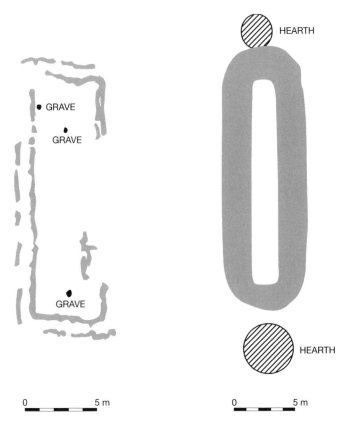

Figure 2.15 Outline plans of the Bronze Age cult houses at Sandergergård, Denmark
(left), and Hågahögen, Sweden (right). Information from Kaul (1987) and
Victor (2002).

although querns are often found, these are also associated with burials. A recent
excavation close to the great round barrow of Hågahögen in Sweden established that there were unusually low levels of phosphate inside one of these
buildings (Victor 2002: 195). Another example at Sandergergård in Denmark
supplies additional information (Kaul 1987). Again this took the form of
a rectangular structure defined by a considerable stone wall. It was located
within a short distance of a Late Bronze Age settlement but included an
unusual range of contents. Within the building were three urned cremations
and a number of crucibles and moulds from metalworking, but, in contrast to
a normal domestic assemblage, there were no flint artefacts on the site. Beyond
the southern end of the building were two standing stones and, in between
them, four decorated slabs. Each depicts the human hand, a motif that is widely
distributed in Bronze Age rock art.

71

Rather similar issues are raised by work in the Netherlands, Here it is possible to compare a series of mortuary monuments of the Late Bronze Age and Iron Age periods with the form of the domestic buildings on which they were based. In this case there is the added advantage that both can occur on the same sites.

The monuments in question are known as long-beds, and that name is used here in preference to the alternative term 'long barrow', which could lead to confusion with the Neolithic monuments mentioned earlier (Roymans and Kortelag 1999). These structures are elongated parallel-sided enclosures whose chronology extends from the Late Bronze Age into the Early Iron Age (Figure 2.16)

Long-beds form part of larger cemeteries in which the dominant rite was cremation and may be accompanied by a variety of other features, including round barrows and flat graves. They account for roughly 10 per cent of the monuments in any one complex. Some of the largest belong to the earliest phases in particular cemeteries, and they enclose a number of adult burials, mainly, but not exclusively, those of men. The oldest examples, which occur in the Northern Netherlands and North-West Germany, also contain rectangular post settings and may include both inhumations and cremations. Some of these earthworks are associated with quantities of pottery which is interpreted as evidence of feasting.

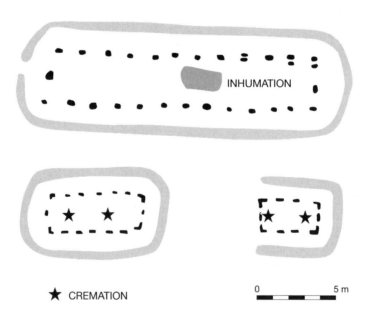

Figure 2.16 Outline plans of Late Bronze Age and Early Iron Age long-beds in Northern Europe, showing the positions of the associated burials. Information from Roymans and Kortelag (1999).

The post settings inside these earthworks are generally between six and twenty metres long and had an entrance at one end. It is not clear whether they had been roofed. In the Netherlands they are described as mortuary monuments because they enclose the sites of graves, but comparable structures in North-East France have been interpreted as cult buildings. Among the most notable of these is the structure already discussed at Acy-Romance.

Roymans and Kortelag have suggested that these monuments are transformations of the domestic buildings of the same period:

> The interpretation of the long graves can be taken further if we see them as a symbol for a house, which in its turn is a metaphor for the basic family-unit. In the world of the living, the house formed the domicile of each family and was the symbol of the social position of a family head. After the death of a family-head, he was buried in his 'house', thus providing for continuity between the world of the living and the dead. The hypothesis that long-beds were associated with houses is based on the elongated form of the earthen grave monuments, which reminds us of the long house of the North-West European plain.
>
> (1999: 49)

There are several reasons for accepting their argument. This particular way of commemorating the household seems to have been adopted during the period when domestic buildings were abandoned and relocated every generation, and it had lapsed by the time that this practice came to an end. The early timber settings inside long-beds are of roughly the size and proportions of the larger long houses of the same date and their orientations seem to be rather similar (although this can also apply to other kinds of mortuary monuments on the same sites). In some cases they were aligned with the local relief or followed the long axis of the cemetery, but at the extensively excavated site of Someren-Waterdael in the Netherlands this explanation may not be justified. Here it is possible to relate the Iron Age cemetery to the houses of the same period (Roymans and Kortelag 1999: fig. 3). It is interesting that, although the long-beds were located well away from the dwellings of the same period, both sets of features had the same alignment. They were obviously related to one another.

So far I have limited this discussion to rectangular buildings. Do similar arguments apply to the round house? Here it is worth recalling an example considered in Chapter 1. Much of the difficulty of interpreting the henge monument at Durrington Walls in Southern England arose because there were few criteria for distinguishing between an assemblage of domestic artefacts and the material deposited at a ceremonial centre. But one characteristic was the enormous scale on which the timber circles within this enclosure had been built (Wainwright and Longworth 1971). Like the earthwork that surrounded them, these were massive undertakings, and yet they are not altogether different from other features of the same period (Figure 2.17). They include free-standing timber settings like those on Machrie Moor (Haggarty 1991) and the structures associated with other henges and palisaded enclosures in Britain. The essential elements are a circular perimeter with a well-defined entrance, and an internal setting of uprights, normally arranged in a square. Some of these buildings are so large that again it may have been difficult to roof them. Variants of this scheme can be found, but that is less important than identifying their original prototypes which seem to be the insubstantial dwellings of the Late Neolithic period. The small wooden buildings at Trelystan (Britnell 1982) show the same organisation of space as these massive structures. So do a number of stone-built houses. In some cases the central post setting was replaced by a hearth, bounded by a square setting of slabs, but even then the basic principle was the same. There was a continuum among Late Neolithic structures from small round houses to the enormous timber settings found inside henges and similar enclosures. The fact that some of the largest examples were replaced by rings of upright stones suggests that they assumed a specialised role, as does the architecture of Stonehenge which represents the features of a timber circle in a more durable material (Gibson 1998). If these connections are any more than a coincidence – and they involve virtually the entire sample of domestic buildings of this period – it suggests that the metaphor of the 'big house' may be relevant again here. Indeed, it may be no

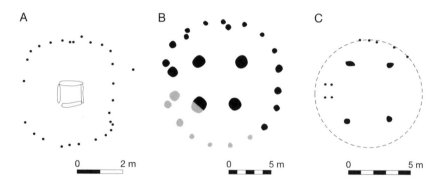

Figure 2.17 Late Neolithic timber buildings at (A) Trelystan, Wales, (B) Durrington Walls, Southern England and (C) Woodcutts, Southern England, showing how structures of very different sizes conform to the same ordering of space. The example at Trelystan forms part of a settlement, whilst that at Durrington Walls is interpreted as a public building and is located inside a massive henge monument. The building at Woodcutts is one of a pair found just outside two small henges of similar date. Information from Britnell (1982), Wainwright and Longworth (1971) and Green (2000).

accident that the complex deposits of artefacts and animal bones associated with some of these monuments are themselves more elaborate versions of those found on settlement sites.

Earlier in this section I commented that some of the massive rectangular buildings erected in prehistoric Europe looked so similar to one another that they had been difficult to date. A number of plausible comparisons had proved to be entirely misleading. Something similar may have happened in Ireland, where a group of circular monuments, looking very like henges, was constructed at the end of the first millennium BC. In this case there are some indications of how they might be understood.

A number of the 'royal sites' of the Iron Age have been identified on the basis of literary evidence, although these sources relate to a period long after these structures had been built. Among the most famous of these is Navan Fort, the legendary capital of Ulster (Waterman 1997). On excavation, these monuments have two striking characteristics. Like Neolithic henges, they are defined by an external bank and an internal ditch, and they also resemble those structures because they contain enormous timber circles. In the circumstances it has been tempting to suggest direct links between them and to postulate a continuous tradition of henge building extending over two thousand years.

It is certainly true that monuments with some of the attributes of these 'royal sites' existed during the later part of the Bronze Age, just as the Iron Age earthworks could be created at sites with the remains of much older monuments, but there is a danger of taking these connections too far (Newman 1998). Unlike their British counterparts, the Neolithic henges in Ireland rarely had internal ditches. Nor does it seem likely that Neolithic ceremonial centres were reused in their original form. In fact, the putative henge at Navan dates from the first century BC (Waterman 1997).

The timber circles inside these enclosures raise similar problems, for again they have been compared with the buildings of the Late Neolithic. This is quite unnecessary, and, if more distant comparisons are required, they are better made with the structures found within the Late Bronze Age ringworks of Eastern England, some of which were of comparable size (Needham and Ambers 1994). It seems more likely, however, that these are simply enlarged versions of the houses of the same period in Ireland. Indeed, the excavator of Navan Fort assumed that the first timber buildings on the site were ordinary dwellings. In his opinion only the later, more elaborate structures played a specialised role (Waterman 1997).

Two areas were excavated inside the principal enclosure at Navan and both revealed traces of timber buildings of a rather similar form. Each had been enclosed by a small circular earthwork. These structures consisted of two conjoined rings of uprights, one of them significantly larger than the other. Unlike the Neolithic buildings with which they have sometimes been compared, the timbers were set in continuous trenches rather than individual post holes. This type of construction was first built on the site during the Late Bronze Age or

Early Iron Age, but it may have a lengthy history, for almost exactly the same arrangement is evidenced at settlements of the first millennium AD (Edwards 1990: chapters 2 and 3).

The most complex sequence comes from the excavation of Navan Site B, where a long succession of circular trench-built structures, surrounded by a ring of posts, was finally replaced by a massive set of concentric timber circles, no less than forty metres in diameter (Figure 2.18). There was a huge upright at its centre. It is this building that has compared with those inside English henges. It had been encased within an enormous cairn and then burnt down.

Two observations are important here. Any links with henge monuments are significantly weakened because it is only the latest post setting at Navan that resembles the timber circles found on those sites. The earlier structures took a quite different form and are more like the buildings found at other royal centres in Ireland. Second, the excavator of Navan Fort considered that the site had originally been that of a settlement associated with a number of circular houses (Waterman 1997). It is possible to question this interpretation, but the fact remains that the massive structure that was eventually built on the site replaces a series of much simpler buildings. Surely this is another case in which a ceremonial centre was regarded as the 'house' of the entire community: an interpretation that is compatible with its role in later literary sources.

That prompts a final observation. Not only was the sequence at Navan Fort characterised by a series of conjoined circular buildings, the earthworks on the site take a similar form. Inside the bank and ditch which define its outer limits are a ditched enclosure and a mound, built side by side. The same arrangement is found at other royal sites, including Tara (Newman 1997). It seems as if the layout of the entire complex exhibits the same organisation of space as the separate buildings within it. Could it be that the hill itself was conceived as one great house?

Such connections are not peculiar to the regions with a tradition of circular buildings. Another example comes from the Northern Netherlands. Here Waterbolk (1977) has identified a distinctive group of square or rectangular enclosures whose dates extend between about 350 BC and AD 100. They are defined by ditches or fences, and two of them are bounded by several palisades. They were built in places that had already experienced at least one phase of open settlement, defined by the presence of granaries and occasional long houses. At Rhee, the construction of the first enclosures also followed a period in which the site had been occupied by burial mounds and possibly shrines. At least one of the sites saw a renewed phase of domestic activity after the enclosure had gone out of use.

The excavated material from these enclosures is the same as that found in the settlements of the period, but the associated buildings have an unusual character. In contrast to those in use before the enclosures were built, they did not include any houses 'with clearly separate living and stable parts' (Waterbolk

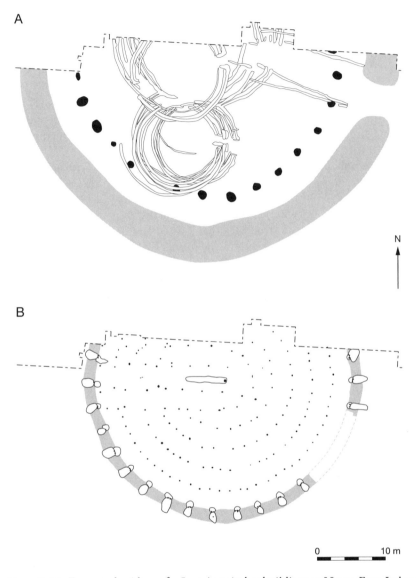

Figure 2.18 Excavated evidence for Iron Age timber buildings at Navan Fort, Ireland. The upper drawing (A) shows the original form of the monument, with a sequence of conjoined circular structures approached from the entrance of a circular earthwork enclosure. In a second phase (B), the buildings were replaced by series of concentric post circles. These were buried beneath a massive circular mound. Information from Waterman (1997).

1977: 168). There were large rectangular structures that Waterbolk has interpreted as barns, and all the enclosures contained raised storehouses or granaries. In his view these sites possessed an exceptional character, and he compared them with two groups of monuments which I considered briefly in Chapter 1, the hill forts of Southern England, and the Viereckschanzen of Central Europe. The first comparison was tempting because these hill forts contain so many storage structures, and the second because the Dutch enclosures were either square or rectangular and in one case had been built on the same site as a cemetery. Neither parallel is particularly convincing, and I would like to suggest yet another context.

As Waterbolk pointed out, these enclosures were associated with occupation debris and yet none of the domestic dwellings belonged to the same phase as these monuments. On the other hand, the large barns that he identified inside one of the enclosures at Zeijen did contain hearths. Is it possible that these were really halls, like the structures that I discussed in the first part of this chapter? At the same time, a second enclosure at Zeijen had a most unusual ground plan (Figure 2.19). It was approximately rectangular and had been defined by as many as seven palisades. It was entered by two gateways in its longest side. Towards either limit of the enclosed area there were groups of timber buildings, but the structures within them were of different sizes from one another. Nowhere was there any sign of a house. In some ways this curious arrangement epitomises the unusual nature of these sites, but in one respect it has a more individual character. I have already suggested that the earthworks at Navan and Tara were organised according to the same design as the post settings inside them. Could it be that the rectangular enclosure at Zeijen was laid out on a similar principle to a long house, so that once again it was considered as the 'dwelling place' of an entire community? That interpretation is illustrated in Figure 2.19.

Summary: the consecration of the house

'The Consecration of the House' is the title of a piece of music by Beethoven, but it is appropriate to use it here because so many of the activities associated with prehistoric dwellings seem to have assumed a special significance. This chapter has considered some of the possibilities. The first section brought together evidence from three different disciplines – Medieval archaeology, Classical archaeology and social anthropology – to suggest how the dwellings of particular people or groups in society could take on additional functions in public ceremony. That was especially obvious with the feasting halls at Gamla Uppsala, but it was also apparent from the ways in which Iron Age buildings in Greece and Maori meeting houses had changed their character over time.

Two particular features of the New Zealand meeting house were especially revealing and they were compared with some of the characteristics of prehistoric buildings in Europe. These had biographies of their own, rather like living

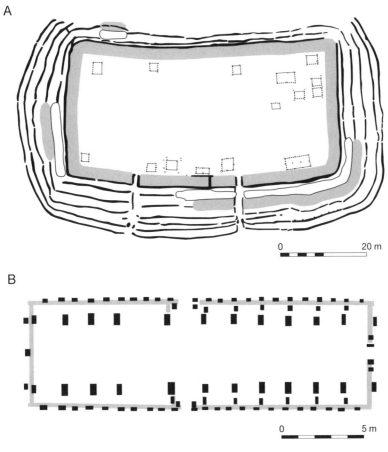

Figure 2.19 Iron Age enclosure at Zeijen and a long house at Fochteloo, Northern Netherlands. Both seem to exhibit the same organisation of space. Information from Waterbolk (1977 and 1995).

creatures, and the ways in which they were used, and the offerings that were deposited there, may have reflected the history of the household and marked the passing of time. In the course of this discussion I noted an important contrast between the circular houses found in the British Isles and the rectangular buildings that are so characteristic of Northern Europe. That distinction was mirrored by important differences in the ways in which they developed: a point that is considered again in Chapter 6.

The abandonment of houses may be marked by the deposition of cultural material, but in some cases it was commemorated in a much more obvious manner. That may have happened because one of the inhabitants had died. In such cases the house could be burnt down and replaced on another site.

79

Sometimes human remains were placed amidst the ashes and, on other occasions, the entire structure might be covered by a burial mound. This seems to have happened quite widely, but the discussion paid most attention to the well-preserved evidence from Scandinavia. Another course was to commemorate the abandoned house by reproducing some of its features in a more durable medium, and this may account for the similarities between the forms of Neolithic dwellings and the configuration of long mounds and passage graves.

Lastly, this chapter considered two other ways of registering the significance of the house. First, the forms of individual buildings might be reproduced on a massively enlarged scale. This seems to have happened across much of Europe where large rectangular buildings, not unlike later feasting halls, were constructed in a variety of different periods, from the Neolithic to the Iron Age. A clear illustration of this principle came from Late Bronze and Early Iron Age cemeteries in the Netherlands. The same idea led to the development of outsize circular buildings too, and these were illustrated by the henge monuments of Neolithic Britain and the royal sites of the Irish Iron Age. Not only were round houses reproduced on an extraordinary scale, the same prototype seemed to underlie the form of some major earthworks of the same period. Again those were circular structures, but the discussion ended by suggesting that a similar principle might be extended to a group of rectangular enclosures in the Iron Age of Northern Europe. In every one of these cases the features of the domestic dwelling were imbued with a heightened significance.

But such houses, and the buildings around them, also provided the framework for a set of everyday activities that archaeologists all too often take for granted. Is it possible that these underwent a similar transformation? Chapter 3 investigates that question.

3

A DUTY OF CARE

How everyday activities assumed
a special significance

The rite of spring

Few books on prehistoric archaeology reach a large audience, and those that do are rarely written by specialists. One of the exceptions is P.V. Glob's account of *The Bog People* which has been translated from the original Danish (Glob 1969) and has gone through several editions.

Glob was Professor of Northern Archaeology and European Prehistory at Aarhus University when, in 1960, he became Director of the National Museum in Copenhagen. This appointment posed a challenge. It became his responsibility to explain the significance of Danish archaeology to the general public. Two subjects seemed to catch their interest more than any others. There were the well-preserved corpses excavated from Bronze Age round barrows which Glob described in *The Mound People* (Glob 1983), and the human remains found in peat bogs which formed the subject of his most famous work. *The Bog People* was well received because it brought his readers face to face with the past with an immediacy that no other archaeological material could achieve. They also became acquainted with practices and beliefs that lay far outside their own experience. It was those beliefs that Glob set out to document.

Bog bodies are not peculiar to the archaeology of Denmark. Well-preserved human corpses are also known from the Netherlands, North Germany and, to a lesser extent, from Britain and Ireland (Van der Sanden 1996; Turner and Scaife 1995; Coles *et al.* 1999). It seems as if they may represent a single phenomenon, for most of the examples date from between 800 BC and AD 200, with an emphasis on the Late pre-Roman and Roman Iron Ages. Human remains had been deposited in similar locations during much earlier periods, but these do not take the form of preserved corpses.

Glob put forward the theory that they had been human sacrifices, but this particular interpretation is not always accepted. Whereas he emphasised the importance of a long tradition of making offerings in bogs, other scholars have placed more weight on the treatment of the people whose bodies have been found there (Van der Sanden 1996: chapter 12). Some of them had been shaved and stripped of their clothes before they were put to death with exceptional violence. This suggested the alternative interpretation that these were criminals and outcasts whose remains had been deposited in such places to keep them away from the living. Both explanations derive from the writings of Tacitus and each may apply in specific situations (Todd 1987: chapter 6). What is clear is that in either case the deposition of human bodies involved an awareness of the supernatural (Figure 3.1)

The final chapter of Glob's book emphasises the importance of other finds from Danish bogs and relates them to Tacitus' account of the sacrifices made to Nerthus, the goddess of fertility, who received these offerings as she crossed the country in a special vehicle:

> At Rappendam – an elongated fen, once a lake . . ., parts of no fewer than twenty eight wheel[s] . . . were found during peat cutting in 1941 and 1942. Some other parts of wagons were also recovered, and the share of a plough which was the agricultural tool of the Early Iron Age. These objects lay in groups, indicating that they were deposited on a number of different occasions. Near one group was the skeleton of a man lying on his back with knees bent. The left arm was down by his side, the right lying obliquely across the chest, a posture known in other bog people. Parts of the skeletons of at least five sheep and bones of cows, horse and wild pig were also found . . . We can see at once that this is a sacrificial deposit which matches Tacitus' description.
>
> (1969: 120)

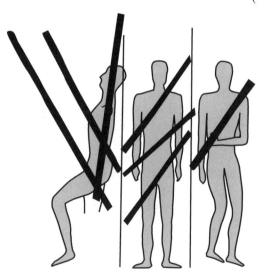

Figure 3.1 Schematic outlines of human bodies in Northern Europe, showing the way in which the corpses were held in position by pieces of wood. Information from Van der Sanden (1996).

Before his appointment to the National Museum, Glob had written a more technical monograph on some of this evidence, the title of which can be translated as *Ard and Plough in Prehistoric Scandinavia* (Glob 1951). This was a pioneering account of the early agricultural tools found in Northern Europe, many of which had survived because they came from bogs. Although Glob's main concern was with their importance for agrarian history, he was well aware of the curious circumstances in which they must have been deposited (Figure 3.2). His account prefigures what he would write in his most famous book:

> The numerous discoveries of prehistoric ards and ploughs within the Scandinavian cultural area and the areas bordering it to the south have been interpreted . . . as the outward signs of a definite custom of making offerings in connection with the ritual spring 'ploughing', after which ards and parts of ards were deposited in sacred bogs as gifts to the higher powers . . . The circumstances of the discovery of the ards here published, together with a large number of the details of the ards themselves, show that they were deposited in the bogs for a special purpose . . . Of highest importance for the correct interpretation of the discoveries is Hjørdlunde where many wagon wheels and bones of domestic animals and human beings were found.
>
> (1951: 131)

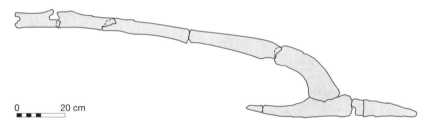

0 20 cm

Figure 3.2 A wooden ard from the bog at Vebbstrup, Denmark. Information from Glob (1951).

There were several reasons for him to take this view. These remains were not found in every kind of bog. Rather, 'a very large proportion of them are found in quite small, often high-lying saucer bogs. . . . Eight of the Jutland ards were discovered in [these] areas' (1951: 131). Only three came from more extensive deposits of peat. One of the ards had been placed at the end of an alignment of stones, two more were covered by a deposit of boulders and a third had been buried in a pit together with prehistoric pottery.

Since Glob's original account, a number of these artefacts have been dated by radiocarbon (Lerche 1995). Although a few examples belonged to the Late Neolithic and the Early Bronze Age, the other finds of ards were deposited between about 1000 BC and the early first century AD, with the largest number

83

in the pre-Roman Iron Age. Thus their history will have overlapped with that of the bog bodies, although their chronologies do not coincide exactly.

It is important to understand the methods by which Glob came to interpret these finds. There were three strands to his argument, each of which has wider implications for archaeology.

The first is the most traditional. This is the use of written sources to illuminate activities in the past. Here he and his colleagues worked on a number of different levels. As we have seen, his interpretation of the bog bodies was influenced by the writings of Tacitus, which were roughly contemporary with the phenomenon that he was investigating. It was on that basis that he suggested that the corpses were the remains of people who had been sacrificed to the goddess of fertility. His critics appealed to exactly the same source, arguing instead that the victims were social outcasts who had been humiliated before they were killed. Their interpretation was strengthened because the proponents of this view were able to appeal to local folklore, although nothing is known of when those ideas developed.

When Glob considered the ploughs that are also found in North European bogs, he employed a more varied range of sources. Besides the reference in the *Germania* to a goddess of fertility, he drew on the literature of other parts of the world to talk about the special significance of cultivation. His account ranges widely. It refers to rituals recorded in Egypt, China, India, Thailand, Greece and Cyprus. He also makes use of folklore, drawing on the beliefs documented in Denmark, Sweden and North Germany, but he employs these sources in the way that other prehistorians have utilised ethnographic texts, as a source of inspiration that can inform a purely archaeological analysis.

Today such an analysis might be called 'contextual' archaeology, but the concept had not been articulated at the time when he was writing. His work on early ploughs dates from the 1940s and 1950s and *The Bog People* was first published in Danish in 1965. The contextual approach was most explicitly developed in two books by Ian Hodder, *Symbols in Action*, which dates from 1982, and an edited collection, *The Archaeology of Contextual Meanings*, of 1987. These books argue that material culture is used in an active manner and that the meanings that were once assigned to ancient things can be inferred from the contexts in which they are found and from the items that are associated with them. Material culture behaves rather like a language in which concepts are defined and articulated through a process of juxtaposition, comparison and opposition.

Glob's approach follows a similar procedure. He emphasises two key elements: the unusual contexts in which human bodies and the remains of ploughs have been found; and the ways in which certain types of material might be associated together in these settings, whilst others were excluded. Thus the finds of corpses are only part of a wider pattern connected with the Iron Age use of watery locations. Certain items might be discovered there more often than on dry land. Obvious examples include the remains of wheeled vehicles which he relates to Tacitus' account of Nerthus, and pots containing food (Becker 1971). Some traces of these would have survived in other contexts, but they are poorly represented. Other items were made from perishable materials, so that Glob could consider their associations within the deposits found in bogs but could not compare them with their representation in other environments. Among these items are spades, troughs, anthropomorphic wooden figures and, of course, the remains of ploughs. He was able to suggest that they possessed a special significance because they were often deposited together.

Such deposits were not confined to the Iron Age, as the radiocarbon dates for these ards make clear. There are examples whose history extends across the whole of the first millennium BC, and there are others which are considerably older. The tradition of placing ploughs in bogs and pools extends into later periods also. In the same way, the association of human remains with such locations has a lengthy history, with another group of finds which dates from the Neolithic period (Koch 1998). Again these were placed there at the same time as offerings of food. Still more important, numerous stone and metal artefacts seem to have been deposited at sites of this kind in Northern Europe, and when the practice was at its most expansive these finds included many items made of bronze, including, tools, weapons, personal ornaments and a variety of specialised types like musical instruments (Levy 1982). Such collections of metalwork are less common in the Iron Age, but, when Glob came to study the significance of the finds of ards, he knew very well that they might represent just one manifestation of a longer tradition.

In some cases Glob was able to take his analysis even further through a detailed examination of the artefacts themselves. Had they been used, or were they made specifically as offerings? Could they have functioned as tools, or did they simply mimic their outward forms? The evidence provided by the ards is especially important here. In some cases 'the implements cannot have been made for normal use' (Glob 1951: 131); they were formed from such soft wood that they would never have worked, and in one instance an artefact was obviously left unfinished. Other examples exploit the natural shape of the raw material so that they resemble a cultivation tool. For example, 'the Svarvarbo ard is made of a naturally bent piece of wood, which can never have been able to plough straight, [and] shows scarcely any signs of wear' (ibid.: 132). Glob sums up the evidence in this way:

> The objects show . . . that the offerings consisted of complete but worn-out ards, ards of woods which were unsuited to agricultural work . . . [and] ards of poor or simplified construction, rendering them unsuitable for serious employment . . . [In some cases these deposits contain] the most important part of the ard, the share, again in several cases so fragile and with so little sign of wear as to suggest that they were intended from the beginning as offerings.
>
> (1951: 132)

Finally, he supports his interpretation by referring to the depictions of ploughing found in prehistoric rock art. The first point to make is that these are widely distributed. If they were simply scenes from daily life, why had so much trouble been taken to render them in a durable medium, and why were the same scenes carved so often? For example, it provides one of the dominant themes of the art of Valcamonica and Mont Bégo in the Southern Alps where its sheer repetition from one panel to another suggests that it may have enjoyed the same significance as the drawings of weapons (Anati 1961, 1976 and 1984; De Lumley 1995). There are fewer ploughing scenes in Scandinavia where this activity is depicted on less than a dozen sites. In fact it is a particular feature of the west coast of Sweden. To quote Malmer:

> [It cannot] be claimed that the distribution of ploughing scenes in rock art could significantly reflect the extent of agriculture in the Bronze Age. Today agricultural land in Bohuslän represents 18 per cent of the whole area, while in Denmark the figure is 65 per cent, and there is no reason to believe that Bohuslän was relatively more important as an agricultural area in the Bronze Age. It is perhaps even possible that the interest in ploughing scenes in Bohuslän was stimulated by the fact that the prevailing conditions for agriculture left a lot to be desired.
>
> (1981: 47)

In fact his argument may be understated, as the extent of cultivable land in Bohuslän could have increased as the sea level fell *after* these carvings were made. He also observes that drawings of ards occur in the same small area – and sometimes on the same carved surfaces – as representations of wheeled vehicles. In one case, at Backa, 'within a group of six carts is an ard pulled . . . by two . . . draught animals. As with three of the cart designs nearby, the feet of both draught animals are turned inwards towards the beam' (Malmer 1981: 47). This may suggest an attempt to form a closer connection between these groups of images. Such drawings date from the Bronze Age, but it may be more than a coincidence that in Northern European bog deposits finds of wooden ards should be associated with the remains of dismantled vehicles. Again this recalls Tacitus' account of Nerthus who travelled in a special carriage and received sacrifices in the course of her journey.

Glob's discussion of the Swedish rock carvings draws attention to other characteristics of these images:

> The fact that a horse was harnessed to the ard, as shown in the rock carvings at Tengeby . . . is alone sufficient to underline the special character of this carving, as the horse was [rarely] used for this type of work [during the prehistoric period], whereas it is often portrayed in Scandinavia as drawing the divine sun.
>
> (1951: 132)

Figure 3.3 The carving of a ploughman at Litsleby, Western Sweden. Information from Glob (1951).

Again, at Litsleby 'we see a crook ard drawn by oxen and driven by a potently phallic man who holds in one hand a branch or tree' (Glob 1951: 132; Figure 3.3). Naked ploughmen may also figure in the rock art of Mont Bégo (De Lumley 1995), suggesting that the same link between human and natural fertility was important there. Again that connection is present in folklore.

I have stressed these details because it is important to trace the stages in Glob's reasoning. It is not enough to interpret the deposits of wooden ards through an appeal to the writings of Tacitus, for some of the evidence that Glob presents comes from an earlier period. His case is strengthened precisely because these deposits form only part of a much longer tradition of making offerings in watery locations. It is just as important that some items occur together in such places whilst others apparently do not.

A more detailed analysis of the ards themselves reveals the limitations of purely practical arguments, for they are unlikely to have been agricultural tools that were discarded when they were no longer serviceable. In the same way, the small body of rock carvings depicting plough teams at work shows a number of anomalies which it would be difficult to explain in utilitarian terms. Taken together, these separate arguments allowed Glob to put forward a more balanced interpretation. In doing so, he was ahead of his time.

It was in a paper published in 1942 that Glob originally suggested that ards had been employed as votive offerings. This article was one of the sources cited by Grahame Clark a decade later when he discussed ancient farming in his book *Prehistoric Europe: The Economic Basis* (Clark 1952). It is striking that nowhere in this account does he consider why these artefacts had survived; he treats them simply as part of the development of farming. This is typical of a more widespread attitude to prehistory. In effect, the bog bodies of Northern Europe contribute to the study of ritual and belief, but the primitive ploughs that were deposited in similar locations form part of an economic archaeology.

The faultlines in archaeological reasoning identified in Chapter 1 come to the surface again. Clark is not alone in adopting this attitude. His book was written over fifty years ago, but even now prehistorians can show the same reluctance to consider food production as more than a technical exercise.

Garden magic

It is surprising that archaeologists pursued such a narrow path when social anthropologists had long been aware of the interplay of ritual and practical affairs in the course of daily life. A good example of this approach is illustrated by the work of one of the founders of the discipline, Bronislaw Malinowski.

Like Glob, Malinowski wrote books that reached an audience outside his own field, and again their titles were chosen to attract attention. The most famous are probably *Argonauts of the Western Pacific* (1922) and the book that I shall be considering here, *Coral Gardens and their Magic* (1935).

This study is divided into two volumes, each with a more specific title: *Soil-tilling and Agricultural Rites in the Trobriand Islands* and *The Language of Magic and Gardening*. His treatment is exhaustive and, in combination, the books run to over eight hundred pages. They are lavishly illustrated and the first part contains nearly a hundred photographs. These are supplemented by eight 'documents' and two substantial appendices. The shorter volume includes a corpus of linguistic terms related to gardening, and a catalogue of magical formulae.

Malinowski was one of the pioneers of anthropological fieldwork. As Edmund Leach has said:

> The most crucial innovation was that he actually pitched his tent in the middle of the village, learned the language in its colloquial form and observed directly at first hand just how his Trobriand neighbours behaved throughout the 24 hours of the ordinary working day. No European had ever done this before and the kind of ethnography that resulted was completely new.
>
> (Leach 1966: ix)

Leach also described Malinowski as 'a unique and paradoxical phenomenon – a fanatical theoretical empiricist' (ibid.: vii). Although Malinowski regarded himself as the founder of a distinctive approach to anthropological theory, it is for the quality of his fieldwork, rather than his wider interpretations, that his work is celebrated today. In that respect *Coral Gardens and their Magic* is very like the monographs which describe archaeological excavations and it shares the same concern with detailed documentation.

It would be impossible to summarise all the results of Malinowski's project, and I shall have to be extremely selective here. Perhaps the obvious starting point is provided by two observations that he made towards the start of his project. First, a particular aesthetic characterises the gardens of the Trobriand islanders:

> The gardens of the community are not merely a means to food; they are a source of pride and the main object of collective ambition. Care is lavished upon the effects of beauty, pleasing to the eye and the heart of the Trobriander, upon the finish of the work, the perfection of various contrivances, and the show of food . . . A further complexity is added . . . by the diversity of crops, the various kinds of gardens, and the differentiation of plots according to their magical, aesthetic and practical function.
>
> (Malinowski 1935: 56)

Second, Malinowski observes that the production of food goes well beyond the needs of a subsistence economy, for the inhabitants of the Trobriand Islands were growing far more food than they could possibly have consumed. As he wrote in *Argonauts of the Western Pacific*:

> Half of the native's working life is spent in the garden, and around it centres perhaps more than half of his interests and ambitions. In gardening the natives produce much more than they actually require, and in any average year they harvest perhaps twice as much as they can eat . . . They produce this surplus in a manner which entails much more work than is strictly necessary for obtaining the crops.
>
> (1922: 58–9)

These two observations are directly related to one another because gardening provides a medium for competitive display, and much of the produce that results is put on show in the settlement, often in special buildings. Although some of the surplus may eventually be left to rot, the giving and receiving of foodstuffs is central to social relations among the islanders.

Linking these two characteristics – the aesthetics of gardening and the extraordinary amounts of food that it produces – is the role of magic, which forms one of the principal themes of Malinowski's study. This is a specialised procedure and involves the participation of an expert, whom he calls the 'garden magician' or 'wizard'; the Trobrianders themselves call him the towosi. The towosi is generally the headman of a village, his heir or a close relative. In most respects he resembles other members of the community:

> In the carrying out of a magical act the performer looks very much like an ordinary native bent on practical work . . . The rites are simple and direct, and only the fact that some of the spells are chanted aloud in the field or in the village would lead you to enquire what the man was really after.
>
> (1935: 12)

In his study Malinowski provides an account of the activities involved in food production and the different kinds of magic with which they are associated. A 'chart of magic and work' shows how complex these can be (1935: 436–43). He enumerates no fewer than twenty 'technical and social activities' that take place in the course of the year and lists them along with the forty episodes of garden magic that sustain them. His summary also identifies the people involved in such processes and the times when these are carried out. Some of the events have a rather arcane character, but others are easier to comprehend. They include the 'charming' of axes and torches, the ceremonial burning of the vegetation and the planting of taro. There are also a number of taboos which prevent any use of the gardens over a prescribed period of time. Malinowski's summary lists the participants in each of these events. They extend from the magician and his acolytes to the workmen and the gardener himself.

These simple rituals serve a number of purposes, and Malinowski traces the sequence through the entire cycle of food production. The first involve the preparation and selection of the land and play an important part in bestowing fertility on the soil. Then there are events that facilitate the burning of the surface vegetation, the exclusion of wild pigs from the cultivated land and the growth of crops. Weeding is accompanied by further acts of magic, and taro from the garden is offered to the ancestors. The first fruits are deposited on their graves and, finally, there are rites which accompany the harvest and its display. Every stage in the process of food production is ritualised.

The most obvious evidence of the importance of food production is provided by the Trobriand storehouse or bwayma (Figure 3.4). This building serves several purposes and can take more than one form. It has

> a dry well-ventilated interior, protected alike from rain and from sun, and lifted sufficiently above the ground to exclude obvious pests . . . Commoners' bwayma designed to preserve the most everyday yam in good condition must be easy of access to the owner and sufficiently in view of the community and the owner to safeguard it from pilfering . . . Yam-houses of commoners are as a rule placed inconspicuously next to the dwellings.
>
> (Malinowski 1935: 242)

These play a role in the subsistence economy.

They can be distinguished from the more elaborate storehouses which are used for public display. They may be associated with people of higher status. Malinowski describes them in these terms:

> Since wealth, especially accumulated vegetable wealth, serves not only as a practical means of sustenance, but also as an index and symbol of

power, the show storehouses must express this in their lofty and imposing dimensions, their decoration, their elegant shape and their conspicuous position. Also, since the direct impression of food has a combined aesthetic and economic fascination to the eyes of the Trobriander, their contents must be visible.

(1935: 242)

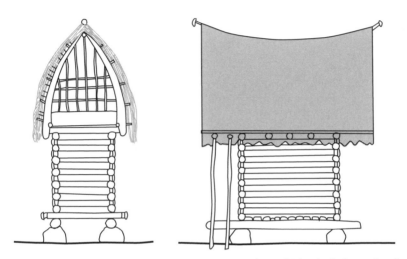

Figure 3.4 A raised storehouse or bwayma in the Trobriand Islands. Information from Malinowski (1935).

In fact Malinowski observes that yams are better housed than the inhabitants of the settlements in which they are stored. This may be why they are consecrated in a magical ceremony which accompanies the filling of the bwayma. This is not the only time when these buildings assume a special significance, for the distribution and display of food happen on a series of different occasions. They play a crucial role in the rituals that punctuate human life, including marriages, funerals and mourning feasts. Food is also distributed at dances and presented as 'ceremonial tribute' to the ancestral spirits when they return each year to the living. As we saw in Chapter 1, what may be interpreted by archaeologists as a simple storehouse could have had many other connotations.

I make this comparison because the Trobriand bwaymas are structurally rather similar to the Galician hórreos discussed in the opening section of this book. Again they provide a medium for social display and seem to be integrally involved in the spiritual life of the community. Malinowski's comments on the differences between individual structures are very relevant here, as he emphasises the important variations in their size and decoration. He also points out how the storehouses of the elite may be differently sited from the simpler structures of the commoners. That is because

> harvesting . . . is a quite definitely festive occasion . . . In the manner in which food is handled and displayed, in the custom of admiring and counting the yams and the yam heaps, in the filling of the painted yam-houses, in the . . . ritual of prosperity – in all this we [are] constantly . . . faced with the emotional appeal of . . . stored food.
>
> (1935: 82)

To a large extent that was because its accumulation was the outcome of successful magic.

So far this chapter has compared two very different situations. In the first case, the deposition of agricultural tools in the peat bogs of Northern Europe could be interpreted according to purely archaeological methods, although these received some support from ethnographic analogy. The second example showed how food production in the Trobriand Islands was attended by ritual and magic. In this case, the interpretation of these processes depends on anthropological fieldwork, although the remains of the storehouses that played such an important part in these processes would surely be found by excavation. In considering the evidence from Scandinavia I drew attention to other sources used by Glob. I would like to explore them now. His study of the ploughs and ards found in the wetlands of Denmark focused on three features: their relationship to the images found in rock art; the ways in which these artefacts had been made; and the circumstances in which they were deposited. I shall consider each of these in turn.

Picturing prehistory

People in later prehistory represented their worlds in visual images, but these pictures can easily be misunderstood. That is because they are studied as ancient 'art', and all too often the styles and techniques that they employ command more attention than their contents. This is particularly true in studies of Neolithic and Bronze Age Europe. It happens for several reasons. More recent images are compared unfavourably with those made during the Palaeolithic period, which at first sight come closer to the canon of Western painting. At the same time, the later designs are often treated in the same manner as portable artefacts; they are broken down into their smallest components and investigated as part of culture history. Alternatively, they are taken literally and treated as illustrations of daily life.

Recent research on Palaeolithic art should have shown the dangers of that procedure, but few of the scholars who study later images have taken much interest in this material. It has long been acknowledged that the paintings and engravings of the Palaeolithic period are mainly concerned with animals.

People are sparsely represented and very few elements of the natural landscape can be identified. Although it would be easy to describe this as hunters' art, the idea is not altogether helpful (Clottes 1996), for there are serious disparities between the different species represented in these media and the animals that were actually killed. Moreover, some of the images were extremely stylised, they could be located in places that were difficult to reach and there are instances in which the features of humans and animals were combined. Therianthropes are also found in the art of the Mesolithic period (Bradley 2001b).

Such evidence should warn us against taking these images too literally. In many parts of Europe, post-Palaeolithic art is also dominated by pictures of animals, but this time it features agricultural production. It would be advisable to approach these scenes with caution, for again they may provide an unbalanced interpretation of reality. A number of features stand out. Perhaps the most revealing is the clear distinction that was now made between humans and animals. This applies to depictions of domesticates, but it extends to wild species, too. In the art of late hunter gatherers, in Northern Russia, North Scandinavia, Southern Spain and the Danube Gorge, it was not uncommon for their features to be combined. This echoes the ethnographic observation that not all hunters distinguish between themselves and their prey; people and animals form a continuum and their identities overlap (Bird-David 1990 and 1992). More recent depictions are quite different, and, in them, these species are distinct. This separation is maintained throughout the Neolithic and Bronze Age periods but breaks down with the combinations of human and animal shapes that typify Iron Age art (Megaw and Megaw 2001).

People and animals are clearly distinguished from one another in the paintings and carvings found at monuments and on natural surfaces in the landscape, but this is also true of ceramic models and stone sculptures. The adoption of domesticates was not only an economic development. Livestock had become a kind of property, and it seems as if this new concern was reflected in the making of artefacts; individual people or animals were portrayed in the form of pottery vessels (Bánffy 2001).

We should consider this development in its wider context. It happened mainly in Central and Eastern Europe, where the Neolithic way of life seems to have been introduced by settlement from other areas. In regions further to the north and west, the adoption of farming may have been a more protracted process and seems to have involved a period of contact between farmers and local foragers. Such regions include the shores of the Baltic, the Atlantic and the North Sea. Again the use of domesticates provided a source of visual imagery.

One of the clearest examples of the new relationship is provided by Late Mesolithic artefacts in South Scandinavia. These were used during a period in which hunter gatherers were in contact with farmers. Such connections are attested by the objects that were introduced across the agricultural frontier, but one of the most striking features of this period is the depiction in Ertebølle art of what seems to be a sheaf of corn (S. Anderson 1980). North-West France was another region in which agriculture may have developed through contacts between the local population and early farming communities, and their interaction may be signified by a series of visual images that were carved on statue menhirs. They included domesticated animals, bows and arrows, axes, crooks and, possibly, yokes (Le Roux 1984). A few of the menhirs were shaped to look like polished axeheads, whilst fragments of broken carvings were incorporated in the fabric of megalithic tombs (Le Roux 1992; Cassen 2000). A number of the same motifs appear on pottery (Constantin 2003). Such designs are very much a feature of Atlantic Europe, and drawings of crooks also characterise the menhirs of Southern Portugal, which may belong to the beginning of the Neolithic sequence (Calado 1997).

Some of the designs on Breton Neolithic pottery appear to show cattle horns, or bucrania (Le Roux 1992; Constantin 2003). Carvings of a similar motif are widely distributed in European rock art but usually developed at a later date. These are well known among the petroglyphs of the Southern Alps, where they occur in large numbers at Valcamonica and Mont Bégo (Anati 1984; De Lumley 1995), but their distribution is much more extensive. They are a striking feature of the decorated outcrop at Escoural in Portugal (Figure 3.5; Gomes *et al.* 1983) and are also found in the megalithic tombs of Sardinia (Bray 1963). They have been identified inside a gallery grave at Warburg in North Germany (Günther 1990).

It is difficult to interpret the portable artefacts that assumed the forms of people or animals. Most are known from settlements, although a number of examples have been found in earthwork monuments. The evidence from the

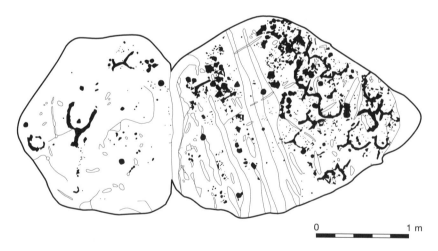

Figure 3.5 Carved bucrania on the rock outcrop at Escoural, Portugal. Information from Gomes *et al.* (1985).

margins of Neolithic Europe is more clear-cut, for here the images formed part of the very fabric of menhirs and megalithic tombs. It seems as if the components of the new economy, and the artefacts associated with their exploitation, took on a special power through this association.

The distinction between these different traditions of depicting animals and artefacts corresponds to a broader division in Neolithic archaeology. Towards the south and east, it seems as if the main focus of ritual activity was the settlement and the house, and it was here that many of these artefacts were deposited. At the same time, both contexts provided the source of inspiration for the development of the first monuments, although that did not happen until a later phase. In other publications I have discussed the idea that long mounds symbolised the dwellings of the past and earthwork enclosures the settlements of earlier generations (Bradley 1998b: chapters 3 and 5). The models of animals might be understood in relation to this emphasis on domesticity.

By contrast, in the west it seems as if monuments were an early development and that the origins of 'megalithic' architecture are perhaps to be found among the indigenous population of Atlantic Europe (Scarre 2003). Here the first Neolithic settlements and houses have left little trace, but the public monuments of the same periods are omnipresent. From Portugal to Brittany they include chambered tombs and menhirs, and the process of shaping and decorating them provided an ideal opportunity for portraying the artefacts and animals associated with a Neolithic way of life. Across large areas of Europe the same concerns were expressed in visual form, but the choice of media depended on more general ideas about the relationship between ritual and domestic life.

Those concerns were not confined to the Neolithic period. The case of the bucrania is especially interesting here. On one level, this image has been traced through a series of contexts from the Near East to Western Europe. Its local contexts are no less revealing. As we have seen, this motif is especially characteristic of the rock art of the Southern Alps, where it appears frequently at Valcamonica and Mont Bégo (Anati 1984; De Lumley 1995). The use of this particular design might refer to the importance of upland pasture, and it certainly seems as if some of the carved panels on the latter site were located in relation to paths. On the other hand, these drawings of bucrania are sometimes found with carvings of weapons and with anthropomorphic figures that closely resemble the statue menhirs in the region (L. Barfield and Chippindale 1997). The details of the bucrania are important, too. I have already mentioned the importance of ploughing in the Bronze Age rock art of Sweden. It seems hardly surprising that so many of the drawings of cattle at Mont Bégo should be associated with similar scenes. In this case there is less room for ambiguity (Figure 3.6). The Scandinavian examples are found in places where cultivation would have been difficult, but those at Mont Bégo are well above the areas in which crops can be grown and could never have depicted activities that were

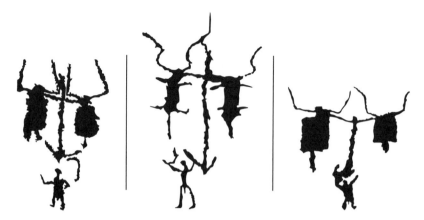

Figure 3.6 Scenes of ploughing among the rock carvings at Mont Bégo, Southern France. Information from De Lumley (1995).

taking place in the vicinity. In that respect they contrast with the situation at Valcamonica.

This observation is important for another reason. The rock carvings at Mont Bégo seem to have been created over a shorter period than their counterparts on the latter site. Their chronology may not extend beyond the Early Bronze Age, whereas those at Valcamonica continue into the Late Bronze Age and even the Iron Age. Although the two groups have many features in common, the North Italian site has certain characteristics of its own. Lawrence Barfield describes its later phases in this way:

> In contrast to the religious nature of the Bronze Age engravings, the rock artists were now concerned with scenes of everyday life.
>
> (1971: 142)

We can question this assumption. Even at Mont Bégo there is a suggestion that some of the carved panels depict an agricultural landscape. A number of rectilinear designs have been interpreted as views of fields and the smaller motifs set amongst them as the positions of houses (Fossati 2002; Arca 2004). Such compositions have even been compared with maps. It is impossible to be sure whether these ideas are correct, but, if they are, any areas of cultivated land would have been located a considerable distance away. Similar panels can be recognised at Valcamonica, where field systems could well have existed, but the very fact that they are found at both sites may be reason enough not to take these representations literally. Exactly the same applies to the scenes of ploughing. Again these are common in both these groups of rock art, but the occurrence of such images at Mont Bégo means that they would have referred to an activity that was happening somewhere else. Another reason for caution is that some of the ploughmen shown at Mont Bégo appear to be naked, as they are in certain of the Swedish petroglyphs discussed by Glob. This feature is less common at Valcamonica but not altogether absent.

Some of the carvings found at Valcamonica are reproduced in archaeological textbooks as illustrations of later prehistoric settlements. Again there are doubts over the directness of this link. Anati places a special emphasis on the numerous depictions of roofed buildings in this group (1961, 1976 and 1984). He interprets them as houses, distinguishing between unfinished examples, structures in which particular people are performing domestic tasks, 'ritual huts' and 'houses of the spirits'. This impressionistic approach is confusing enough, but is there any reason to believe that most of these buildings were domestic dwellings in the first place?

Many of the drawings share certain features (Figure 3.7). The buildings seem unnaturally tall and narrow and may have been raised on stilts. Often the upper storey projects out over the ground floor so that they look top-heavy. This impression is heightened by the presence of a prominent gabled roof. Some of the 'houses' were entered by ladders leading directly to the first floor. It is hard to see how such structures would have been used on a day-to-day basis.

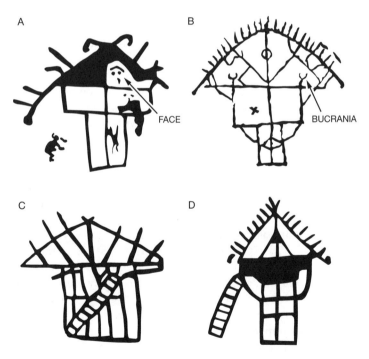

Figure 3.7 Four of the structures identified as houses among the rock carvings at Valcamonica, Northern Italy. Information from Anati (1961 and 1976) and Pauli (1984).

There are other difficulties in interpreting them as domestic dwellings. They bear no resemblance to the Late Bronze Age and Iron Age houses that have been excavated on dry-land sites in Northern Italy or Switzerland, some of which were really log cabins based on a stone foundation (Wyss 1971). Anati (1961) prefers to compare them with the palafites known from wetland contexts in the Italian lakes (Simone 1992). Again there are problems with this comparison, for it is not always clear which dwellings had been raised above standing water and which were simply built on wet ground consolidated by a network of piles (Schlicht-Herle 1997). In any case the comparison seems inappropriate. These sites are some distance away from Valcamonica and there would be no reason to erect such peculiar structures there. Pauli was surely right when he said that 'it is more likely . . . that these [drawings] were meant to represent granaries rather than actual "lake dwellings"' (1984: 80). His argument is particularly persuasive as granaries of much this form are built in the Alps today.

The effect of these arguments is to make the rock drawings of Valcamonica almost as problematical as their counterparts at Mont Bégo. That is hardly surprising since these sites had shared the same range of specialised imagery during an earlier phase. Perhaps it is too simple to suggest that the later petroglyphs at Valcamonica depicted 'scenes of everyday life'. There are two reasons for taking this view. It is hard to see why the settlements in which people lived should have been represented so sparingly, compared with the storehouses in which they kept their grain. At the same time, details of some of the drawings suggest that even these buildings might have played a specialised role (Figure 3.7). For example, one of the structures seems to be associated with bucrania, which look rather like trophies mounted on its outer wall. In another case, giant horns seem to have been attached to the top of the roof, and, in a third instance, a raised building is associated with two pairs of eyes. This is something which it shares with statue menhirs, and it has the effect of turning it into a living creature.

This is not to doubt the relationship between the images at Mont Bégo and Valcamonica and the workings of the agricultural cycle, but just as the carved panels at Mont Bégo could only have referred to processes that were happening many kilometres away, the petroglyphs at Valcamonica do not provide a balanced commentary on the events of daily life in the way that Anati has claimed (Anati 1961, 1976 and 1984). Rather, they stress certain aspects at the expense of others. In particular, they emphasise the importance of crop production. The building and occupation of houses play only a limited role, for the drawings present a partial image of the world. These supposedly mundane scenes may have been just as significant as the designs made during earlier periods. The important difference is that the art of the previous phase had expressed the importance of warriors and weapons. Now it was the growing and storage of food that seem to have been ritualised.

At a number of points I have compared this evidence with that from Northern Europe, and, in concluding this section, I should like to do so again.

In a curious way the difficulties of characterising the 'houses' at Valcamonica are echoed in the archaeology of Poland, North-East Germany, the Northern Netherlands and South Scandinavia, but in this case the problem is posed by a portable artefact. In Chapter 2 I mentioned the Later Bronze Age 'house urns' that are found in Italy and Northern Europe (Behn 1924; Bradley 2002b). At the southern end of their distribution these resemble the forms of dwellings that are known from excavation, but towards its opposite limit the situation is very different.

House urns are ceramic models of buildings that portray details of their architecture such as doors, roofs and external decoration (Figure 3.8). They originated in about the tenth century BC and continued in use until the eighth century or a little later. That means that their currency could have overlapped with the scenes of ploughing depicted in Scandinavian rock art and also with some of the deposits of ploughs discussed by Glob. The house urns in Northern Europe have been found in cemeteries and contain human cremations. They are by no means common. For example, they are recorded with only a tenth of the burials in extensively excavated cemeteries in Southern Sweden (D. Olausson 1986). When they do occur, they may be associated with small items of metalwork, particularly razors and pins.

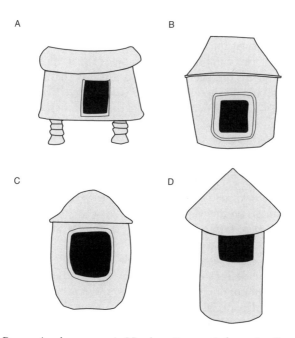

Figure 3.8 Bronze Age house urns in Northern Europe. Information from Behn (1924) and Bergmann (1973). The illustration on the bottom right shows the reconstruction of an excavated granary in North Germany according to Gebers (1985).

The term 'house urn' was devised in the mid nineteenth century, long before the settlements of the same date had been identified and excavated. It no longer seems appropriate, for there is little in common between the forms taken by these ceramic models and the timber dwellings recorded in modern field-work. Although the distribution of these vessels extends across an area with more than one style of domestic architecture, most of the buildings were quite substantial rectangular structures, whereas the house urns suggest a slighter construction that was often circular, or square with rounded corners (Bradley 2002b). These models have other unusual features. The doors of some of the house urns do not open at ground level but are located part way up the wall, as if their prototypes had raised floors. This is even more obvious in the case of some examples from Poland which represent small rectangular buildings raised on pedestals.

In 1959, Oelmann offered a new interpretation of these objects. They were not models of prehistoric dwellings, but copies of storehouses or granaries of a kind that was being recognised in excavation. There is every reason to accept this view, but it does have interesting consequences. If the house urns of Northern Europe were actually model granaries, it suggests that these build-ings – or the ideas associated with them – must have carried a special significance. This is even more obvious as these distinctive vessels were asso-ciated with cemeteries in which they were used to hold human remains. When we consider the peculiar significance that seems to have attached to ploughs and the act of cultivation during the same period in Northern Europe, it is hard to resist the view that certain stages in the production of crops were ritualised during the Late Bronze Age, just as they may have been at Valcamonica. Malinowski's account of *Coral Gardens and their Magic* gives some indication of the ways in which this might have been happened, but to take the comparison further would be misleading. Instead I shall turn to another of the methods used in Glob's analysis.

Behaving with style

Glob's account of the wooden ploughs found in the wetlands of Denmark places a particular emphasis on the ways in which they were made and the materials from which they were formed. Some of these objects were *representations* of ploughs that could never have been used.

Other prehistoric artefacts raise the same issues. They may be profusely decorated and these designs can extend from one kind of object to another. They may be created out of unusual materials, and it even seems possible that they were made under special circumstances: an issue that I raised in Chapter 1 when I discussed the production of metals and personal ornaments. In each case particular objects or activities may have been imbued with a distinctive style, by which I mean that they were intended to communicate a message. They were related to characteristic ways of making and doing things that could have been understood by other people.

An obvious example recalls the subject of the previous section, the different styles of visual imagery that are thought of as prehistoric 'art'. It is not un-common for these to have been translated from one medium to another. As this happened, they may have carried their original significance with them. Thus the distinctive style of paintings and carvings known as Schematic Art extends from Iberian caves and tombs to a variety of portable items including idols and decorated pots (Garrido and Muñoz-Atilleros 2000). Copper axes in parts of North-West Europe may share their characteristic decoration with Bell Beaker ceramics, and the same motifs may also be associated with necklaces and gold lunulae (J. Taylor 1970). Razors and other metal artefacts in Bronze Age Scandinavia carry some of the same designs as the rock carvings of the region (Kaul 1998). Similarly, the distinctive embellishment of La Tène metalwork also occurs on decorated querns in Ireland (Figure 3.9; Raftery 1984: 244–6). In some cases it may be appropriate to think in terms of a specialised style associated with restricted knowledge or social status, but the last example seems to extend from the products of skilled craft workers to the domestic arena where the grinding of grain would have been a regular occurrence.

In other cases artefacts had special qualities because they were made out of particular substances. In the case of fine metalwork this is hardly surprising, but the same is true of artefacts whose forms are based on those of everyday objects. Perhaps the classic case is Pliny's account of the way in which the Druids used gold sickles to cut mistletoe (*Natural History* XVI: 251). In prehistoric Europe a variety of unusual materials were exchanged over long distances, including obsidian, spondylus shells and amber, but only occasionally

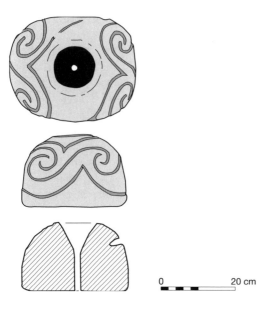

0   20 cm

Figure 3.9 Decorated Iron Age rotary quern from Ticooly-O'Kelly, Ireland. Information from Raftery (1994).

101

were they made into objects of types which were familiar in daily life. For example, amber beads in the shape of axeheads are known from Neolithic Sweden (Runcis 2002).

In fact some of the best examples of this process come from the Neolithic period. Perhaps the most obvious case concerns the jadeite axeheads which were produced in the foothills of the Alps and distributed across large parts of Europe (Ricq-de Bouard 1996). There are certainly instances in which objects of this kind were deposited in specialised contexts. Others were converted into personal ornaments, like those depicted on the walls of the chambered tomb at Gavrinis in Brittany. These artefacts were not suited for practical tasks but were easy to recognise because of the distinctive materials of which they were composed. What seems especially important is that they should have been modelled on the form of a domestic tool.

Another extensive exchange network concerns the movement of Grand Pressigny flint from its source near Poitiers in Western France (Giot *et al.* 1986). Artefacts of this distinctive honey-coloured rock were distributed as far as the Netherlands. This is usually explained because the stone bears a certain resemblance to metal, perhaps suggesting that it was a substitute for copper or bronze. One reason for taking this view is that objects originating from this source resemble the daggers found in graves. Recent research in France has questioned this comparison, for microwear analysis has shown that these flint 'weapons' had actually been used as sickles (Plisson *et al.* 2002). The relationship observed in the case of jadeite axes seems to have been reversed. Rather than a specialised object imitating a familiar type, an everyday activity was carried out using artefacts of an unusual form and raw material. By doing so, people may have invested an everyday procedure with an additional layer of meaning. These unusual objects would have allowed the harvesting of grain to be performed in a distinctive *style*.

In all these instances the nature of the raw material would have been apparent. A more complex situation arises in studies of the bone artefacts of the Neolithic period. Sidéra (2000) has recently analysed those of the Linearbandkeramik, Michelsberg and Chasséen complexes between the Paris Basin and the Rhine. In certain phases she observes that a significant proportion of the food supply was acquired by hunting. In other periods, the remains of domesticates are better represented. That seems quite straightforward, but the evidence of bone tools reveals a more complex pattern. During the periods in which domesticates provided most meat the bone industry emphasised the significance of wild animals. When game was more important, the relationship was the other way round. This example is revealing for it might have been quite difficult to distinguish between these groups of tools. There are some obvious exceptions – artefacts made from red deer antler would have been easy to recognise, and so would those made out of teeth – but what seems to have been more important than their appearance was the knowledge of how the material had been obtained. Some of these objects were grave goods, but others were used in daily life. The distinction between the domestic and the wild was obviously important.

Similar conventions might have influenced how and where artefacts were made. Again this is a topic which has created some confusion, for prehistorians sometimes write about it using terms that are more appropriate to the modern economy. I shall illustrate this process using the evidence of Neolithic flint mines and quarries. The problems of metalworking will be discussed in Chapter 5.

A study of the evidence from Southern England has emphasised the problems involved in understanding flint mines (Barber *et al*. 1999). Adequate raw material for making axes and other artefacts could have been obtained from superficial deposits within the same region – and sometimes it was – whilst the actual locations where raw material was extracted were apparently cut off from the main areas of settlement and may have been selected because they could be seen from a distance. Those in mid Sussex may have been intervisible, whilst others could have been viewed from causewayed enclosures, and, like those sites, may have been located on the edges of the landscape. The contents of some of the mines are curious too. They seem to include placed deposits of pottery, the remains of animals and antler tools. There are also human remains. Although formal burials are rare, the shafts contain isolated bones similar to those from earthwork monuments. It even seems possible that in one case the opening to a gallery had been decorated with drawings of animals which have no equivalents in other contexts (Russell 2001: 186–9). Animals also feature as burials on these sites.

The artefacts made at flint mines may have had a special importance in Neolithic society (Barber *et al*. 1999). Axes were produced at the early sites close to the south coast of England, and a specialised form of discoidal knife originated from the later stone source at Grimes Graves. Finished artefacts of both these types can be found in specialised contexts, including hoards. The emphasis on tool production is particularly striking as one of the burials at Cissbury was accompanied by a flaked axe, whilst a ground stone axe, apparently imported from a distance, was used to trim the face of a gallery at Grimes Graves before it was deposited in the filling of the mine. Similar contexts on other sites contain placed deposits of artefacts and animal remains. In Sussex it seems as if small mounds or cairns of mined flint were constructed in between the shafts, and in a few cases they may have been positioned directly above an abandoned working. These features are difficult to date, but some of them certainly originated during the operation of the mines and were associated with human burials (Russell 2001).

The evidence from Southern England is not unusual, although less attention has been paid to the interpretation of Continental flint mines and more to the technological procedures involved in extracting and working the raw material (Weisberger *et al*. 1981). At the French site of Jablines, however, the filling of a mine shaft contained the same range of personal ornaments as the burials of the same period (Bostyn and Lanchon 1992: 124–5). Similarly, the famous mine complex at Spiennes in Belgium included three inhumations and a series of human skulls (De Laet 1982: 266–8). There were further finds of skulls at Ryckholt-St Gertruid in the Southern Netherlands (Werkgroep Prehistorische Vuurstenmijnbouw 1988; Felder *et al.* 1998). In this case there were also hoards of miners' tools which seem to have been brought together as offerings after they had been used. Most of these collections consisted of flint picks and hammerstones.

Of course it is possible to take the evidence too far and to suppose that flint mines were dedicated to ritual activities. That interpretation is tempting because a proportion of the axes made there do seem to have been imbued with a special significance. This is most apparent from their occurrence in other contexts. On the other hand, the evidence that has been presented simply shows that certain activities at flint mines were carried out with a greater degree of formality than might once have been anticipated. In that sense we can suggest that they were *ritualised*.

Similar problems affect the interpretation of the quarries where raw material was extracted for making axes. Sometimes it was selected because of its distinctive appearance when other sources would have provided better work tools. This is a point that has been made in the archaeology of Britain and North-West France. Again the extraction sites could be located at conspicuous points in the landscape – a particularly impressive example is the thin spike of rock called Le Pinnacle in the Channel Islands which became the focus for a series of votive deposits during later periods (Patton 2001). Fieldwork in Cumbria has shown that the outcrops selected for making axes there were at greater elevations than other exposures of the raw material and that they were usually located above steeper ground. This is unlikely to be fortuitous when the stone source was in a remote upland landscape (Watson 1995). Other quarries could be located on islands even when similar raw material was being taken from accessible sources on the mainland. Two examples are particularly revealing, for again they suggest that stone-working was not a straightforward procedure.

On Lambay Island near to Dublin an axe quarry contained a number of placed deposits of artefacts and debitage which had been covered by cairns (Cooney 1998). A very similar arrangement is found at Goodland, an earthwork enclosure on the mainland (Case 1973). The form of these mounds recalls another excavated example at the axe production site of Graig Llwyd in North Wales (Williams and Davidson 1998) and the small round barrows associated with Sussex flint mines (Russell 2001). The other case was at Beorgs of Ulyea in Shetland (Scott and Calder 1952). Here two distinctive structures are recorded at the stone source (Figure 3.10). One was a small passage grave which had been dug down into the natural surface against an outcrop. Nearby was a deeper trench of roughly the same proportions. This followed the edge of another exposure of the rock. One side of the excavation was retained

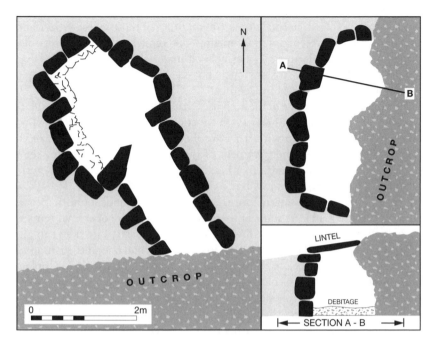

Figure 3.10 The passage grave and the nearby Neolithic quarry at Beorgs of Ulyea, Shetland. Information from Scott and Calder (1952).

by a drystone wall before it was roofed by a series of lintels. The first monument was clearly a chambered tomb of a well-known type, but the second contained a quantity of stone-working debris and was apparently a quarry whose products may have been transported as far as Orkney and the Scottish mainland. Surely the cross-references between these two structures were intentional. Perhaps they served to emphasise the significance of axe production.

Axes do not seem to have been ground and polished at the stone source, yet the later stages of production may also have been invested with a particular importance. In France, polissoirs are so often discovered in the vicinity of chambered tombs that they are recorded in the inventory of the country's megalithic monuments. In Britain and Ireland axe-polishing stones were incorporated in the fabric of a number of such tombs and traces of the same activity have been identified on monoliths in the stone circle at Avebury (Gillings and Pollard 1999). A polissoir also occurs in the causewayed enclosure at Etton. This is important because it was here that axes imported from the Cumbrian quarries 250 kilometres away were deliberately destroyed before their remains were deposited in pits (Pryor 1998: 266–8).

These are simply examples of what may have been widespread practices. What they have in common is that they involved special skills and special processes. Only by these means could the raw material be transformed.

Sometimes it seems as if such activities needed to happen in special places – in locations cut off from normal domestic activities, or those whose significance was marked by the presence of monuments – and often they were accompanied by the provision of offerings. The associated material is very varied and even includes human remains. It is obviously not enough to consider the making of artefacts as a set of technical procedures.

The same applies to some of the activities that took place within settlements. In recent years a number of writers have commented on the way in which domestic activities overlap with what are thought of as specialised rituals. In most cases these involve the treatment of the dead. In Scandinavia one set of associations links the preparation of food and the use of cremation cemeteries through a series of processes involving the use of fire (Kaliff 1997 and 1999). This may provide an explanation for the burnt stone mounds found at Bronze Age sites (Figure 3.11). As some of them contain a mixture of animal remains and pottery they are interpreted as the remains of feasts, but they can also include human bones. There is considerable diversity, and not all these mounds of burnt material are associated directly with living sites. Moreover, in Uppland their contents seem to have changed over time. The earlier examples have fewer associations with other kinds of material, whilst those dating from the Late Bronze Age are more likely to include human bones and metalwork (Karlenby 1999). That may be consistent with a more general change from inhumation

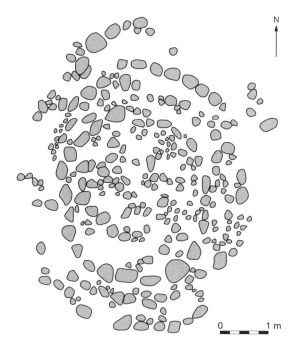

Figure 3.11 A small stone setting beneath a Bronze Age burnt mound at Rinkeby, Eastern Sweden. Information from Runcis (1999).

to cremation. One of the clearest examples of such relationships is found at Hallunda near to Stockholm, where the same part of the excavated area contained wooden houses, deposits of burnt stone, cremations and pieces of bronze metalwork (Jaanusson 1981). Although this has been interpreted as an industrial area, it may be another instance in which craft production was ritualised.

A further link between activities within the settlement and the treatment of the dead is the occurrence of querns in cemeteries (Skoglund 1999). These do not seem to have been used to process the ashes of the dead and it may be more helpful to think in terms of an association between the agricultural cycle, death and regeneration (Fendin 2000). That might also explain the association between cremations and the model granaries discussed earlier in the chapter. It seems possible that the dead were thought of in similar ways to the harvest which lay dormant over the winter before it came back to life.

If there is a complex relationship between human cremations and mounds of fire-cracked stones, the links between burial mounds and clearance cairns are just as complex. In this case they apply to the Bronze Age in Scandinavia and the British Isles (Högrell 2002; Johnston 2000). For many years it has been difficult to account for the enormous numbers of small cairns that survive on marginal land. A few of these are associated with orthodox mortuary monuments and others can be found close to panels of rock art. The problem is that the smaller piles of boulders may result from land clearance. That could be why some of them were built on small outcrops or accumulated around large earthfast boulders. On the other hand, it cannot be the entire explanation, for a number of these structures seem to have been associated with deposits of artefacts, with fires or even with human burials. How are we to resolve the confusion?

Johnston (2000) has argued that the ambiguity was intentional. Land clearance involved the removal of stone from the cultivated plots, just as the completion of a funeral required the provision of a cairn. But this was not a compromise in which the requirements of ritual were met with a minimum of labour. Rather, these cairns were directly linked to the working of the land and for that reason they assumed a wider significance. It was those associations that made them appropriate places in which to deposit the dead. Again the fortunes of the deceased were linked to the agricultural cycle.

In this section I have considered a number of practices and the ways in which they seem to have been ritualised. I began with the evidence of artefacts and the processes by which some quite elaborate objects echoed the forms of ordinary domestic tools. I then considered the circumstances in which they were made and the difficulties raised by production sites. Lastly, I looked briefly at some of the domestic tasks that took place within the settlement: cooking, processing cereals, grain storage and land clearance. At certain times and in certain places all of these were caught up in the treatment of the dead. Again it is impossible to distinguish between rituals and domestic routines.

Making offerings: monuments and the deposition
of domestic artefacts

The last strand in Glob's argument is perhaps the easiest to comprehend. This is the question of deposition. It seemed very unlikely that ploughs and other agricultural implements would be left in watery locations by chance, especially as the same kinds of places might include pots containing food, dismantled vehicles, metalwork and human remains. There is an enormous literature on the 'votive offerings' from such contexts, but these finds may confuse the wider picture because they would have been difficult to retrieve. For that reason the following discussion is based on the material associated with monuments on dry land. To achieve a broad geographical cover, a number of sites mainly in Scandinavia are juxtaposed with similar examples in Iberia.

There are two ways of thinking about the artefacts that prehistoric people employed in their daily lives. One is to consider the functions of these items and the other is to study the circumstances in which they were deposited. But problems arise if we confuse those two procedures.

Consider the evidence of grave goods. Among the burials of the Bell Beaker tradition there may be many kinds of cross-reference between the objects that feature in the funeral rite and those associated with domestic life. Although there is considerable variation from one region of Europe to another, these relationships can take several forms. Exactly the same object may have been buried with the dead and deposited in settlements, for example arrowheads or decorated pottery. In some cases there are differences in the quality or style of these particular items – the arrowheads in burials may be especially finely made (Bailly 2001), the pottery vessels could be more fragile than the others (Boast 1995) – but still there is a clear relationship between the two assemblages. Alternatively, the objects deposited with people in the grave may reflect their position in society. Thus particular sets of grave goods might refer to the activities of hunters, warriors, leather workers and smiths. In this case a particular selection of objects evokes the role that someone could have played in life (Case 1977). It may be an idealised portrait, for these objects would have been chosen by the mourners, but it does maintain a close connection between the living and the dead. Archaeologists have no difficulty in accepting that artefacts whose distinctive forms refer to the domestic world might sometimes be deposited in more specialised contexts. Perhaps that is because some activities were imbued with a particular significance.

That example is familiar to prehistorians, but what if we consider a second question? If particular kinds of artefact played a part in funeral rites, how were they to be treated in the settlements of the same period? And if certain tasks were so significant that they were symbolised by grave goods, was their importance also acknowledged in the domestic assemblage? Here we come to the problem of deposition.

Not all the deposits that are found in settlements can be treated as chance accumulations. As Hodder argued twenty years ago, it is too easy to impose modern conceptions of 'rubbish' on the societies of the past (1982: chapter 8). In Chapter 1 I mentioned the confusion that had been caused by the presence of human burials in prehistoric storage pits in Southern England, and I shall consider this evidence further in due course. It is surprising that such discoveries should have seemed unusual as finds of human remains are common-place in the Bronze Age settlements of Central and North-East Europe. They have been studied in a monograph edited by Rittershofer (1997).

In this case human bones, and even whole skeletons, have been found within the occupied area and sometimes they seem to be directly associated with animal bones. They may represent a minority burial rite rather than the chance accumulation of unwanted material. These finds can be associated with some types of settlement rather than others – for example, such deposits may be particularly characteristic of hill forts – and specific body parts may be over-represented, especially skulls. A number of the bodies had undergone special treatment. They may have been dissected or burnt, and only certain parts could have been deposited. Alternatively, individual bones might have been modified at some stage before they entered the archaeological record. A good example is the production of masks out of human crania. There is also evidence that deposits of human remains were associated with particular kinds of feature within the settlement. In the Laustiz Culture, for instance, human and animal

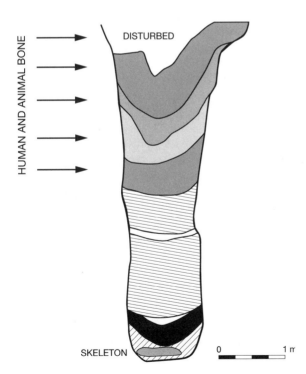

Figure 3.12 Section of a Late Bronze Age shaft or well and associated deposits of human and animal remains at Frankfurt-Lossow, Eastern Germany. Information from Bukowski (1999).

109

burials were placed in shafts that may originally have been wells (Figure 3.12; Bukowski 1996 and 1999). In some regions these deposits existed in parallel with cemeteries, but in other areas they provide practically the only evidence for the treatment of the dead. Although there is considerable diversity, it seems clear that they were purposeful deposits and that it was necessary to connect them with the places where people lived.

The corollary is equally important. For some time it has been obvious that certain kinds of object may have been associated with the domestic sphere but had to be deposited beyond its limits. In the Southern Netherlands, for example, Fontijn suggests that pins and sickles may be associated with houses and farmyards, and axes and spearheads with the edge of the settled land. These are often found in streams and marshes. Swords and more elaborate personal ornaments entered the archaeological record at a still greater distance from the occupation site, and they are known from major rivers (Figure 3.13; Fontijn 2003). Clearly, objects that may have been connected with daily activities need not have been discarded in the places where people lived. Again there is an important difference between the ways in which an artefact was used and the context in which it was deposited. Thus the axe was a domestic artefact which

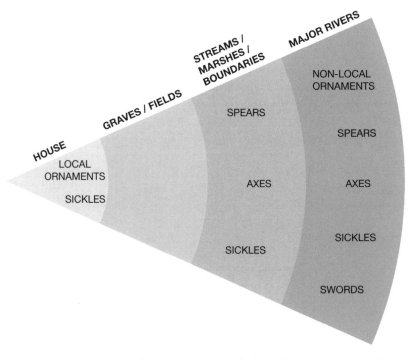

Figure 3.13 The contexts of Bronze Age metal finds in the Southern Netherlands in relation to distance from the settlement. Information from Fontijn (2003).

was probably meant to work timber, but it became a votive offering when it was buried in a marsh.

What do these examples have in common? In every case the items found in specialised contexts were of types that were directly associated with the domestic domain. They were not a special class of artefact. Moreover the same types that occur in these different deposits can sometimes be found within the settlements themselves. Thus the crucial distinction to make is not between different kinds of object or between the roles that they had played in daily life. Rather, it concerns the manner in which they were deployed when their use came to an end.

A good example of this process is found at El Pedroso, on the border between Portugal and Spain (Delibes *et al.* 1995). This site has two main components: a walled settlement on a hilltop with a group of houses, and what seems to have been a cave sanctuary located on the lower ground (Figure 3.14). They are associated with radiocarbon dates in the mid to late third millennium BC. Here I shall be referring to the excavations that I carried out together with Rámon Fábregas and Germán Delibes.

At first glance, the different components of the site could hardly be more different from one another. Inside the enclosure wall there is a group of circular houses, including a workshop where arrowheads were made. The defences comprise a massive wall, a gateway and a tower, and the settlement seems to have extended beyond the fortifications to a series of terraces on the side of the hill. But the cave is located beneath a massive outcrop and its position can only be recognised from the defences because a cairn was built on top of it. The cave has two chambers, separated by a narrow passage. Both of these were decorated, the first chamber entirely with cup marks and the second with a series of carved anthropomorphs and other motifs typical of Iberian Schematic Art. Outside the entrance there was a terrace, revetted by a massive wall built in a similar technique to the main enclosure. At a late stage in its history this was overlain by a roughly circular platform. It is possible that the outer chamber of the cave was used first and that may have happened during the same period as the construction of the terrace wall. In a subsequent phase the inner chamber may have come into use and perhaps it was then that the platform was built (Bradley 2002c).

Two points are relevant to my argument. First, it seems most unlikely that the cave was a living site. No trace of any house was found on the terrace immediately outside it, and space inside each of the decorated chambers was far too limited for domestic activities to have taken place there. In fact the presence of carved decoration suggests that this site had played a specialised role. The second point is critical. There seem to be few distinctions between the kinds of artefacts found in and around that cave and those from the fortified settlement at El Pedroso. Despite some differences of chronology, both include large amounts of ceramics, worked quartz, stone axe heads, arrowheads and querns. Of course there are minor distinctions to observe, but these are far

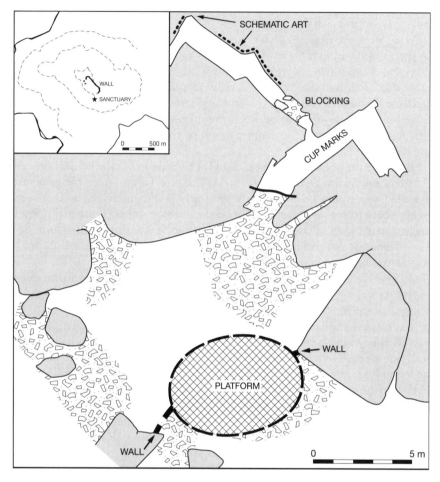

Figure 3.14 The decorated sanctuary at El Pedroso, Northern Spain, showing the two areas of carved decoration inside the cave, the extent of the walled terrace and the position of an external platform. The inset shows the position of the sanctuary in relation to the hill fort.

outweighed by the similarities. How could this have come about when one part of the site included the remains of houses, whilst the other seems to have been unsuitable for occupation?

In some respects the different parts of El Pedroso recall elements that have been found separately at sites of the same period in North and Central Portugal (Jorge 1998). The hill fort, with its houses, is one of a number of examples which seem to be associated with domestic occupation, but the decorated cave is like Crasto de Palheiros and Fraga da Pena where in each case a striking rock formation has been enhanced by platforms or walls (Sanches

112

2001; Varela 2000). But that is not the only possibility, for the cave can also be compared with other examples associated with hilltop settlements. In the same way, the platform that was built towards the end of the sequence at El Pedroso is very similar to one outside the walled enclosure at Castelo Velho (Jorge 1999 and 2002) which was associated with human bones (similar material would not have survived in the acid soil at El Pedroso). There are other comparisons between these sites. There are considerable terraces or ramps at Fraga da Pena and Crasto de Palheiros, and a large circular platform built around a rock outcrop in the centre of the enclosure at Castelo Velho might have played a similar role to the cairn above the cave at El Pedroso.

Some of these sites are enclosures and seem to have been used as settlements. Others are interpreted as ceremonial monuments, but both groups raise the same problem, for it is by no means easy to characterise the differences between them. The clearest distinctions concern the architecture of these places. Thus one group features terraces and platforms but lacks many obvious dwellings. The other has defensive walls and houses, but sometimes their features overlap. El Pedroso includes a fortified settlement but has a decorated cave with an artificial terrace immediately outside it. There is a similar terrace or ramp at Castelo Velho, but in this case it is just beyond the enclosure wall. In the same way, the structures at Fraga da Pena and Crasto de Palheiros emphasise the position of a striking rock formation. So does the sanctuary site at El Pedroso, but here there is a defended settlement on the mountaintop. Fraga da Pena introduces a further variation, for two small enclosures built against the granite tor contain a specialised assemblage, including a number of Beaker vessels, a copper artefact and an idol, whilst a less specialised assemblage is associated with a domestic site beyond their limits. It shares yet another distinctive feature with El Pedroso, for the rock outcrop at Fraga da Pena has painted decoration.

El Pedroso and Fraga da Pena emphasise the difficulty of distinguishing between a class of monumentalised settlement and a ceremonial site, for both components occur together where they might be found in separate locations. At the same time, the artefact assemblages from the different parts of El Pedroso have a similar composition. The apparently 'domestic' material associated with the houses on the hilltop is like that found inside the cave, which was too small to have been inhabited.

How could the same kinds of material have been associated both with ritual and with daily life? That is a question that goes to the heart of the matter. Castelo Velho is especially relevant here, for Susana Oliveira Jorge has written about the way in which her interpretation of the site has changed (1999 and 2002). What first seemed to be a fortified settlement she now describes as a ceremonial monument (Figure 3.15). This is consistent with the results of excavation, but one element must not be overlooked. A number of the structures on the site do have an unusual character, not least the external platform with its deposit of human bones, but the enclosure itself replaced an open settlement

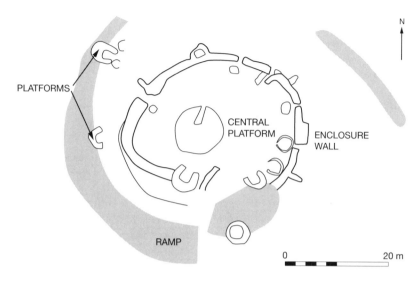

Figure 3.15 Outline plan of the Copper Age and Bronze Age enclosure at Castelo Velho, Northern Portugal. Information from S.O. Jorge (1999 and 2002).

and may include the remains of houses. Moreover most of the material associated with this site makes an explicit reference to the concerns of daily life. Thus there are finds of loom weights and broken pottery, quernstones and a copper axe. There is also evidence of burnt grain. These seem to have been deposited with some formality. They were usually placed within stone-lined containers or larger structures which were filled on a number of occasions before some of them were sealed by slabs. These deposits may refer to the domestic sphere, but in this context they assume a special significance.

The problem is not peculiar to Iberian archaeology. There are many similar cases, but in the interests of brevity I shall confine myself to two examples. The first concerns the causewayed enclosures of the Neolithic period. The second takes the argument into the Late Bronze Age.

I begin with the causewayed enclosure at Sarup in Denmark (N. Anderson 1997). This went through five phases of activity, the first two of which involved the creation and use of an earthwork perimeter. There were obviously many formal deposits here, including finely decorated pots, axes, animal remains and human bones, some of which were purposefully located in relation to the enclosure ditch. In fact individual segments of the perimeter were carefully screened by palisades. But the excavator also attempted to characterise the deposits found inside that enclosure, distinguishing between those associated with domestic occupation and what he called 'ritual pits' (Figure 3.16). The first group consisted of storage pits containing artefacts in their secondary filling, whilst the 'ritual pits' were those dug specifically to receive offerings

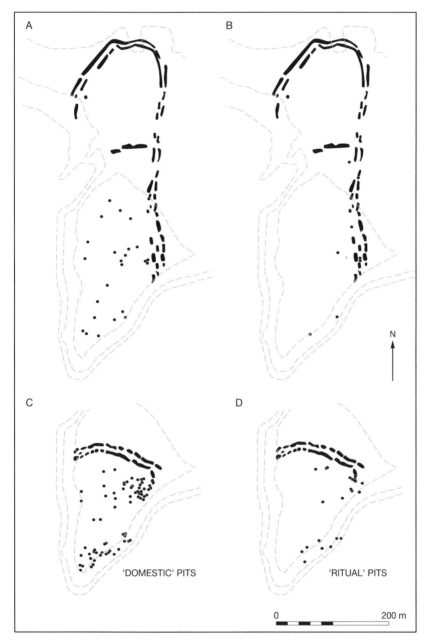

Figure 3.16 Two phases of the Neolithic enclosure at Sarup, Denmark (A and B and C and D). The plans follow the excavator's distinction between 'domestic' and 'ritual' pits. Information from N. Anderson (1997).

115

of complete pots or axeheads. During the enclosure phase about 30 per cent of the pits were associated with 'ritual' and 70 per cent with 'occupation', but in subsequent phases, when the perimeter was no longer maintained, the proportion of specialised deposits apparently fell, suggesting that domestic occupation became more important.

This analysis depends on a simple distinction between the practical and the non-utilitarian. A limited range of intact objects are regarded as special and ritually charged and the remainder as refuse which was casually discarded. This is an entirely subjective scheme. For example, caches of tools or raw material are interpreted as occupation debris, where they would be treated as specialised deposits if they were found in isolation. In the same way, axe heads are considered to have been important in ritual life, but quernstones are denied the same significance.

It is interesting to compare Anderson's interpretation with the results of excavation on a similar enclosure at Etton in Eastern England (Pryor 1998). In this case the site had been buried beneath a layer of alluvium, with the result that it was very well preserved. Detailed analysis of the ground surface inside the earthwork showed that the enclosure had not been inhabited and there were no signs of any domestic buildings. Rather, the environmental evidence from the project suggested that the monument had been used only intermittently, perhaps on a seasonal basis. It was obviously set apart from the normal pattern of settlement.

Like Sarup, the interior of the enclosure at Etton contained a large number of pits, but this time they were not interpreted in functional terms. They contained unusual quantities of burnt animal bones as well as the remains of non-local axes, which may have been deliberately destroyed. These compare with the contents of the 'ritual pits' at Sarup, but similar deposits at Etton included querns. Again they were interpreted in terms of ritual activity.

The interrupted ditch at Etton provided the focus for a series of placed deposits, which were covered over and renewed on several occasions. Different segments of that ditch contained different kinds of offerings, and individual assemblages may have had a distinctive layout, with items of particular significance placed against the causeways providing access to the site. The excavator has suggested that these collections of material were provided by particular groups of people, who came to the monument for that purpose. Individual segments of the earthwork may have been created and maintained by separate parts of the community, but not all these lengths of ditch need have existed at the same time. Such features had probably been surrounded by a rim of spoil so that people could view the material displayed within them. Indeed these deposits varied so much from one part of the site to another that Pryor describes them as purposeful 'statements' (1998: 357–8). Again such statements were composed from the items that were familiar in domestic life. Indeed, a recent study of the lithic artefacts from a similar enclosure in Southern England could not identify any major differences between them and the material from other sites of the same date (Saville 2002). It seems likely that the real difference concerns the circumstances in which these items were used and deposited.

The last example concerns a completely excavated Late Bronze Age enclosure at Odensala Prästgård, near Stockholm (Figure 3.17; M. Olausson 1995). This occupied a low but conspicuous hill and consisted of two approximately concentric enclosures, each of them defined by a rubble wall. Like the causewayed enclosures of the Neolithic, they seem to have been built in segments, but in this case they were used during the first millennium BC. The inner circuit was sub-circular and the outer circuit roughly square, although neither defined a continuous perimeter. A series of stone settings occurred against the inside of both enclosure walls and had often formed around a conspicuous boulder. Beyond the outer limit of the monument were a series of other structures and deposits.

The central feature of the site was a circular stone setting which contained the burials of four adults and a child; these were associated with bronze tweezers and with fragments of three knives. Another human burial was discovered in a similar feature against the limit of the inner enclosure, whilst the last example came from an open area beyond the monument altogether. The burials on the

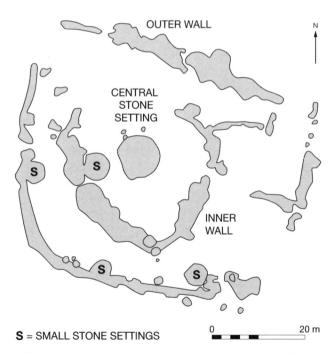

Figure 3.17   Plan of the Bronze Age enclosure at Odensala Prästgård, Eastern Sweden. Information from M. Olausson (1995).

hilltop are Middle Bronze Age, but the wall that was built around them probably dates from the ninth century BC. The interior contains no evidence of any structures of other kinds, but the irregularities in the exposed rock were filled in to create a level surface.

The most striking evidence was of fire, and this extended to the material of the walls and to the surrounding area. There were a number of hearth pits, and beyond the enclosure there seems to have been an oven. The large quantity of burnt stones may provide evidence for large-scale cooking, as it seems to do on other sites of this period in Sweden. Nearly all the evidence of burning came from the outer part of the monument. In addition to the hearths, the excavation located the positions of twenty-six features that were identified as graves, half of which contained burnt animal bones which had apparently been cleaned before their deposition. Only one animal was represented in each of these features and the parts with most meat were absent. One of these burials was against the inner wall and also contained human remains. With that exception, the human burials tended to be found at the centre of the site and the animal graves towards the periphery.

Beyond the limit of the enclosure there were two terraces, each of them occupied by a wooden 'cult house' of the type that is sometimes associated with barrow cemeteries. These were accompanied by numerous hearths, concentrations of fire-cracked stone and by layers of cultural material containing many animal skeletons. There were also deposits of burnt grain which seem to have been brought there fully processed. Just as the cremated bone had a different distribution from the other burials of animals, they were also separate from the levels of grain, which may be rather later in date. The excavator interprets the site as a ceremonial monument at which feasts probably took place. It saw the sacrifice of foodstuffs brought in from nearby settlements, but it does not seem to have been inhabited. What is particularly significant here is the way in which domesticated plants and animals were being offered – and probably consumed – at a site which was associated with older human burials.

What do these different places have in common? They share certain structural features, for all of them can certainly be described as monuments. In some cases they were defined by walls and in others by earthworks, but a characteristic that they share is that in every case particular activities or deposits of cultural material seem to have been put on display. The separate lengths of ditch at Etton were surrounded by a bank of excavated soil, and at Sarup they were enclosed by wooden fences. At Odensala Prästgård there were numerous stone settings, as well as two specialised buildings of a kind that is sometimes associated with a cemetery. The site has a complex layout which shows a superficial resemblance to that of Castelo Velho, whilst other Bronze Age earthworks in Southern Sweden actually have interrupted perimeters in the manner of a causewayed enclosure. One of the Scandinavian enclosures at Draget focuses on a massive rock outcrop like some of the Iberian monuments. It encloses a number of stone settings, but excavation has shown that it was not a settlement (M. Olausson

1997). In the same way, sites like Castelo Velho, Crasto de Palheiros, Fraga de Pena and the cave at El Pedroso all include terraces, ramps or smaller platforms which would have given added emphasis to the activities that were taking place there. Indeed the granite outcrop at El Pedroso would have highlighted the position of anyone who was standing in front of the cairn on its highest point. The architecture of these monuments is like that of a theatre, emphasising the positions of certain actors and events and displaying them to a wider audience.

Conclusion: the ritualisation of domesticity

It would be easy to describe such performances as public rituals, but archae-ologists have been reluctant to do so because so much of the excavated material from these places is similar to the finds from settlements. Why is the field evidence so ambiguous? As I suggested in Chapter 1, prehistorians face this situation because they have been working with an unsatisfactory conception of ritual. They are used to contrasting the sacred and the secular as if they were categorically opposed. As a result, their accounts of prehistoric Europe are not sufficiently subtle. Artefacts, monuments and deposits are considered to be either ritual or functional, as if this simple dichotomy were the only way of interpreting them. Like the much-criticised distinction between culture and nature, these schemes say more about the concerns of Western society than they do about people in the past.

What the sites discussed in the previous section have in common are structures and deposits which utilise the components of domestic life but pro-vide them with a new emphasis. It is because these elements all form part of a wider settlement record that their deployment in specialised contexts has been so difficult for archaeologists to understand. Perhaps the problem is of their own making. Should they distinguish so sharply between the sacred and the profane or between the ritual and the domestic? Instead they ought to place more emphasis on the process of ritualisation, for this is a form of behaviour which is often used strategically. As we have seen, it may be employed by specific people to attain specific ends. Ritual itself is a form of action which can leave certain physical traces, and these are among the features that make up the archaeological record, yet particular excavated contexts are not imbued with special qualities in themselves. Rather, they result from distinctive kinds of performance. Such performances may have been composed out of elements that had a wider resonance, for this is how they would have gained their social significance and why they could have been understood.

I suggest that one way of reconsidering some of the problems identified in Part 1 of this book is by studying how rituals were constructed out of the materials of domestic life. Elements taken from everyday activities seem to have been emphasised and acted out in the past. This could happen at a variety of scales, from an individual action to a public ceremony, and in a whole range of contexts from a house to a hill fort. Particular activities were highlighted

119

through the manner in which they were performed, and such performances were distributed along a continuum from the local and ephemeral to the large scale and highly structured. Ritualisation is a process which can extend from the everyday to the arcane. It permeates the prehistory of Europe, but it has to be understood in its local contexts.

Many of the rituals practised in ancient Europe selected and emphasised the components of domestic life in a kind of theatre. This could have happened in many locations: in settlements, in 'natural' places, at production sites or in specially built monuments. The connecting links, however, are clear. Some of the elements of daily life were played out with an added emphasis, in special contexts and, perhaps, before a special audience. The modern distinction between the sacred and the profane is meaningless here, and so is any attempt to divide the archaeological record on the same lines. In prehistory ritual gave domestic life its force, and domestic life in turn provided a frame of reference for public events. Ritual and domestic life were not two halves of a single phenomenon, to be picked apart by the archaeologist. Instead they formed two layers that seem to have been precisely superimposed.

Part II

WHERE THE STRESS FALLS

4

A HOUSE WITH A POOL

Rituals and the materials of farming

The names

There are at least two ways of investigating the roots of Neolithic Europe, each of which involves a different kind of archaeology. In some cases there has been an emphasis on the process of colonisation. That is appropriate where there is little evidence of indigenous people in the areas that were settled. Obvious examples include the investigation of tells and research on the Linearbandkeramik. The strength of the argument can, of course, be exaggerated, but it certainly makes it easier to consider Neolithic culture in its own terms.

This is not so clear along the shores of the Mediterranean or the Atlantic, where it has been necessary to study a complex interplay between the use of domesticates and that of wild resources. In this case the adoption of agriculture was more problematical and had to be negotiated between different groups of people. The problem is still more severe in the prehistory of Sweden and Norway, for here the expansion of Neolithic farming ended. No matter how cereals were first introduced, there were limits to the natural conditions under which they could be grown. There were many places in which hunting, gathering and fishing would provide more reliable sources of food (Prescott 1996; Bergsvik 2001).

As a result of these physical limitations, it has not been easy to characterise the Neolithic of Scandinavia. During the Ertebølle period the local inhabitants were in contact with farmers across the agricultural frontier. They exchanged portable artefacts with their neighbours to the south, they made pottery in a distinctive style and they may even have occupied certain locations all year round (Fischer 2002). But there is little to suggest that they exploited domesticated plants and animals. Hence they are rightly described as 'Mesolithic'. On the other hand, there are 'Neolithic' populations whose archaeology is equally problematical. In Bohuslän, in the west of Sweden, there are megalithic tombs, but there is little evidence that agriculture played an important part in the lives of those who built them. Still further to the north, the problem is even more severe. The Neolithic of Western Norway is characterised by coastal settlements, some of which may have been occupied by sedentary communities.

They could have participated in alliances with people in other areas, but the local inhabitants were not farmers, nor did they build monuments (Bergsvik 2001 and 2002). To the east, along the Baltic, there are other problems, for in parts of Southern and Central Sweden it has been claimed that the groups who had practised farming during the TRB (Tricherbecher, or Funnel Beaker Culture) period returned to hunting, gathering and fishing during a subsequent phase in which they adopted Pitted Ware from their neighbours (Malmer 2002: chapters 3 and 5). Again the terminology is confusing. The earlier use of wild resources is characterised as 'Mesolithic' and the first use of domesticates as 'Early Neolithic'. That is logical, but, in apparent contradiction, this reversion to an older economic system began during the 'Middle *Neolithic*' period and is sometimes described as '*sub-Neolithic*'.

Although such schemes raise problems, it is in situations like these that it is possible to compare the ritualisation of domestic life in two different patterns of settlement. For that reason this chapter is mainly concerned with the TRB and Pitted Ware sites of Scandinavia and, in particular, with the archaeology of Central and Southern Sweden.

Skumparberget and Skogsmossen

My initial focus is on the TRB settlements at Skumparberget and Skogsmossen (Apel *et al*. 1997; Hallgren *et al*. 1997). They were about ten kilometres apart towards the landward end of what was a peninsula during the Neolithic period. Both are approximately 150 kilometres west of Stockholm but they would originally have been close to an inlet of the Baltic (Figure 4.1).

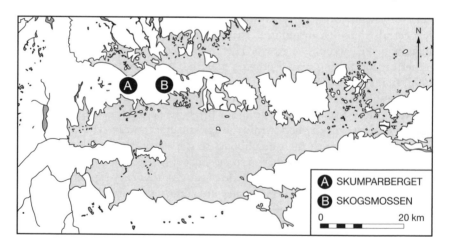

Figure 4.1 Locations of the Neolithic settlements at Skumparberget and Skogsmossen, Eastern Sweden. Information from Apel *et al*. (1997) and Hallgren *et al*. (1997).

In certain respects these sites are very much alike. The main feature at Skumparberget was an oval house defined by a setting of post holes and a clearly defined area of burnt daub. This building was approximately twelve and half metres long and six metres wide and was aligned from north-east to south-west (Figure 4.2). It shares the same features with a more damaged structure on the nearby site at Skogsmossen (Figure 4.3). They would have been approximately contemporary with one another and at Skumparberget large-scale excavation suggests that the house may have been an isolated structure rather than one component of a more extensive group of buildings. There were perhaps three phases of occupation at Skogsmossen but it seems likely that separate residential units changed their positions over time. Even so, each of these occupation sites may have taken a similar form to that at Skumparberget. Both sites were associated with evidence of cereals, and the burnt bones that survived at Skogsmossen are dominated by cattle and pig, with smaller numbers of ovicaprids, fish and seals. Those at Skumparberget were rather similar but may have included a greater range of wild species.

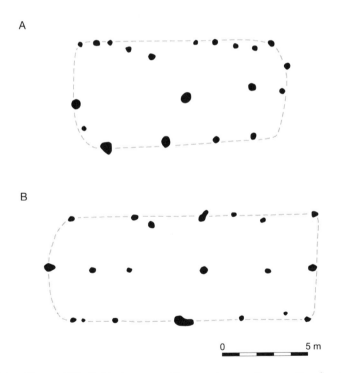

Figure 4.2 Plans of Neolithic houses at Skumparberget, Eastern Sweden (A), and Dagstorp, Southern Sweden (B). Information from Apel *et al.* (1997) and M. Andersson (2004).

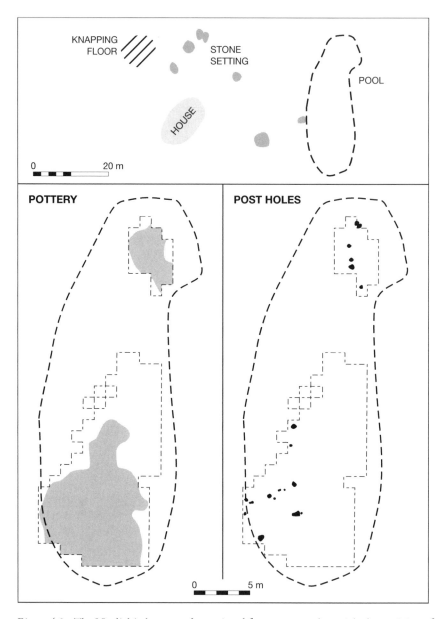

Figure 4.3 The Neolithic house and associated features, together with the position of the nearby pool at Skogsmossen, Eastern Sweden. The detailed plans illustrate the distribution of pottery and post holes found in the excavation of the pool. Information from Hallgren *et al.* (1997).

There were other features in the excavated area at Skumparberget and the excavators suggested that there was a certain order in the way in which they were distributed:

> The food processing area was located immediately north-west of the [house] . . . It was composed of hearths, small fragments of funnel beakers and stone tools traditionally associated with domestic duties, such as different kinds of millstones from the processing of grain. The refuse areas were located on the edge of the site and were defined by large amounts of pottery sherds, fragmented stone tools, lithic-production debitage and burnt animal bone. On two of the specific-activity areas, thin-butted axes were produced . . . On a third, cattle were butchered.
>
> (Apel *et al.* 1997: 42)

At Skogsmossen, the position of the house was again marked by a concentration of burnt daub. Like its counterpart at Skumparberget, it was surrounded by an orderly arrangement of deposits associated with the settlement. In the excavators' words:

> There is a quite clear picture of a . . . house [flanked] by different, spatially separated activity areas, which can be interpreted as a farmyard . . . North of the house, there is an area with three hearths, high phosphate values, and a relative abundance of burned animal bones . . . All parts of saddle-shaped grinding stones, including the only intact example which was found in the settlement, were located in this area . . . To the west [of this was] a knapping floor, where porphyrite axes were manufactured . . . To the south-east of the house, a concentration of burned animal bones, together with high phosphate values . . . indicate that the area has been used for rubbish disposal.
>
> (Ibid.: 100–1)

There is another element which is shared by both these sites. So far they have been characterised as isolated houses surrounded by the residues of everyday activities. Different tasks were undertaken in different areas and space within the settlement may have been carefully organised. There are a number of anomalies which suggest that all this evidence cannot be explained in functional terms.

The main anomaly at Skogsmossen is an arc of stone-settings which seem to have supported upright posts. These were on one side of the Neolithic house, in between the building and a pool. Their fillings contained pottery, lithic debitage and burnt animal bones, but in two cases they also included some intact objects. In one instance these consisted of a greenstone axe and an axe roughout in the same material, three fragments from burnt flint axeheads, a stone chisel, a quernstone, a polissoir, and parts of two arrowheads. The green-stone axe had been set in the ground, blade uppermost, while two more examples in the same raw material had been deposited nearby. Two axeheads, a polissoir and a quern were found in a similar feature. This distinctive group of structures was closely related to the overall distribution of activities in the settlement at Skogsmossen:

> If one draws a line between the three constructions, a boundary between the house and the different activity areas in the farmyard is created. All the saddle-shaped grinding stones were found north of this line, whilst almost all the greenstone and flint axes . . . were . . . to the south . . . In the same area as many of the axes were found there was also a large quantity of highly fragmented pottery.
>
> (Ibid.: 101)

There are similar anomalies at Skumparberget, although these do not take such an obvious form. Axeheads and roughout axes were found in a series of clusters within the excavated area, and in two cases there is evidence that they were being made on the site itself. Both working floors are associated with finds of TRB collared flasks, a rather unusual form which also occurs in a marked concentration outside the house itself. There are other indications that axes of various kinds were of special importance at Skumparberget. A ceramic amulet took the form of an axehead, whilst part of a battle-axe made of diabase had been deposited in a pit within the settlement. Its context stood out from that of the other artefacts, a point which was emphasised by the excavators:

> In the area where the . . . battle-axe . . . was found the remains of some kind of structure involving post holes and two parallel rows of fire-cracked rocks was uncovered. Adjacent to the structure, complete pottery vessels had been deposited. It is likely that this area can be regarded as some kind of ritual space within the site.
>
> (Ibid.: 25)

Other axes at Skumparberget had been treated in a distinctive manner. Although artefacts of different raw materials could be found together, all the thin-butted axes were represented by broken fragments. All but one of the pecked axes were complete. It may be no accident that the only exception was the battle-axe buried in the pit.

Again it is worth emphasising the common elements. Both settlements were engaged in agricultural production. Axes were also made there. The artefacts that seem to have been selected for special treatment were similar at both sites: axeheads, the polissoirs employed in their production, the quernstones used to prepare food, and the ceramic vessels that may have served it. Animal bones were perhaps employed in a structured manner at Skogsmossen, but there are too few of them to substantiate this claim.

On a still broader scale both these sites have exceptional characteristics. The most obvious feature of Skumparberget is acknowledged in the title of an article about the site: 'Burning down the house'. It describes what the authors refer to as 'the transformational use of fire' (ibid.). This is particularly important as the domestic building at Skogsmossen may have been destroyed in the same way, although the argument is not so clear-cut. It was not only the building at Skumparberget that had been burnt, for many of the excavated artefacts, including pottery and worked flint, had also been affected.

The publication of Skogsmossen has an equally arresting title, and this introduces a further element into the discussion (Hallgren *et al.* 1997). The paper refers to Skogsmossen as 'an Early Neolithic settlement site *and sacrificial fen*' (my emphasis). As the writers explain, this is one of the few examples of such a site to have been excavated, and it was the first of its kind to be identified in Central Sweden.

It consists of a shallow hollow which contains two pools of water and extends over approximately 300 square metres (Figure 4.3). The bog was located only twenty-five metres from the house, but they were separated from one another by the stone-settings mentioned earlier. The cultural deposits extended to a depth of about 60 cm and, on the basis of radiocarbon dating, have been assigned to three distinct episodes within the Early Neolithic period.

The deposits of cultural material were found in the deeper parts of the natural depression where there is standing water today. A little structural evidence was found in these areas, as there were post holes in the bottom of the hollow and finds of clay daub from its filling. The larger pool may have been associated with a rectangular platform between 15 and 20 square metres in extent, but the post holes in the remaining part of the site cannot be interpreted in detail. The excavators suggest that one purpose of the wooden platform was to facilitate access to the pool.

It is never easy to distinguish between the by-products of human settlement and intentional offerings of the kind that are suggested here, but Hallgren and his colleagues present a compelling case. They compare the material from the bog with the deposits associated with the house. There are a series of contrasts between the two assemblages. The pottery from the settlement site is fragmentary, but it seems likely that ceramics entered the bog as complete vessels, which may have been broken deliberately. The percentage of decorated pottery is higher among the collection from the bog than in the settlement site: 18 per cent from the excavated areas of the pool, compared with 9 per cent from the dry-land deposit associated with the dwelling and its surroundings. Clearly the fen was not a domestic midden.

Similar contrasts extend to other kinds of artefacts. There are also a number of axeheads which seem to have been deliberately destroyed either by breaking them or by exposing them to fire. It is clear that they had been in good condition before that happened. Some had been burnt so severely that they had changed their colour and texture, and in certain cases fragments of the same artefact had been distributed across different parts of the bog. One of the burnt objects was a polygonal battle-axe, not unlike the fragmentary example from the pit at Skumparberget. There were other flint and stone artefacts in the Skogsmossen bog, but, like the axeheads, they had a distinctive character. There were a series of flint tools, including arrowheads, knives and scrapers. The latter were unusually large and almost half of them had been burnt. In the same way, the pool contained a series of flakes which were significantly bigger than their counterparts in the settlement assemblage. It also included most of the quartz cores on the site, and once again these were deposited when they could still have been used. There were a few exotic items which were restricted to this part of the excavation. The most notable was a fine slate knife of a kind associated with hunting communities in Northern Sweden, as well as projectile points of the same material.

The slate artefacts are very different from the finds associated with the settlement, but there are similarities between some of the other tools from the separate parts of Skogsmossen. The pool contained the remains of a number of querns, but again some of these stand out from the material found in the occupation site as three of them were 'intact and fully functional' (Hallgren *et al*. 1997: 70). They were found amidst a deposit of other stones, some of which had been burnt. These rocks had obviously been brought to the site deliberately and were associated with the greatest concentration of artefacts.

Bone hardly survived in the filling of this feature, although there were traces of grain. Otherwise it seems as if the material deposited in the pool was similar in kind to the contents of the nearby settlement, or, indeed, to the finds from Skumparberget. In certain cases the artefacts found on dry land might have been part of formal deposits, and in that case it may be more than a coincidence that the main emphasis was on a restricted range of types: axes, querns and entire ceramic vessels. The main contrast concerns the polissoirs from Skogsmossen, but even these could have been used in making some of the artefacts deposited in the pool. The evidence from Skumparberget is far more limited, but again the settlement seems to have included some specialised deposits, including a battle-axe and several complete pots. That is not the only connection that stands out. At both sites it seems likely that the houses had been destroyed by fire, and the same interpretation extends to a significant proportion of the artefacts from the excavations. The votive pool at Skogsmossen also contained a number of burnt axes and other stones. It hardly needs adding that nearly all these deposits contain material of kinds associated with land clearance and food production.

These features have their counterparts at other Neolithic sites in Southern Scandinavia, the Netherlands and North Germany, but in most of these regions the situation is complicated by the presence of monuments. Skumparberget and Skogsmossen provide such an instructive case precisely because they are located well beyond the northern limits of their distribution. Nonetheless it is worth making the point that all the practices that seem to be evidenced at these two sites also occur in places with a more varied archaeological record. We can consider this evidence under three categories. First, there are the specialised deposits associated with settlements in areas further to the south; then there are other examples in which pools and similar locations were selected as the focus for deliberate deposits; and, finally, there is evidence of comparable practices associated with specialised monuments. These were mainly enclosures and tombs.

Wider relationships

Economy and material culture

The settlements described so far both date from the Early Neolithic period. As we have seen, they were also occupied by farmers. If we are to consider the significance of votive offerings over a wider area, we must come to terms with some important differences of chronology and economy.

Skumparberget and Skogsmossen were occupied by people whose material culture belonged to the TRB or Funnel Beaker tradition, but during the same period there were settlements in Central Sweden which had a very different character. These were often located on the coast and were associated with Pitted Ware (M. Larsson and Olsson 1997; Malmer 2002: chapter 3). The people who lived there practised hunting, gathering and fishing rather than agriculture. Some kept a few domesticated animals, but they do not seem to have engaged in cultivation.

The relationship between those two traditions is controversial, but it appears to have changed during the Middle Neolithic period. The frequency of Pitted Ware sites apparently increased and, with it, the importance of wild resources. Eventually, the Battle Axe Culture saw some reversion to farming, although the evidence is patchy and it may not have been a uniform process. This tradition extended over a large area and involved long-distance contacts between Sweden and regions to the south. The main trends are identified in a useful paper by Ahlfont *et al.* (1995) which maps the distribution of early domesticates in Sweden.

Deposits in settlements

These relationships are important as they are reflected by differences in the character of votive deposits. Since there is so much regional variation, the simplest procedure is probably to treat the agricultural settlements separately from those inhabited by hunter gatherers.

In one sense the settlements at Skumparberget and Skogsmossen are a little unusual for they lie beyond the distribution of most of the votive deposits

131

associated with farmers. There is also evidence from the settlements sustained by wild resources, but on the whole this took a different form. The main groups of offerings associated with early agriculture are found in Southern Sweden where they occur on sites with wooden houses not unlike those just described. For the most part they avoid the buildings themselves and focus on some of the pits within the occupied area (Figure 4.4; Malmer 2002: 40–1 and 71–3; M. Andersson 2004). Their contents stand out for a number of reasons. They contain intact or undamaged artefacts, including ceramic vessels, but they can also include items that had been burnt. These are just the kinds of material that featured in my previous discussion. Karsten (1994) has argued that the location of such deposits changed during the Neolithic period so that the later deposits are more closely associated with individual houses and were sometimes placed in their foundations. Their distribution tends to favour the position of the outer wall rather than the internal roof supports.

A few examples illustrate the main points. A number of the pits found in settlements share a distinctive configuration (Rogius *et al.* 2001). Large stones were placed on the bottoms of these features and over them people laid out ceramic vessels, axeheads and deposits of burnt material before the excavation was refilled (Malmer 2002: 41). In other cases it seems as if objects had been burnt after they had entered the ground; Karsten describes these as 'fire offerings' (1994: 192). In another instance a large funnel beaker had been smashed against a conspicuous rock. Such cases stand out because complete pots and axeheads are unusual on domestic sites. Malmer suggests that complex artefacts were also deposited on the surface within the settlement area. The clearest example was at Karlsfät where 'a thick-butted flint axe lay in a rectangular stone kerb, beside a stone setting which is presumably associated with a house' (2002: 73). This was the one complete example on that site. Settlement deposits can be even more distinctive. A recent study of Western Scania shows that human bones are sometimes found in Early Neolithic pits (M. Andersson 2003). A few of the houses are also associated with flat graves (Figure 4.4).

It is interesting that Malmer's recent synthesis of 'The Neolithic of South Sweden' contains a section on the 'offerings and offering-places' of the TRB Culture, and another on 'offerings and votive sites' in the Battle Axe tradition, whilst 'settlements and votive sites' are treated together in the chapter concerned with Pitted Ware (Malmer 2002: 39–43, 71–6 and 97–126). That is not a criticism of the book. Rather, it reflects an important contrast between the deposits associated with agricultural settlements and those on sites used for hunting, gathering and fishing. That is particularly true in those areas in which the economy may have changed. Ceramics became less elaborate and their social importance was probably reduced. The same could apply to other objects. Malmer describes the situation in Central Sweden:

This ceramic regression, and the resistance [to] new TRB innovations, has direct consequences in several other spheres: no megalithic graves were built . . ., offerings declined or ceased, and animal husbandry and the . . . cultivation of grain decreased in favour of hunting and fishing . . . [T]he frequency of flint objects and flint waste is lower at [Pitted Ware sites] than TRB settlement[s] . . . In addition, a smaller percentage of the flint is burnt, which was probably because flint was in short supply, but especially also because the ritual burning of flint known from the TRB . . . did not occur . . . Generally speaking, it may be said that an important part of the transition . . . is that ritual gave way to practical considerations.

(2002: 102)

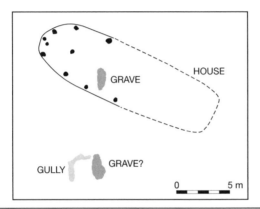

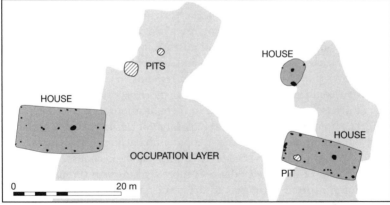

Figure 4.4   The relationship of Neolithic houses to graves and pits at Tofta (upper drawing) and (below) Dagstorp, Southern Sweden. Information from M. Andersson (2003).

That may not provide the complete answer, and at a number of points in his text Malmer acknowledges the problem. Thus 'the settlement at Häggsta . . . includes a structure that was no doubt built for ritual purposes' (2002: 98); a hearth surrounded by flat stones at Djupvik 'is most likely a ritual structure' (ibid.: 98); and 'the Hedningahällan site . . . evidently had a partly ritual function' (ibid.: 101). The problem is not that 'ritual gave way to practical considerations', but that it was so closely bound up in domestic life that it may be impossible to recognise as a separate sphere of activity. The ambiguity is most apparent at the 'pile dwelling' of Alvastra, a site which raises so many problems that I shall consider it in a section of its own.

The strongest argument for specialised activities is provided by the abundance and variety of archaeological evidence at certain points on the coast. Some unusually large and productive settlements have been identified as aggregation sites, for they include numerous hearths and evidence for large-scale food consumption. Sometimes these places show few signs of domestic buildings. Occasionally, there are other features which draw attention to their exceptional character: house floors at Fräkenrönningen that had been stained with red ochre (a material more commonly associated with graves): an occupation site at Siretorp in which successive deposits contained the bones of golden eagles; and another at Bua which produced a notable collection of axes (Malmer 2002: 100, 115 and 118).

There is also some compelling evidence for an association between Pitted Ware settlements and human remains (Malmer 2002: 91–7). Formal cemeteries are best evidenced on Öland and Gotland where it seems as if they were established in places which had already been occupied. This suggests a close connection between the living and the dead, and it is clear that in some cases domestic activities continued very close to the burial ground. On the Swedish mainland, however, the evidence is less clear-cut. It is certainly true that flat graves would be more difficult to recognise where bone artefacts do not survive, but that does not explain why archaeologists should overlook other distinctive grave goods, such as arrowheads, axes and amber beads. Nor does it account for the discovery of disarticulated human remains in settlements. No doubt some of these could have been reworked from older deposits, for a small number of intact burials have been recognised in these locations, but the contrast with the evidence from the two islands is too striking for this to provide a satisfactory answer. For example, there is one case, at Fräkenrönningen, where a body associated with red ochre had been buried in the floor of a house. At the Pitted Ware settlement of Åby the evidence is more striking still (Figure 4.5). Here bones belonging to at least two adults were found in the same small area as domestic buildings, two chisels, an axe, an arrowhead and a concentration of imported flint. There was no sign of a grave, but the excavator suggests that this had been a formal deposit (M. Larsson 2003). It seems likely that the same applies to other finds of human remains on Pitted Ware sites. Not all of these need be later in date than the period of occupation, and there is little evidence

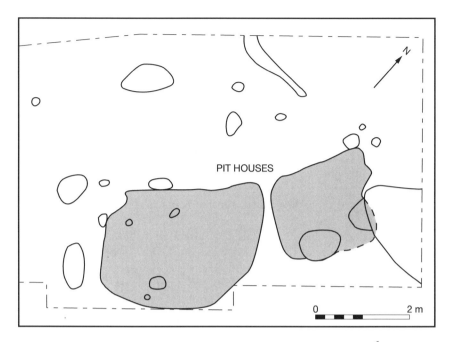

Figure 4.5 Outline plans of two pit houses in the Neolithic settlement at Åby, Eastern
Sweden. Information from M. Larsson (2003).

that they came from disturbed burials. Rather, the relics of the dead were
incorporated in the settlements of the living, as they may have been during
the Ertebølle period (Brinch Petersen and Meiklejohn 2003).

Deposits in 'natural' places

Skogsmossen is important because it is one of the relatively small number
of ritual pools investigated in recent years. It also lies a little outside their main
distribution, which focuses on Scania and Denmark. But, like Skumparberget,
it also produced finds of burnt axeheads. These are another characteristic
of votive deposits in South Scandinavia, but because so many of their contents
are restricted to lithic artefacts it is impossible to distinguish between the
activities of farmers and those of hunter gatherers.

There are a large number of specialised deposits from the bogs, rivers and
lakes of Northern Europe, but their components are much the same as those
of occupation sites on dry land. There is a broad contrast between the Danish
evidence, which includes many finds of pots (Koch 1998), and the record
from Sweden in which stone artefacts are far more common (Karsten 1994;
M. Andersson 2004: 170–2), but both areas show a similar emphasis on various
forms of axe, as well as occasional human and animal bones. There are

135

important distinctions on a more local level, so that we see striking contrasts between the representation of polished and unpolished axes, multiple finds and single finds, and pots with more or less elaborate decoration. Nevertheless the material deposited in these contexts is not altogether different from the finds associated with settlements.

This may seem an obvious point, but comparison with the evidence from the Scandinavian Bronze Age soon helps to put these observations in perspective, for here it is apparent that a number of metal items are found in votive deposits and practically nowhere else (Levy 1982). Indeed, it would not be too much to suggest that the contents of settlements and those of bog deposits were almost mutually exclusive. Examples of this contrast include the presence of elaborate weapons in water deposits rather than settlements, and the restriction of specialised types like musical instruments to the deposits associated with bogs.

The Neolithic evidence is very different, although it shows some patterning of its own. A number of the ceramic vessels in Danish peat bogs contained traces of food, and the remains of sacrificed animals, however uncommon, seem to have observed a clear distinction between domesticates and wild species (Koch 1998: 153–4). Particular kinds of artefact were deposited in particular contexts, so that the axeheads found in isolation might be larger than those in groups (Karsten 1994). Similarly, pots were placed in open water whilst it seems as if axes, including what may have been roughouts, were more closely associated with bogs. Perforated stone artefacts seem to be especially frequent in rivers.

Similar distinctions extend to deposits on dry land where there may be a distinction between the Swedish finds of isolated axes and the multiple finds that are usually described as hoards. Some of these appear in relative isolation, whilst others seem to have been located beside a prominent stone which could have acted as a marker. These deposits were certainly located within the settled landscape, but it is clear that they were not uniformly distributed, as the main concentrations of multiple and single finds are separated by areas in which these finds are absent.

Nor were these artefacts deposited at a uniform rate, either on land or in water. The process began in the Mesolithic and votive offerings were relatively uncommon early in the Neolithic period, but they soon increased in frequency before the process was checked (Karsten 1994). The practice resumed during the currency of Battle Axes and one extraordinary feature is how often the same places were used for making offerings after a lapse of several hundred years. To a smaller extent, the same pattern applies to the deposits of ceramic vessels in Denmark (Koch 1998).

At Skogsmossen it seemed likely that the process of making offerings was facilitated by the construction of a wooden platform. Similar features have been observed at other sites in Sweden and Denmark and it seems as if these places were used repeatedly (Karsten 1994; Koch 1998; Svensson 2004: 212). Human remains are relatively uncommon but include a few bodies which have been interpreted as sacrifices, as well as deposits of skulls which tend to be associated with rivers. Some of the artefacts had been broken before their deposition but only a limited proportion had been burnt.

Again there is a contrast with the evidence from dry land. As we have seen, there are deposits of burnt artefacts, particularly axeheads, from the excavation of Neolithic settlements, and it has often been observed that an unexpectedly high proportion of the domestic assemblage seems to have been affected by fire. During the last few years two remarkable sites have been excavated in Scania. The first is at Svartskylle (Figure 4.6; L. Larsson 1989). This is a low hill whose setting recalls the positions of causewayed enclosures in Denmark. The site is characterised by considerable numbers of burnt axeheads, found in apparent isolation. This impression has been confirmed by fieldwork which has shown that it was neither a settlement nor a monument. It was simply a specialised location in which one particular kind of artefact was consumed by fire.

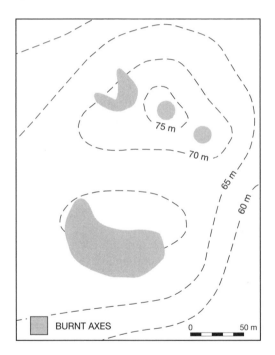

Figure 4.6 Deposits of burnt flint axes on the hilltop at Svartskylle, Southern Sweden. Information from L. Larsson (1989).

Just as many of the practices that typify Early Neolithic water deposits in Sweden were resumed during the Battle Axe period, Svartskylle has its counterpart during the latter phase. Recent excavation at Kverrestad has identified a very similar site, but this time it dates from the opposite end of the sequence. Again this was not a settlement or a monument but a specialised location

137

devoted to the destruction of artefacts by fire. There were certain contrasts, for some of the burnt artefacts at Kverrestad had been buried in pits and in a few cases they were accompanied by human and animal remains (L. Larsson 2000a and b). Again it seems as if artefacts that had been directly involved in the clearance and cultivation of farmland were sacrificed in conspicuous locations. Very similar practices took place at Neolithic monuments.

Deposits in monuments

Again there is evidence of a punctuated sequence of deposits at the Neolithic monuments of Southern Sweden. The commonest are megalithic tombs, and here the evidence can be divided between the construction of dolmens and passage graves during the earlier part of the Neolithic and a later stage when some of these sites were reused for individual burials. Monumental tombs were no longer built during this second phase and in fact there seems to have been a period in which such structures were redundant. Chambered tombs date from the Early Neolithic and the first part of the Middle Neolithic and regained some of their significance during the Battle Axe Culture. They are a feature of the TRB Culture and were not built by the people who made Pitted Ware (Tilley 1996; Malmer 2002).

It remains to be seen whether the regions with megalithic tombs also saw the construction of earthwork enclosures, as happened in Denmark and North Germany. At present only one example has been identified in Sweden (L. Larsson 1982), but comparison with the evidence from other parts of Scandinavia suggests that the number may increase. In any event, it is clear that Scania and Bornholm did see the construction of what has been described as a 'second generation' of enclosures (Svensson 2002 and 2004; Kaul et al. 2002). They date from the very end of the TRB Culture and the Battle Axe Culture, which means that this happened after a period in which votive deposits had been less common. It may be no coincidence that the newly constructed enclosures were often close to flat cemeteries of the same date.

It is easiest to characterise the first group of enclosures by reference to the evidence from Denmark and, in particular, the monument at Sarup which featured in Chapter 3 (N. Anderson 1997). These sites belong to a widely distributed category of earthwork characterised by large deposits of cultural material, human remains and animal bones. These sites are generally defined by interrupted ditches, and few of them provide convincing evidence of settlement contemporary with the use of these earthworks; it is a moot point whether they became domestic sites during a subsequent phase. The main types of artefacts associated with these places were decorated pottery vessels, flint and stone axeheads and saddle querns. Sarup itself was near to a number of megalithic tombs and the excavator suggests that the enclosure played a part in mortuary rituals. It seems to have been a place where collections of cultural material were put on display before they were buried. In some cases there is evidence that objects had been destroyed, often by fire. In Scania similar activities perhaps took place at open sites, as deposits of the same kind have been identified at Hindby Mosse. Again these may have had a special character.

In this case the excavated area included a dense deposit of TRB material marking the limits of an almost circular area approximately 70 m in diameter. Although many of the artefacts are of kinds which occur in settlements, this particular site also contained a series of structured deposits of pottery, animal bones and axeheads. Some of the axes had been burnt. There were also human bones belonging to at least twenty individuals (Svensson 2002 and 2004). It may be no coincidence that nearby there was a votive pool containing further deposits of animal bones and axes. This had a longer history, as the finds extend from the Mesolithic period to the Early Bronze Age (Nilsson 1995; Svensson 2004: 197–203). There was also a megalithic tomb accompanied by a large amount of pottery (Burenhult 1973).

In fact concentrations of material were assembled outside many of the tombs. At one time it was supposed that these were grave goods which had been cleared from the burial chamber during a subsequent phase, but now it is accepted that the dead were accompanied by personal ornaments and a limited range of smaller objects. By contrast, the collections found outside these monuments include large numbers of decorated vessels, as well as axeheads and some human bones. It seems likely that these vessels had originally held food and drink, and there has been much discussion of the relationship between the pots selected for this purpose and those associated with settlements. There is a substantial overlap between the two groups, but there are also minor variations (Hulthén 1977; Tilley 1996: 292–315), as there were between those associated with the house at Skogsmossen and the finds from the votive pool on the same site. Another link is that very large quantities of flint could be burnt at the megalithic tombs (Madsen 1997). This included not only artefacts but unused raw material.

The 'second generation' of Neolithic monuments in Sweden is represented by palisaded enclosures (Svensson 2002 and 2004) and, despite the chrono-logical hiatus mentioned earlier, these replicate many of the characteristics of the older sites. They are a recent discovery and it is too soon to say much about them. Nevertheless they do not seem to have been settlements and yet they are associated with formal deposits of the same kinds of material as we find on habitation sites. Axeheads were buried beneath some of the upright posts and a number of these monuments had been set on fire. A particular feature of the examples in Scania is that they are associated with the production of flint axes. The monuments can be quite impressive, for they are between two and six hectares in extent and made considerable use of timber. One example at Rispebjerg on the island of Bornholm was defined by no fewer than fourteen palisades, although it is not clear whether all of them were in use at the same time (Figure 4.7; Kaul *et al.* 2002). The construction of the enclosures at Dösjebro and Hyllie may have taken between 2,500 and 6,000 worker days.

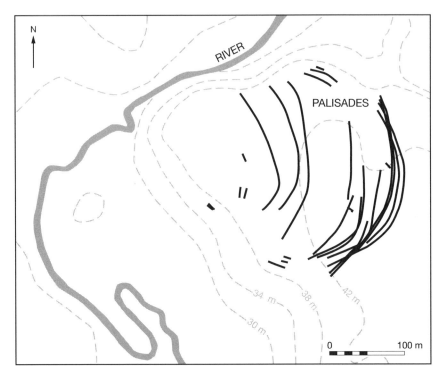

Figure 4.7 Outline plan of the Neolithic palisaded enclosures at Rispebjerg, Bornholm. Information from Kaul *et al*. (2002).

Alvastra

I said that monuments are not associated with Pitted Ware, although there were obviously specialised deposits at some of the settlements belonging to that tradition. There is one place which epitomises many of the issues that have been considered in this chapter.

This is the unusual site of Alvastra in South Central Sweden (Browall 1986 and 1987; Malmer 2002: 103–12). It consists of the well-preserved remains of two timber platforms which were constructed in a mire at the foot of a conspicuous mountain. The structure underwent many modifications which have been traced by dendrochronology, but its essential features were clear even from the earliest excavation. The site had been built in a low-lying situation and would have been damp during the summer months and inundated during the winter. It could not be defended and was a most unsuitable place in which to live. Indeed, domestic sites of the same period have been identified on dry ground in the surrounding area.

140

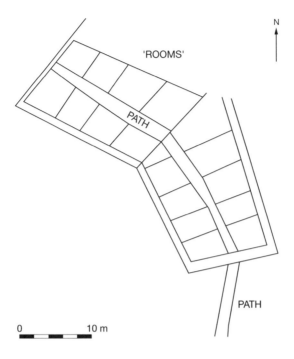

Figure 4.8 Simplified plan of the Neolithic platform at Alvastra, South Central Sweden. Information from Browall (1986).

The two platforms were organised around a central path which divided them into approximately equal parts, each of which consisted of a series of small compartments or 'rooms' (Figure 4.8). Although there is no evidence that they had been separated by partitions, each seems to have had its own hearth, which was often renewed. The excavated assemblage from Alvastra is most unusual. The ceramics suggest that it was associated with Pitted Ware, although there is a smaller contribution of TRB vessels. This is consistent with the radiocarbon dates from the site. The lithic artefacts have many of the characteristics that have already featured in this chapter: virtually all the flint axes had been broken and many of them were burnt; their counterparts in other raw materials were left intact. There were many animal bones, suggesting a mixture of wild and domesticated species, and the botanical remains provide a similar impression, with the remains of cereals as well as those of wild plants. Other elements were more unusual. At an early stage the timber structure had been burnt down. Moreover, there were the remains of many unfinished battle-axes. Later deposits on the site contained human remains, including the disarticulated bones of adults and children, some, and possibly all, of whom were male. There was also the skull of a man who had probably been scalped.

141

The most recent excavator of Alvastra is ambivalent about the correct interpretation of the site, for he describes it as a 'pile dwelling' and sometimes even as a 'settlement', yet he also comments that its purpose 'must have been social solidarity, feasting and worship. The participants in the feasts and ceremonies . . . were men. The reason for locating the feasting place in a mire must have been privacy; but above all the dramatic topography' (Malmer 2002: 112). The separate compartments on the timber platform may have been used by different groups from the surrounding area.

Discussion: water and fire

The ambiguity is revealing. Alvastra contains many of the same artefacts as the settlement sites of the period and yet it combines two of the key attributes of Swedish votive deposits: water and fire. It includes the axeheads that are found with Neolithic houses and may even provide similar evidence for the production of elaborate artefacts. The deposits of cereals and domesticated animal bones connect it not only to habitation sites, but also to the monuments where human remains occur. Yet the timber platforms could hardly be less monumental. The contrast is especially important since its period of use may have overlapped with that of a megalithic tomb located only 1,500 metres away (Janzon 1984).

At the same time, Alvastra is associated mainly with Pitted Ware and also provides evidence of game animals and wild plants. It includes many hearths but no obvious domestic dwellings, and it is associated with a significant number of disarticulated human bones. All these features characterise the aggregation sites of hunters and fishers on the Baltic coast. These were communities who do not seem to have built any monuments.

In fact Alvastra occupies a pivotal position in a number of quite different interpretations. It characterises some of the settlement deposits, and many of the votive deposits, of the TRB Culture. Its contents also overlap with those of megaliths and causewayed enclosures. At the same time, it has much in common with other Pitted Ware sites. There is abundant evidence for the use of wild resources; the platforms were in no sense monumental; there are indications of large-scale food consumption; and, mixed in with the material that might be found on a domestic site, there are human bones. The platform – and some of the artefacts – had been burnt, like those at the monuments of the TRB Culture, yet the practice of making offerings in wet places is one that may have had its origins in the Mesolithic period (Karsten 1994).

In fact it is important to consider the Swedish evidence as a whole. At its simplest this can be characterised in terms of four components: the Ertebølle period, when people were entirely dependent on wild resources; the TRB Culture, when they first adopted farming; the currency of Pitted Ware when some communities practised an economy based on hunting and fishing; and, finally, the Battle Axe Culture, when agriculture maintained its importance in certain areas.

All these groups are mirrored in the archaeology of votive offerings. It is clear that the first deposits of animal remains and artefacts do not date from the Neolithic period. Sites like Hindby Mosse show quite clearly that they originated in the Mesolithic period (Karsten 1994; Svensson 2004). Some of those practices were augmented by the activities of the first farmers in Southern Scandinavia, and the number and variety of votive offerings increased during the early part of the Neolithic period. They also extended to new contexts – enclosures and chambered tombs – and to new kinds of ritual involving the use of fire. Pitted Ware sites provide less evidence of this kind of activity, and most of the indications of ritual come from settlements or the locations interpreted as aggregation sites. In either case, no monuments were built. Finally, during the Battle Axe Culture something of the sheer diversity of the first Neolithic system seems to have reasserted itself. Chambered tombs were reused for burials and a novel kind of enclosure was constructed where activities similar to those associated with older monuments took place. It was during this phase that the deposition of artefacts in bogs and pools resumed with any intensity. Once again it seems as if many kinds of material were consumed by fire.

There are two observations that we can make about this remarkable pattern. The first is that water deposition began before the adoption of domesticates and in its initial stages it reflects the world view of Ertebølle communities. That connection is not unexpected since so many of the sites occupied by hunters, fishers and foragers in Southern Scandinavia were located on the coast or along the margins of rivers and lakes (Fischer 2002). Nevertheless, that link between votive deposition and water was to prove extremely long-lived, for it did not come to a conclusion until the first millennium AD (Bradley 1998a). During the Neolithic period it ran in parallel with a quite different phenomenon: the deliberate destruction of artefacts – and occasionally of entire structures – by fire. This practice has a more restricted chronological distribution. It is clearly evidenced on the sites of the TRB and Battle Axe Cultures when farming was important, but it is seldom associated with Pitted Ware. Again there is a possible explanation. A number of writers have suggested that this may be a reference to the processes involved in cereal growing (Madsen 1997). Perhaps the burning of artefacts and monuments referred to the importance of fire in preparing land for cultivation. The results of pollen analysis in Denmark support this view (S. Andersen 1993), although they need not imply the use of swidden agriculture (Rowley-Conwy 2003). Fire was a potent force in maintaining the well-being of society.

If that is so, it may not be surprising that much of the material deposited in monuments or votive deposits during the Swedish Neolithic refers to the processes involved in clearing land, raising domesticated animals and growing crops. That may be why it has been hard to tell the difference between settlement assemblages and more specialised contexts. Indeed, it provides one reason for doubting whether the distinction between ritual and domestic life can contribute much to the Neolithic archaeology of Northern Europe. As the excavations of Skumparberget and Skogsmossen demonstrate, these two elements are closely intertwined.

5

MULTIPLICATION AND DIVISION

The problem of utilitarian bronze hoards

The question of classification

Librarians are rather like archaeologists, for they must classify their material in order to make it accessible. Prehistorians categorise the remains of the past and present the results in print. Then libraries organise that work according to its subject matter.

Sometimes this raises problems. Consider the series of monographs published as *Praehistorische Bronzefunde*. The separate volumes have a quite specific format. They list the metal artefacts of Bronze Age Europe, region by region, one type at a time. Thus there are entire books on pins, brooches, bracelets, axes, spearheads and swords. The intention is that eventually these will provide a catalogue of all the metalwork that survives. This has still to be achieved, and we may be forgiven for wondering whether interpretations of this material can be deferred any longer.

In the Reading University library all the volumes of *Praehistorische Bronzefunde* are shelved together following the scheme worked out by the editor when the series was founded. They are organised according to different kinds of artefacts and different regions. The Sackler Library in Oxford adopts a different principle. It locates them according to their subject matter. This is a sensible procedure and one that shows a genuine comprehension of the fields covered by individual books. But it can produce unexpected results. For example, most of the volumes cataloguing Bronze Age swords are located among accounts of early warfare, but one of the books is shelved in the section documenting the cultures of prehistoric Europe. That is entirely appropriate, for it is on the sequence of sword types that the local chronology depends. Following that precedent, one might suppose that the volumes concerned with bronze axes would be found in the same place, but again they are divided between different parts of the library. As expected, one group is among the texts on material culture and chronology, but the other occupies a section concerned with metalworking. Since so much raw material was distributed in the form of axeheads it was logical to adopt this procedure. It would seem possible to organise the books on Bronze Age sickles according to the same criterion, for again these artefacts may have provided standard units of metal. On the whole that is what happens, but another volume in this series is located among the works on early farming. That can also be justified, as sickles were agricultural tools.

If this seems confusing, the uncertainty is created by the authors themselves, for in the archaeological literature metal artefacts are employed in all these different ways. They provide the foundation for regional chronologies and distributions; they offer vital evidence for the exchange of raw material; and they play a part in reconstructions of ancient social life. How can we bring these different concerns together? One approach is to discuss the contexts in which this material occurs.

The question of context

Prehistoric metalwork can appear in many guises: as artefacts associated with burials, as the residues of craft production and in the curious collections known as hoards. Such features have come to dominate archaeological writing during recent years, and nowhere more than in accounts of the Later Bronze Age. To some extent this is an understandable reaction to the large amounts of material available for study, but in another way it is because its very existence poses new kinds of problems for archaeological research. As I commented in my discussion of Viereckschanzen, it is difficult to recognise a special class of 'votive artefact' because so many different types of object were removed from circulation with some formality. It is to that process that we owe their survival to the present day.

This is particularly true of bronze artefacts, although their interpretation is hampered by the ways in which research has been divided between a series of specialist fields. Thus there are reviews of grave goods, settlement finds, single finds and the groups of metalwork described as hoards, but until quite recently there were few discussions of the links between these categories. This was because it was so tempting to think in terms of dualities. Thus the finds from graves were contrasted with those from settlement sites, and the metalwork from rivers, bogs and lakes was sometimes distinguished from that found on dry land (Levy 1982; Bradley 1998a; Fontijn 2003). Behind all these divisions there was a broader agenda at work. In certain cases it could be assumed that metalwork had been discarded voluntarily, whilst in others it might have been lost or stored for later retrieval. Artefacts associated with burials were taken out of circulation permanently, although in fact there is some evidence of Bronze Age grave robbing (Rittershofer 1987). In the case of metalwork deposited in rivers recovery was rarely an option, so ritual activity was postulated on the basis of negative criteria: it could be recognised because these cases departed in such obvious ways from what appeared to be practical concerns.

The corollary might seem to be that those artefacts that could have been retrieved would not be interpreted as votive finds, but in fact that position has rarely been adopted in recent years (Dickens 1996). It seems entirely implausible that during some phases of the Bronze Age the positions of stored or hidden objects should have been forgotten, while in others they were recalled with so much accuracy that little metalwork survives, and in any case this approach would not take into account a number of other observations. Some of the metalwork found on dry land is associated with animal bones or, occasionally, with human remains, whilst there can be a direct relationship between the kinds of places where it was deposited and the types of object that were selected for this purpose (Bradley 2000: chapter 4).

Again the discussion has been influenced by a distinction between ritual and the everyday. Thus deposits of metalwork that seem to be closely related to those found in graves occupy a privileged position in the debate, and collections of this kind of material are usually interpreted as votive deposits. This may happen where particular kinds of weapons or personal ornaments are found in burials in one phase and in different deposits during the succeeding period. Alternatively, the same kinds of artefacts might be employed as grave goods in one region but deposited in hoards or rivers in a neighbouring area. As both groups of material had complementary distributions, the interpretation of one came to influence the interpretation of the other (Torbrügge 1971).

That approach left the deposition of a large body of metalwork to be explained. Often it consisted of those kinds of artefacts which were not associated with rivers or graves in the first place. In many areas finds of tools were the principal category, and these fell outside this simple scheme because they were often associated with other objects of the same kind. Sometimes artefacts of types that occurred in specialised contexts were also found as fragments in these collections. For example, the groups of axes in dry-land hoards might be associated with broken ornaments and weapons. It seemed as if such items had played a dual role in the past. In some contexts they might be used as grave goods or as votive offerings, whilst, in others, they appear to have been accumulated as scrap metal. In certain areas these two kinds of deposit had mutually exclusive distributions, so that it seemed possible that objects which had played a restricted role in one region might have lost their original significance when they were accumulated in another area. Here they could be treated as a source of raw material (Bradley 1998a: 144–50).

On one level this scheme seemed quite plausible. Groups of intact metalwork could have been discarded as part of a ritual. The same types can be found in fragments in the hoards which may have been associated with smiths. Not only did some of these deposits contain what might be regarded as scrap, such finds could also be associated with ingots, slag, crucibles and casting jets. This interpretation was supported by the evidence of metal analysis which showed that very few of the objects that entered the archaeological record could be linked with particular sources. That was because the bronze out of which they were made had been recycled.

This evidence suggested a simple contrast in the character of Bronze Age metal finds. Certain types were deliberately deposited in specialised locations, which might be burial mounds or entirely unaltered places in the landscape. Often they were contexts from which these artefacts would have been difficult or impossible to retrieve. They were usually interpreted as votive deposits. Other kinds of object were buried singly or in groups in places from which it would not have been difficult to recover them. Although there is considerable variation, two kinds of hoard were often identified amongst this material: 'merchants' hoards', which contained groups of unfinished objects that might have been stored there by a smith; and 'founders' hoards', which comprised accumulations of scrap metal which was awaiting transformation when it entered the ground. The dry-land deposits, then, were often associated with craft production.

In this way many different types of deposit were grouped together as 'hoards'. At first this happened because they formed what were described as closed associations – groups of artefacts that had been deposited simultaneously. They provided vital evidence out of which to build a chronology. This was a perfectly proper exercise, although it soon became clear that some associations were more closed than others. The problems arose when different questions were asked, for there was no reason to suppose that these collections had been formed for identical reasons.

Ritual hoards, utilitarian hoards

There is an inevitable tension between those studies which consider the social significance of particular kinds of artefact, and accounts of how they were made. Sometimes it seems as if the very same types shifted between two domains. That is to say, objects that played an important role in society may have been formed out of others which had been melted down. Moreover, types which are found in specialised locations, such as the weapons associated with rivers, could also be employed as a source of raw material. They occurred as fragments in the deposits described as scrap hoards together with the by-products of metalworking. This is hard to understand, for it seems as if the same kinds of artefact were used in specialised transactions on some occasions and in everyday affairs on others. That was why Levy's study of Danish Bronze Age metalwork distinguished between 'ritual' and 'non-ritual hoards' (Levy 1982). I followed this distinction in a book first published in 1990, referring to the categories of 'votive' and 'utilitarian' hoards (Bradley 1998a: 10–14). I now think that this was unwise.

One reason for rejecting this division is provided by recent studies of the ways in which particular objects had been made and used. A number of writers have shown that the artefacts found in specialised contexts often played practical roles before their deposition. Thus the axes associated with Early Bronze Age burials in Central Europe had apparently been used and resharpened (Keilin and Ottaway 1998), and the same applied to those discovered in more recent hoards (Roberts and Ottaway 2003). Many of the objects found in the later metalwork deposits of Southern England also showed signs of wear, and in this case its intensity varied over time and from one region to another (R. Taylor 1994). The sickles that are interpreted as standard units of metal in Central and Eastern Europe provide clear evidence that they had also been employed to harvest crops (Figure 5.1; Rychner 1979), and the weapons discovered in graves, rivers and other unusual locations often retain traces of edge damage and resharpening (Kristiansen 2002). Such evidence is widespread and extends from those associated with burials in Northern and Central Europe to the swords and spears deposited in great numbers in the Thames (York 2002). These observations concern their surface appearance, but a recent study of the ways in which different artefacts had been made leads to the same conclusion. In West-Central France, bronzes of the same kind are found in domestic sites and more specialised deposits and have exactly the same composition. There was no question of producing a special class of object for use in ceremonial (Boulestin and Gomez de Soto 1998).

Of course there are exceptional cases. At Flag Fen, for instance, some of the metalwork that was placed in open water may have been made for the purpose, as it would not have stood up to normal wear and tear (Pryor 2001: chapter 10). Such evidence should be distinguished from the traces left when the objects themselves were deposited. For example, in the Southern Netherlands, some of the metal artefacts that seem to have been employed as offerings were sharpened immediately before their deposition (Fontijn 2003). By contrast,

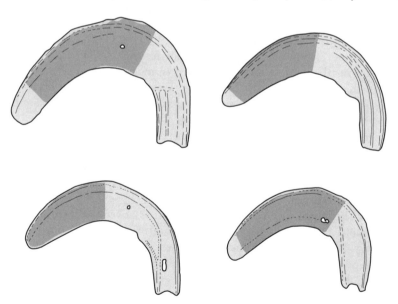

Figure 5.1 Bronze Age sickles showing traces of use from the settlement at Auvernier, Switzerland. The area of use-wear is indicated in dark tone. Information from Rychner (1987).

those discarded in the Thames appear to have been deliberately destroyed, a process that involved an increasing proportion of these objects in the course of the Bronze Age (York 2002). Other kinds of treatment left less obvious traces. For example, studies of the microscopic structure of some weapons suggests that they had been burnt before they entered the archaeological record (Bridgford 1998). This may even have happened because they had passed through a cremation pyre. Such cases do not support the idea that these objects were originally made for use in ritual. Instead, much of this evidence concerns the ways in which they were treated when their other roles had been accomplished.

One way in which we might set about questioning the distinction between ritual and non-ritual hoards is to sever the link between the 'utilitarian' deposits and the activities of smiths. Although this might be possible in individual cases, it does not offer a way forward. As I mentioned earlier, many of these collections include the residues of metalworking, including casting jets, plate scrap, slag and occasional moulds. Moreover, many of the remaining contents of these hoards could have been broken up for recycling, a practice which is clearly evidenced by metal analysis. There seems little prospect of relating these assemblages to the distinctive deposits found in water. In contrast to the collections of broken metalwork considered here, these often include objects which remained intact when they were taken out of circulation.

Another possibility was raised in Chapter 1. This is to suggest that metal-working should never have been regarded as an everyday activity (Barndon 2004; Haaland 2004). The transformation of the raw material may always have been charged with a special significance, and this could have applied to all the material connected with this process – not just the finished products but the scrap metal and even the moulds used to make new artefacts out of old ones. In that case the deposits of metalwork associated with the activities of smiths might have been just as specialised as those found in rivers and bogs. They simply took a different form.

There are several reasons for taking this view. The by-products of metal-working seem to have been imbued with a particular significance. That would explain a number of anomalies in the available evidence. The residues of metal production are occasionally found as grave goods. In Southern Germany, for instance, there are elaborate burials which include copper cake, weights, ingots and unfinished metal artefacts (Winghart 2000). Conversely, there are 'hoards' of half-melted artefacts which have been interpreted as pyre goods, buried separately from the human remains after the funeral was over (Cosack 2003). Some deposits may not have been associated with the dead. In Southern England, deposits of weapon moulds had been placed in the ditch terminals of the fortified settlement at Springfield Lyons (Buckley and Hedges 1987), but others were found outside a hill fort of similar date in Northern Ireland, where they were associated with human skull fragments in the filling of an artificial pool (Lynn 1977). In the same way, there is evidence of metalworking from a number of rather specialised contexts. In Sweden and Denmark bronze working is associated with some of the cult house discussed in Chapter 2 (Kaul 1987; Victor 2002). It is also found together with human and animal remains in mounds of burnt stones of the type considered in Chapter 3 (Karlenby 1999). Again it seems as if the working of metals had unusual connotations. I shall consider this possibility in more detail in the following section.

Multiplication and division

One feature of 'utilitarian' hoards that is normally taken for granted is the presence of incomplete objects. These can be found in a variety of different contexts: in hoards which are dominated by one type of artefact, among single finds or in collections of scrap metal. Although they are rarely discussed, they raise a number of problems.

Sickle hoards

One of the most comprehensive volumes of *Praehistorische Bronzefunde* concerns the sickle hoards of Romania (Petrescu-Dîmbovita 1978). This is important for two reasons. It provides a full record of the contents of these deposits, from intact objects to the smallest fragment, and sickles themselves may be one of the forms in which standard units of metal circulated in Bronze Age Europe.

Many of these hoards do contain broken material and so it is usually supposed that their contents had been brought together for recycling. It is certainly true that many of the sickles are incomplete. That would be logical if they had been broken up as scrap metal, but there is a serious problem. If this took place when the material was buried, all the parts of these objects should be represented, yet it is rarely the case. That raises two possibilities. Perhaps the items found in these collections had been accumulated over a period of time before they were deposited, with the result that some of the fragments had already been melted down. Another interpretation is that these hoards were not the 'closed' deposits that are sometimes supposed. Such collections may have been accessible for a long period of time, with the result that certain pieces were removed and others added. Either hypothesis would account for the mixture of intact and incomplete items found in these deposits.

But it would not explain any imbalance in the representation of different parts of these objects. In two of the largest sickle hoards in Romania we observe a strikingly similar pattern (Petrescu-Dîmbovita 1978). Forty per cent of the artefacts are complete, whilst the socket and lower blade are represented more than fifteen times as often as the remaining section of these artefacts (Figure 5.2). In a third case (the largest hoard of all) only 6 per cent of the sickles are complete, but the same disparity occurs. Among the remaining pieces the butt section of the artefact is represented three times as frequently as the tip.

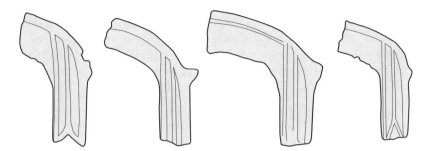

Figure 5.2   Broken sickle fragments from the hoard at Uiorara de Sus, Romania.
Information from Petrescu-Dîmbovita (1978).

A comparable pattern occurs in the smaller hoards and also among single finds. Nearly 60 per cent of the sickles found in isolation are complete, but among the remaining examples butt fragments outnumber tips by approximately three to one. The results are surprisingly consistent in view of the different processes by which these finds have been recovered and documented.

Other items from the same hoards follow a comparable pattern (Petrescu-Dîmbovita 1978). For example, in the largest of all the deposits containing sickles some of the socketed axeheads had been broken. A hundred of these artefacts are complete, but there are parts of another thirty examples. All of these come from the socket and there is not one fragment of a blade (Figure 5.3). The same applies to the swords in this collection. There are seventy of these, but among the incomplete examples hilts outnumber the lower blade by a ratio of 2:1. Similar trends can be identified in other Romanian hoards published in this volume.

One might suppose that this imbalance is due to differential preservation. Were the sockets of the sickles more robust than the remainder of these tools? Would they have survived as well if these broken fragments had been exposed to the elements? At first sight the idea is tempting, but it is not supported by the evidence of occupation sites. Perhaps the best preserved of these are the waterlogged settlements of Southern Germany and the Alpine region, where the archaeological deposits have been protected from later disturbance. Here the evidence shows considerable variation. For example, the large collection of finds from the Wasserburg suggests that few sickles were broken in the course of daily life (Kimmig 1992). The same is true of the finds from Zurich Opera House (Gros *et al.* 1987), but at Auvernier the finds recovered in recent fieldwork reveal a higher level of fragmentation (Rychner 1987). In this case different parts of the broken sickles occur in approximately equal proportions. Swords are rarely found, but axes are commonplace. Many of them are intact, but again the well-published examples from Auvernier suggest that broken blades and sockets occur in similar numbers. It does not seem likely that parts of these objects had been destroyed by ordinary wear and tear.

Figure 5.3   Broken axe fragments from the hoard at Uiorara de Sus, Romania. Information from Petrescu-Dîmbovita (1978).

In any case purely taphonomic arguments fail to explain why the mid-sections of so many sickle blades are represented among the metalwork from Romanian hoards, nor can they explain why the tips of these artefacts appear in such very different frequencies from one collection to another. It is easy to account for the fragmentation of individual artefacts if they were to be melted down, but it is very difficult to understand why certain parts of the broken objects are consistently over-represented whilst others are rare or absent. This suggests that they may have been treated in different ways. Perhaps separate sections of these objects were significant in their own right, in which case even the so-called scrap hoards call for more careful analysis.

The same applies to single finds of weapons. Having said a little about the deposits containing sickles, we can consider Bronze Age swords.

Swords as single finds

Again *Praehistorische Bronzefunde* provides a useful starting point. Different parts of the same object are unevenly represented. For example, in the corpus of British Bronze Age swords (Colquhoun and Burgess 1988) there is a disparity in the representation of broken weapons. Among the many single finds of Ewart Park weapons hilt fragments outnumber the lower part of the blade in a ratio of approximately 2.5:1. For earlier swords the ratio is virtually the same, and among the later Carps Tongue swords it is even wider. There are obvious objections to this kind of analysis – the hilts of swords are easier to recognise than their blades, and this may lead to their preservation and publication – but they do not explain the evidence from well-recorded hoards. In this case it is clear that all the metalwork has been identified, and yet the proportions in which these parts of the weapons are represented are similar to those among the single finds. Here the ratio of hilt sections to the lower blade is 2:1 for the Ewart Park swords. It is virtually the same among earlier swords, and in the Carps Tongue tradition it remains unchanged. This cannot reflect the durability of these different elements, for among the older dirks and rapiers the disparity is significantly reduced; in this case the ratio among the single finds is only 1.5:1 (Burgess and Gerloff 1981). In Eogan's study of Irish swords the numerous examples of Class 4 show a ratio of hilt section to lower blade of only 1.1:1 (Eogan 1965). Again this cannot result from purely mechanical factors, like the differential preservation of fragments in a midden.

As we saw in the case of sickles, the parts of broken swords might have been treated in different ways during the Late Bronze Age. Some fragments continued to circulate or were deposited with a certain formality, whilst others disappear from the record, perhaps because they were melted down. This happened in some periods more than in others, and the British and Irish evidence shows that practice varied widely even over a limited area.

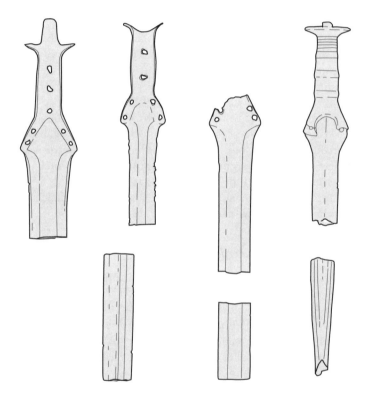

Figure 5.4   Broken sword fragments from the hoard at Szentgáloskér, Hungary. Information from Kemenczei (1989).

Reference to Continental sources reveals a similar situation. Sometimes it is unclear whether all the surviving fragments have been published, yet it seems remarkable that in major corpora of swords the ratio of hilt sections to the lower blade is generally between 1:1 – the situation in Hungary (Figure 5.4; Kemenczei 1989 and 1991) – and 5:1 – that in Southern Germany (Schauer

1971), Austria and Switzerland (Krämer 1985). In each case the different parts of these weapons appear in similar proportions in the local hoards. Yet it is not a universal pattern. In the later hoards of former Yugoslavia, for example, the lower sections of swords are better represented than their hilts (Harding 1995). Again the evidence suggests that cultural selection was important.

It seems as if the separate parts of Bronze Age swords may have possessed a different significance once their original role as weapons was at an end. How else can we account for the survival of so many hilts and upper blades compared with the lower section? This was a widespread pattern in Bronze Age Europe, but it was by no means universal. One possibility is that the hilt was thought to be more directly associated with the original owner. It may have been preserved as a relic whilst the rest of the artefact was used as raw material.

Scrap hoards

Similar conventions may apply not only to individual types but also to the composition of 'scrap' hoards. If objects were being broken up to obtain a set amount of metal, one might expect the process to extend to all the types represented, but this did not always happen. A good illustration of this point is provided by studies of two hoards from Western France, Le Petit Vilatte (Neuvy-sur-Barangeon) and Venat.

The first of these collections is quite remarkable (Milcent 1998). Once again it contains a large collection of metalwork – 628 items – some of which are represented only by fragments. These had been treated as a smith's stock of metal, brought together for recycling, but Milcent's study of this material suggests a more complex interpretation. In fact the stylistic affinities of the individual artefacts suggest that they had been assembled from three different sources. As well as the familiar repertoire of the Atlantic Bronze Age, there was one group of artefacts that is likely to have originated in the Nordic culture area. The third group has close affinities with the metalwork of the North Alpine region (Figure 5.5). These separate components were clearly distinguished from one another. In Milcent's interpretation, each of the exotic assemblages consists of the material equipment of two people – a man and a woman – whilst the metalwork belonging to the local tradition consists of broken objects which cannot be assigned to any particular individuals. That is not to imply that all the foreign material was intact; for example, a Nordic sword is represented only by its hilt and upper blade, whilst one of the axes considered to be of Alpine origin lacks its socket entirely. For the purposes of this chapter, one point is especially significant. Although this was ostensibly a 'scrap hoard', material that had come from different sources or which had been associated with different people was not treated in the same way as the metalwork of local origin. It is almost as if two 'personal hoards' had been combined with the characteristic repertoire of a 'founder's hoard'. Even if some

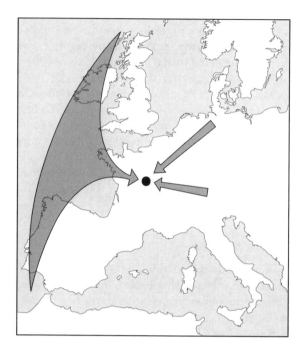

Figure 5.5 The principal sources of the artefacts in the hoard at Le Petit Vilatte, North-West France, distinguishing between artefacts associated with the Atlantic zone, the Nordic culture area and the North Alpine region. Information from Milcent (1998).

of the missing elements had been melted down, it is clear that this process was attended by subtle protocols.

The Venat hoard (Coffyn *et al.* 1981) also contained a large amount of metalwork belonging to the Atlantic Bronze Age (Figure 5.6). Again it has been treated as a collection of artefacts brought together for recycling. Even so, this study makes it clear that different kinds of artefacts had been treated in different ways. At first sight personal ornaments fared better than tools, and weapons were most often broken. Thus 41 per cent of the ornaments in this hoard remained intact, but only 28 per cent of the tools and 16 per cent of the swords, spears and daggers. A more detailed analysis, however, shows that within these categories particular kinds of artefacts might be treated in rather different ways. Thus 70 per cent of the spearheads were incomplete, compared with 92 per cent of the daggers and 98 per cent of the swords. A third of the winged axes were undamaged, compared with only a fifth of the socketed axes. There are similar contrasts among the broken artefacts. Thus there were many pieces of swords and very few intact objects, but hilt fragments outnumbered the lower part of the blade by a ratio of 4.5:1. Among the finds of daggers the equivalent figure is reduced to 1.5:1. There are similar contrasts among the tools in the Venat hoard where winged axes are represented by roughly equal numbers of blades and butts as well as some complete objects, but among the socketed axes blade fragments are under-represented.

156

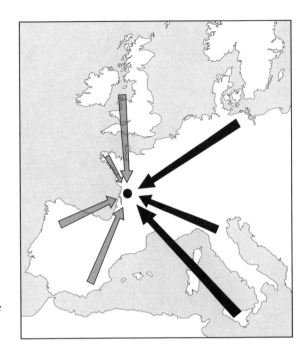

Figure 5.6 The
principal sources of the
artefacts in the hoard at
Venat, Western France,
distinguishing between
the material with
connections to regions
towards the east and the
finds associated mainly
with the Atlantic Bronze
Age. Information from
Coffyn *et al.* (1981).

Of course some of these differences could be due to differential preservation
and also to the sizes of these different objects. Even so, it is noticeable that
the types of artefacts with more extensive distributions in Western and
Southern Europe were not always as badly damaged as those with a restricted
circulation. Among the types that could have circulated over a large area,
66 per cent of the winged axes were broken and 70 per cent of the spearheads (swords, however, were even more commonly fractured). Local types may
be represented by socketed axes and bracelets, and here the proportion of
broken pieces is remarkably high: 80 per cent and 81 per cent respectively.
Again it seems as if the treatment of different kinds of object was far from
uniform.

The Ría de Huelva: a possible shipwreck

The Venat hoard became the subject of a monograph because it provided a means
of bringing together artefacts which had circulated along the Atlantic coastline of Europe, as well as others which occurred in the West Mediterranean.
The great collection of metalwork found in the Ría de Huelva raises rather
similar issues because the site is so close to the meeting point of those two
seas (Figure 5.7; Ruiz-Gálvez 1995). Huelva is located in the Gulf of Cadiz just
two hundred kilometres north west of the Straits of Gibraltar.

157

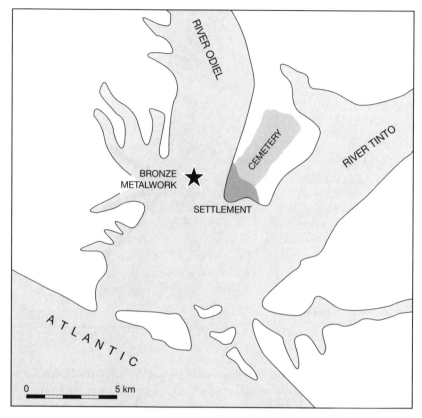

Figure 5.7 The location of the metal finds from the Ría de Huelva, Southern Spain, in relation to the position of the nearby settlement and cemetery. Information from Ruiz-Gálvez (1995).

Like much of the material discussed in this chapter, this collection was found in water, but in this case it came from an estuary close to the confluence of the Rivers Odiel and Tinto. It was found by dredging some distance beyond the tip of a peninsula occupied by an important settlement and cemetery during the first millennium BC. The area provided a sheltered harbour extending inland from the open water of the Atlantic. This deposit probably dates from the tenth century BC.

Because the finds came from a harbour it has always been tempting to consider them as the remains of a Bronze Age shipwreck, comparable with other examples in Mediterranean and Atlantic Europe. The argument is that the metalwork formed part of a cargo of broken and finished items which had been lost at sea. Ruiz-Gálvez has questioned this interpretation and suggested that the artefacts come from a votive deposit. She takes this view for three reasons. The contents of the assemblage are most unusual. In contrast to other wrecks, which can include quantities of broken tools and raw material, the finds from the Ría de Huelva have a specialised character. With very few exceptions, they are either weapons or ornaments, and in her opinion they represent the material equipment of an elite. Second, the find spot is very similar to that of other groups of metalwork found in Bronze Age Europe. It is on a route across the estuary, but it is also located at a confluence. Such positions characterise a number of high-status settlements and groups of river finds. It may be that the Spanish site forms part of a wider tradition. Lastly, she observes that more high-quality artefacts have been recorded from the vicinity of the 'shipwreck'. Chronological considerations mean that they could not have formed part of its cargo, but it is possible that the same location was used for making offerings over a long period of time.

The metalwork was discovered in 1923 and it is no longer possible to reach a firm conclusion on the circumstances in which it was deposited. For our purposes that very ambiguity is revealing, for it shows how difficult it is to distinguish between a collection of artefacts and raw material that had been lost in transit, and an assemblage that was discarded intentionally. It is clear that most of the metalwork survives, as the collection extends from entire swords to the smallest fragments. For that reason the role of incomplete objects seems particularly important (Figure 5.8).

As so often, the collection includes entire swords as well as broken pieces. About 40 per cent of these weapons remain intact, and among the more substantial fragments, hilt sections outnumber blades by a ratio of approximately 1.4:1, a very different proportion from that at Venat. In addition, there are a number of much smaller pieces that come from the hilt or the point. Not many fragments are confined to the middle section of the blade. The broken parts of these swords vary in length, but the hilt sections are generally between 30 and 40 cm long, with a median value of 33 cm. The well-preserved lower sections were more varied, with lengths between 28 cm and 58 cm, but the median is 35 cm. Most of the intact swords are between 57 and 80 cm long with a median of 71 cm. Although these weapons were of various sizes, it seems as if some of them had been divided in half. The two sections had median weights of 380 and 325 grams respectively.

These figures are important when we consider the daggers from the Ría de Huelva. There were thirty of these, but only three were incomplete. Their median weight was 170 grams. They contained the same amount of bronze as the spearheads. This is particularly striking as both these types remained largely unbroken. Again this contrasts with the situation at Venat.

There is a certain logic to the treatment of the weapons from the Ría de Huelva, for it seems to have varied according to their metal content. The larger weapons were subdivided into units of about the same weight, whilst the smaller artefacts were left intact. Interestingly, the daggers and spearheads contained half the amount of bronze represented by the broken swords (Table 5.1).

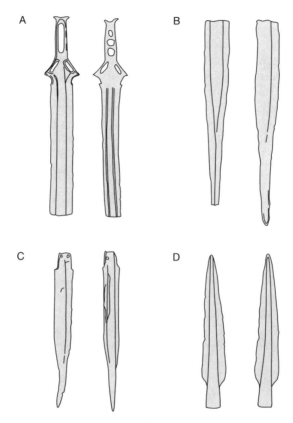

Figure 5.8 Complete and broken Bronze Age weapons from the Ría de Huelva, Southern Spain. Information from Ruiz-Gálvez (1995).

Table 5.1 The treatment and weights of the main types of bronze artefacts from the Ría de Huelva, Southern Spain

Treatment	Type	Median weight
Broken	Sword (*point section*)	380 grams
Broken	Sword (*hilt section*)	325 grams
Intact	Dagger	170 grams
Intact	Spearhead	160 grams

A break with tradition

I have emphasised the fragmentation of different kinds of objects, for they represent a continuum. Broken swords can be found in many of these collections, but they also occur as single finds in bogs and rivers. Fragmentary sickles may have been employed as units of metal, but at well-preserved settlements they are often complete and sometimes it is clear that they had also been used as agricultural tools. In the same way, the deposits of broken metalwork conventionally characterised as 'scrap' hoards may contain particular combinations of artefacts and exclude others entirely. There are many sources of variation, For instance, the bronzes from Le Petit Vilatte seem to combine the personal equipment of individuals from two quite different regions with the normal repertoire of the Atlantic Bronze Age. Again the Venat hoard provides hints that the treatment of different types of artefact was influenced not only by the roles that they had played but also by their distinctive styles in relation to larger regional traditions. In some respects it is the finds from the Ría de Huelva which seem more consistent with a role in the bronze supply and yet in this case there are powerful arguments for regarding the artefacts not as the contents of a shipwreck but as a votive deposit. It is particularly interesting to contrast the treatment of the weapons in this collection with the same process at Venat.

How should we interpret such observations? There are several possibilities. Nebelsick (2000) has taken a radical approach to the analysis of Bronze Age 'scrap' hoards. He studies exactly how their separate components had been treated and makes the point that in some cases objects had not been subdivided to make them easier to melt down; rather, they had been destroyed with unusual violence. What is more, in the collections that he discusses from Southern Germany the extent to which different objects had been fractured varied according to the places in which they were deposited. Thus the collections from hill forts or areas of cultivated land showed only a limited amount of fragmentation, and often none at all. By contrast, the metalwork from what he describes as 'wild' places – cliffs, mountains and a cave – had been badly damaged, and between about 60 per cent and 90 per cent of these objects were broken.

Often the destruction of these objects involved considerable force. In the case of one scrap hoard from Saxony he speaks of: 'a wide range of artefacts in differing stages of mutilation, whereby sheet bronze vessels and wire ornaments show the most spectacular traces of wanton destruction' (2000: 163). He compares the treatment of these objects with that of the human body during cremation. Nebelsick suggests that in certain cases the material categorised as scrap hoards represents the surviving fraction of a sacrifice:

A . . . consequence of seeing the destructive activity in 'scrap hoards' within the context of sacrificial ritual is the redistributive aspect

common to almost all known methods of pagan Mediterranean
sacrifice . . . A putative division of the fragmented material into
a divine and human share would explain why there are so few joins
between fragments in scrap hoards, even when several parts of the same
artefact are included.

(Nebelsick 2000: 169)

But that is not the only way of thinking about fragmentation. Two other
possibilities have been suggested. Perhaps certain kinds of objects were divided
into units of standard weight and were used as ingots. Sommerfeld (1994) has
pursued this hypothesis in a detailed study of the hoards containing broken
sickles. As his research makes clear, the same kind of system could have
involved the subdivision of sword blades.

That may be illustrated by the finds from the Ría de Huelva where the
spearheads and daggers seem to have employed about the same amount of
metal. That is approximately half the quantity of bronze represented by a
broken sword blade, and, if those weapons had been divided into two equal
parts, it is about a quarter of the material required to make one of these
artefacts. The scheme is deceptively neat as there is a wide range of variation
in the sizes of all the objects, but there are similar claims concerning the
weights of entire hoards (Maraszek 2000). More subtle analyses have detected
what may be standard units of metal among the axeheads, personal ornaments
and bronze figurines in different parts of Europe (Briard 1965: 270–1; Ruiz-
Gálvez 2000; Malmer 1992). The overall pattern is convincing no matter
how difficult it is to substantiate the results of any single analysis (Pare 1999).
The problem is that such a system could have developed for more than one
reason. No doubt it would have been important in calculating how much
material a smith would require to accomplish a particular task. At the same
time, if such systems were widely accepted, weighing metal would also have
been one way of establishing its value. Like coinage in the Classical world,
it could have been used to regulate exchange but, like those coins, bronzes
might also have been sacrificed in votive deposits. That is the problem raised
by the finds from Huelva.

Yet another interpretation has been proposed by Chapman (2000). He
summarises his interpretation in this way:

Two people who wish to establish some form of social relationship
or conclude some kind of transaction agree on a specific artefact
appropriate to the interaction in question and break it . . . [Each]
keeps . . . one or more [pieces] as a token of the relationship . . . The
fragments of the object are then kept until reconstitution of the
relationship is required, in which case the part(s) may be deposited
in a structured manner.

(Ibid.: 6)

He describes this relationship between people and objects by the term 'enchainment'. His own study of this process runs from the Mesolithic period to the Copper Age, but he illustrates the same principle with a number of examples which extend from the Classical world to the Middle Ages. This has the great virtue of explaining why parts of broken objects may have followed quite different paths in the course of their careers, but at present it is easier to demonstrate that partial objects retained some importance in their own right than it is to show how they were reunited. At present I know of only one case, from the English Midlands, in which joining fragments of the same sword occur as single finds in different places (Ford *et al.* 1998). They seem to have been deposited within sight of one another on either bank of a river. It would be worth investigating whether the same kind of relationship can be identified in other instances.

All these ideas are useful, although it would probably be misleading to apply any one of them to the entire body of material being studied. For example, Nebelsick's approach might describe one extreme in a continuum of different deposits which involved the mixing of fragmented artefacts of different kinds. Where he stresses the degree of violence with which individual objects had been treated, Chapman's model implies a certain level of formality in the distribution of broken pieces. That is also true of Sommerfeld's interpretation, although this is more closely related to the economic value of the metal. Where these ideas all converge is in suggesting that the transformation of bronze artefacts by the smith was an extraordinary event.

Conclusion: the ritualisation of metalworking

Such approaches to the evidence have the virtue of doing away with the anachronistic distinction between votive and utilitarian deposits. A common process may have extended between those artefacts which are understood in terms of ritual activity, and the hoards of broken objects that have normally been used as evidence of the ancient economy. If certain kinds of metalwork possessed a special significance, it may have been difficult and even dangerous to bring them together to form new artefacts. Perhaps bronze working was associated with rituals which required that a certain fraction of the material was retained as an offering. That is similar to Nebelsick's suggestion that sacrificial deposits would have been divided between the gods and human beings, but in this case the emphasis is on the smith as the agent of transformation. Much the same idea has been suggested by Brück:

> A ritual interpretation does not mean that the deposition of scrap hoards was never associated with metalworking activities. Ethnographic studies of metalworking indicate that ritual is often an integral part of metal production precisely because of the potential danger of this transformative process . . . Votive deposition of scrap

material may have been an essential step in the successful production of bronze.

(2001: 157)

In fact it is no longer possible to maintain any clear distinction between the ritual and functional aspects of metal deposits, for both made considerable use of broken objects. Far from representing opposite poles in the study of prehistoric metalwork, the 'votive' and 'utilitarian' models overlap and on one level their components interlock. Prehistoric metallurgy seems to have been ritualised in the same way as house building and farming and yet at the same time it was a practical skill that was exercised with great virtuosity. There is no need to harmonise the competing models of hoards and hoarding. Each provides a useful perspective on a complex process but none can monopolise its interpretation.

My conclusion, then, is deceptively straightforward. Certain transactions in Bronze Age Europe call attention to themselves through the prominent place that they occupy in the formation of the archaeological record. The deposition of fine metalwork in water is no doubt one example – another is the provision of grave goods. But at the local level there are other processes that have to be understood in the same way. If the deposition of fine objects has long been considered in social terms, I suggest that the same should apply to the practice of metallurgy. This is another field in which prehistorians have been led astray by their own assumptions about the past.

6

THE RITES OF SEPARATION

Domestic rituals and public ritual
in the Iron Age

Settlements and shrines

The history of archaeology is characterised by shifting perspectives. Different types of material move in and out of chronological alignment; seemingly disparate kinds of evidence form unexpected connections. That is not surprising as particular areas of prehistory are studied in detail for the first time.

The same process affects the course of fieldwork and especially that of excavation. In most cases those adjustments are made before the results enter the public domain, but this is less likely to happen when the project is a long one and its findings are issued in instalments. One can hardly complain at this attempt to disseminate information, but it is likely that ideas will change in later stages of the research.

A good example of this process is provided by the Wessex hill fort of Danebury. Excavation took place over no fewer than twenty seasons, but the results of the initial campaign were published after fifteen years (Cunliffe 1984), and the remainder seven years later (Cunliffe and Poole 1991a and b). Although the first report reviewed a decade of fieldwork, it was only to be expected that its successor would offer some new interpretations. One of them is particularly relevant to this chapter.

Towards the centre of the defended area were the remains of four rectangular buildings which could have been recognised on the skyline by anyone passing through the principal gateway. From the start they were identified as shrines, for they looked very like the structures found beneath Roman temples. There were few finds from the examples at Danebury, but elsewhere such buildings are associated with unusual deposits of artefacts.

In the first report on the project all the shrines were attributed to the main period of occupation at Danebury (Cunliffe 1984: 83–7). They might well have been used in sequence, but it seemed likely that they were accompanied by domestic buildings and other features. They were located beside a road that followed the boundary between an area of raised granaries and a zone of pits; indeed, two of these buildings were of similar dimensions to the storehouses. All the shrines were aligned on the main entrance. The final report takes a

165

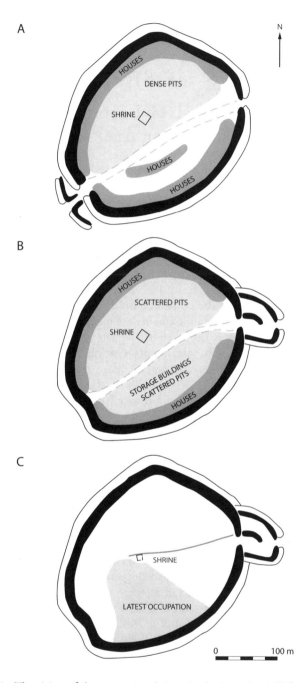

Figure 6.1 The siting of the successive shrines in the Iron Age hill fort at Danebury, Southern England. Information from Cunliffe and Poole (1991a and b).

166

different view. The dating of these shrines is not precise, but now it seems as if the largest example was built when use of the hill fort was over (Cunliffe and Poole 1991a: 238–9). The building dominated a largely empty enclosure (Figure 6.1).

Why is that change of perspective so important? It is because these are exactly the kinds of relationship considered by Venclová (1993) in her discussion of Viereckschanzen. Her views were considered in some detail in Chapter 1, but it is necessary to recall two of the main points here. According to her model, buildings devoted to ritual should be set apart from other structures and ought to occupy conspicuous positions in the landscape. Both those criteria are met by the latest shrine at Danebury, but its predecessors do not conform to her scheme. That sequence introduces some of the issues which need considering here. How far did ritual activity draw apart from domestic life during the later years of the Iron Age?

It is important to recall that Venclová did not base her approach on social theory but on a direct comparison between the Viereckschanzen of Central Europe and a number of Iron Age ceremonial sites in Western Europe. They have certain features in common. Among them is the presence of rectilinear earthworks (Buchsenschutz *et al.* 1989). As she acknowledges, the monuments vary in size and complexity from simple burial mounds to massive ditched enclosures, but most examples date from the same periods, the Middle and Late Iron Ages. In some regions they can be difficult to distinguish from settlements, and the timber buildings found at certain of these sites may have similar characteristics to houses and granaries. But that does not apply to every area, as rectangular structures are uncommon in the British Isles.

Venclová supposes that these sites had a special significance because of the distinctive material associated with them. It can take two forms. In parts of Northern France, Western Germany and North-East England, a number of mounds and enclosures are associated with graves containing weapons, ornaments and, occasionally, the remains of dismantled vehicles (Driehaus 1965; Bretz-Mahler 1971; Haffner 1976; Stead 1991; Demoule 1999). These date from the early La Tène period. The later sites are mainly in North-East France or Southern England (Brunaux 1986; Smith 2001). They are more substantial earthwork enclosures and include deposits of damaged weapons, jewellery, coins and tools. These artefacts may be found within the ditch or in the interior, but in either case they can be associated with animal burials and human remains. Many of the monuments continued in use into the Roman era when the buildings inside them were replaced in stone. Whether or not they were connected with Viereckschanzen, their distinctive character is obvious.

How were they related to the settlements of the same date? That is where the sequence at Danebury is important, for it seems as if the earlier shrines were integrated into the workings of the hill fort, whilst the last of these structures was built when the site was virtually unoccupied. Does this mean that ritual activity was set apart from the domestic world, as Venclová's model implies? And is it significant that this should have happened during a time of political change?

That they may face the rising sun

In some ways the recognition of Iron Age sanctuaries is a recent development. These sites hardly feature in accounts of the period written before 1980, although the existence of rich burials associated with square barrows had already been appreciated over a century before. Modern fieldwork has also shed some light on the ritualisation of daily activities. This chapter compares these two phenomena.

Several writers have suggested a contrast between the votive deposits of the Bronze Age and those of the Early Iron Age. The first period saw the lavish consumption of metalwork, which reached a peak then rapidly fell away. This happened as iron became more widely available, but one metal does not seem to have replaced the other among the offerings in rivers, bogs and lakes. Instead, there was a change of emphasis. Although there are some important finds of metalwork, the void seems to have been filled by different kinds of material, in particular agricultural implements, human remains and deposits of food. These have been interpreted as evidence for a greater concern with fertility (Barrett 1989; Parker Pearson 1984; Lund 2000).

There is a danger of considering these developments in isolation, for many of them were already under way during the Later Bronze Age when deposits of this character ran in parallel with the lavish consumption of metalwork. Others remained important during the Roman period and even into the Early Middle Ages (Bradley 1998a). There is a risk of losing sight of another point as well, for it was during the Iron Age that the centralised storage of food assumed an important role in the political economy (Gent 1983). It may not be necessary to distinguish between the exercise of social power and the performance of public ceremonies. Nevertheless certain basic ideas lie behind the ritual practices of the Iron Age.

Some of these issues have been discussed in a paper by Williams (2003) who has drawn attention to 'the agricultural cycle as metaphor' in later prehistoric Europe. It is worth quoting from his account:

> In prehistory, as in the modern world, most things have a finite life, [including] people, animals, houses [and] even earthworks. Yet the agricultural cycle is perhaps different. A seed, properly sown and cared for, will yield a plant that produces more seeds that can also be sown . . . so that the cycle is unbroken . . . Even when buried in storage pits through the winter, the seeds do not die, but survive to be planted again . . . It is this unending cyclicity that seems to have been the most important aspect behind the agricultural metaphor . . . What [it] attempted to do was . . . to put humans on the same

168

footing as the grain: to allow them to transcend the effects of life and
death and embrace permanence.

(Williams 2003: 242)

He suggests that these developments happened as people came to occupy the
same places for longer periods of time:

Because of the increasing investment that was required as agriculture
intensified, people needed to justify their ownership.

(Ibid.: 243)

If the agricultural cycle went on from year to year, it might provide an
appropriate image of that continuity. Just as crops and animals were renewed
under human management, the lives of the inhabitants extended from one
generation to the next. This created a sense of security quite as powerful as that
provided by the building of hill forts.

How are these beliefs expressed in the archaeological record? There seem to
be three distinct aspects. First, there is evidence of an Iron Age cosmology
which related the agricultural cycle to the movements of the sun through the
course of the year. Second, there is evidence that agricultural facilities, in
particular grain storage pits, assumed a special significance during this period.
And, lastly, agricultural products took over the role of Bronze Age metalwork
in a series of votive deposits. So, to a lesser extent, did agricultural tools. In
the account that follows I shall deal with each of these trends before focusing
on some evidence from France and England.

There is a direct relationship between the agricultural cycle and the progression of the seasons, and this is clearly indicated by the movement of the
sun across the sky. The principal Iron Age festivals are recorded in the Coligny
Calendar (Le Contel 1997) and seem to be related to the main events in the
farming year. They were probably the occasions when assemblies took place.
Their timing could be reckoned from the position of the sun, but the solstices
were important too, for they marked the division between a period in which
the hours of daylight were increasing, and the approach of winter.

These axes are emphasised in a number of different ways. It seems possible
that fields were laid out according to cosmological principles. This evidence
is best known from Middle and Late Bronze Age Britain, where the axes
of large tracts of enclosed land seem to have been orientated on the positions
of the solstices, with little or no regard for the local topography (McOmish
et al. 2002: 54–5 and 153). A similar situation is found in Continental Europe.
Across a large area extending from Belgium to Sweden there are the remains
of 'Celtic' fields which seem to have been laid out according to the same
principles. This is particularly interesting as the majority of these examples
were used during the Early Iron Age when few examples were being created

in England. Therkorn (1987b) has studied this phenomenon in the Netherlands where she comments that Iron Age dwellings share the alignment of these land divisions. That is also true in Britain where Bronze Age and Iron Age round houses usually have their doorways to the south or east (Oswald 1997). In this case it may have been done in order to light the interior, but in Northern Europe, where the doors were located in the side walls of the long houses, this does not seem likely. A larger area would be illuminated by putting the entrances in the ends of these buildings.

In the Netherlands Therkorn (1987b) argues that ceremonial monuments avoid the axis of the houses and fields; instead they face the cardinal points. Thus burial monuments tend to avoid the directions associated with the living. But that was not the case in the British Isles. Here there are a number of regional traditions, but one common element is the appearance of crouched or flexed burials which are often lying on their left-hand side with the head towards the north (Whimster 1981). In contrast to those found in the La Tène cemeteries of France, many of the burials in the British Isles would have faced the rising sun. In doing so, they respected approximately the same axis as the dwellings and land divisions.

Another observation is important here. Although formal cemeteries do occur in certain regions of Britain, they are a local phenomenon and as many human bodies are found in grain storage pits. This choice of location can hardly have been fortuitous, for these features provide an ideal symbol of death and regeneration. As Williams (2003) has observed, the grain is buried in the ground after the harvest, and in the spring it comes to life again. Although there is considerable diversity, most of the bodies found in these pits follow the same orientations as those in other contexts. In that way they add to the connection between the dead and the passage of the seasons.

It is often assumed that pit burials of this kind are a specifically English phenomenon but this is not the case. Over the last twenty-five years increasing numbers have been identified in Germany, Belgium and Northern and Central France, so that now it appears that this practice was shared by communities who lived on either side of the English Channel (Villes 1988; Jeunesse and Ehretsmann 1988; Debiak et al. 1998; Delattre 2000a and b). But such similarities can also be deceptive. The French examples are often found in the same regions as regular cemeteries, and there is a contrast between the treatment of the dead in these two contexts. The cemeteries have a regimented layout, with extended inhumation burials aligned east–west. There is no dominant orientation among the bodies in corn storage pits, as they were put there with a minimum of formality. Most were crouched or flexed, but there is not the semblance of order shown by their English counterparts and their organisation cannot have been governed by the same principles. They may illustrate a similar relationship between death and fertility, but there does not seem to have been any attempt to evoke other aspects of the agricultural cycle or the passage of the seasons.

This relationship between grain storage and the remains of the dead may have a lengthy history. In Chapter 3 I suggested that some of the 'house urns' of the Late Bronze Age and Early Iron Age in Northern and North-Eastern Europe were really model granaries. They could have had a similar meaning to the storage pits, for again they were directly associated with human remains and offerings of food (Figure 6.2; Bradley 2002b). These vessels contained cremations and occur in cemeteries. There are few, if any models of the dwellings of the period.

The same associations extend to animal burials and a variety of other deposits. These are also found in storage pits. As I noted in Chapter 1, they are extremely disparate and are united mainly by the contexts in which they occur. Different species of animals and different parts of their bodies can be placed in these pits, singly or in combination. Certain bones and certain kinds of artefacts might be found in the lower fillings of these features and others at higher levels, and just as particular elements could be combined in these deposits, others would be kept apart. What applies to the fillings of storage pits applies to enclosure ditches too. It is hard to generalise about these practices as they vary from site to site, and broader regional alignments are probably concealed by local traditions of research. In Southern England, for example, much emphasis has been placed on the connections between finds of human and animal remains

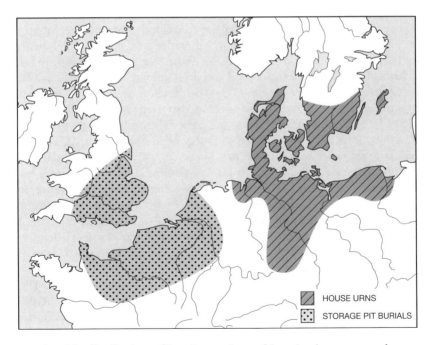

Figure 6.2 The distributions of Late Bronze Age and Iron Age house urns and storage pit burials in North and North-West Europe.

and those of artefacts (Whimster 1981; Wait 1985; Cunliffe 1992; Hill 1995). In France, however, the most detailed analyses have been concerned with the bones (Méniel 1992).

Lastly, we can move beyond the settlements altogether to consider the special treatment afforded to domesticated plants and animals and to agricultural tools. In this case it is worth recalling the contents of Chapter 4. This provided an account of the ways in which the components of domestic life were ritualised in Neolithic Sweden, relating that process to wider developments in the archaeology of South Scandinavia. It may be no accident that some of the same phenomena can be recognised there in the Iron Age. It is particularly striking that again we encounter a series of pots containing food (Becker 1971). Like their Neolithic counterparts, they had been deposited in bogs, but in this case they were sometimes associated with wooden idols (Dietrich 2000). Further components of the ritual system in Northern Europe were described in Chapter 3, for it was in this region that ploughs and other agricultural implements had also been employed as offerings, together with slaughtered animals and human corpses (Glob 1951 and 1969). As we have seen, these may have been sacrificed to the goddess of fertility. Similar finds are recorded from Iron Age deposits over a wider area, extending from the Netherlands into North Germany and Poland and across the North Sea into Britain and Ireland (Makiewicz 1988; A. Andersen 1994; Turner and Scaife 1995; Van der Sanden 1996; Coles et al. 1999; Lund 2000).

They are not the only instances of these distinctive practices and it seems possible that they were adopted over a still wider area. For example, the Iron Age lake deposits best known from the Swiss site at La Tène also provide evidence of human corpses associated with items of metalwork. Although sites like Cornaux and La Tène are famous for their finds of weapons, it is important to remember that these were discovered together with agricultural implements (Vouga 1923; Schwab 1989). It was not only the crops that were emphasised but livestock too. There were a large number of animal bones at La Tène, and these suggest other connections, for they show a striking emphasis on the remains of horses and dogs (Pittioni 1968). Similar deposits have a wide distribution, including the faunal remains accompanying the Bronze Age causeway at Flag Fen in Eastern England (Pryor 2001) and the offerings associated with a prehistoric spring cult in Scania (Stjernqvist 1997). Similar species are also associated with deposits in Swedish settlements (Ullén 1994 and 1996), suggesting that the importance attached to these particular species had been shared across a wide area.

Agricultural tools assumed a special significance in other contexts. Those connected with the processing of grain appear to have been particularly important. As we saw in Chapter 3, some of the querns found in Ireland were decorated in the same style as the fine metalwork of the same period (Raftery 1984: 244–6). Similarly, in North and North-East Europe it is clear that a similar importance attached to sickles during the Roman Iron Age (Penack

1993). In Scandinavia, they are particularly common in women's graves (Figure 6.3). Clearly, they were artefacts with special qualities, and this became even more apparent in the Migration Period when the contexts of such artefacts changed to settlements, hoards and bogs (Figure 6.4).

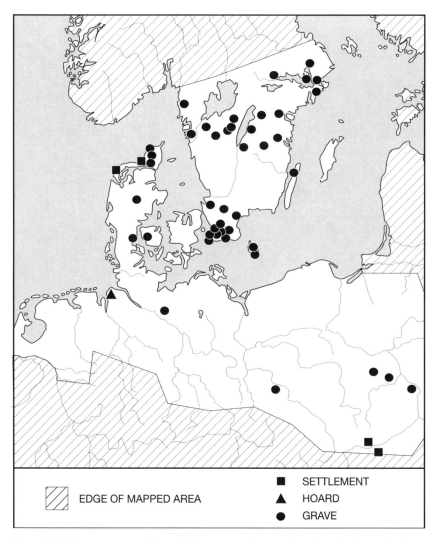

Figure 6.3 The contexts of iron sickles in the Roman Iron Age. Information from Penack (1993).

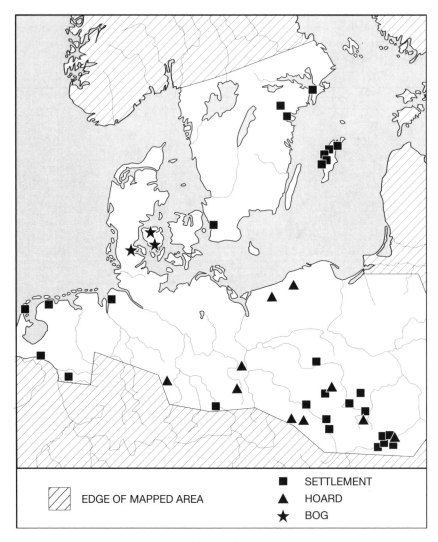

Figure 6.4 The contexts of iron sickles in the Migration Period. Information from Penack (1993).

Death and regeneration

Many of these features are found together, and this suggests that we should consider a common interpretation. Williams has argued that the agricultural cycle provided a dominant metaphor in the Iron Age, as it referred to the continuity of human existence. It may be that even more was at stake. In an influential study, referred to at the beginning of this book, Bloch and Parry consider 'Death and the Regeneration of Life'. The theme is especially pertinent to this chapter for they discuss the association between death and fertility in a series of different societies. In their introduction to the volume they make an important point. Life itself can be considered as a finite resource. It is depleted by death and must be renewed:

> Each death makes available a new potentiality for life, and one creature's loss is another's gain.
>
> (Bloch and Parry 1982: 8)

This is not a question of continuity so much as *substitution*. Through the link between death and regeneration, a fresh life replaces one that has ended. Death releases the fertility that allows human existence to pass from one generation to the next.

The link between death and fertility is surely expressed by the pit burials considered by Williams (2003), but the continuity of life itself may be recognised in another sphere. I have already commented on the relationship between the orientations of Iron Age burials in Britain and those of the houses of that period. I have also emphasised the contrast between the circular buildings on one side of the English Channel and the rectangular dwellings found over much of the European mainland. Perhaps these features are related more directly than it might seem.

In Chapter 2 I commented on some of the features which distinguish these styles of domestic architecture. In the rectangular houses of Northern Europe, there is evidence for two groups of deposits of cultural material. One was associated with their construction and the other with their abandonment. Burials in storage pits are very rare. Until the Late Iron Age these houses seem to have been occupied over a short period – perhaps a generation – and then they were replaced on another site. It seemed possible that the history of the building followed the lives of its occupants and that it was abandoned when the head of the household died (Gerritsen 1999 and 2000). The Iron Age round houses in Southern Britain saw a different development (Brück 1999b). Although they were also associated with cultural deposits, there was little or no distinction between those associated with the creation of the building and those marking its demise. Rather than being replaced somewhere else, new houses were often superimposed on the sites of older ones and, even when this did not happen, their positions might overlap. This relationship is so widespread that it must have been deliberate, especially as work on the new construction could not have started until the remains of its predecessor had been removed.

Whilst the long houses of the Netherlands might be aligned on the position of the sun, their orientations reflected its position at one particular time. By contrast, the sun *moved around* the perimeter of the British houses, so that their characteristic form reflected its daily cycle (Fitzpatrick 1997). Iron Age storage pits illustrate the same symbolic system. Their operation follows another cycle, but this time one that extends from year to year. When the harvest ended, corn was stored underground, and after the winter it was sown. Each new crop was treated in the same way. Then the pits were cleaned and reused until, finally, they became a focus for special deposits (Hill 1995).

If that scheme has any merit, it suggests that in Southern Britain the agricultural metaphor described by Williams (2003) was directly related to the evolution of settlements and the history of the communities who lived there. That is very different from the system in Northern Europe, but how does it compare with the evidence from the north of France where storage pits seem to have been equally significant?

Two features are important here, and again it seems possible that they were related to one another. Although human bodies are found in storage pits, there is no evidence that they adopted a single alignment (Delattre 2000b). They assumed a quite different configuration from the bodies in formal graves (Figure 6.5). In Britain, on the other hand, the orientations of bodies in pits and

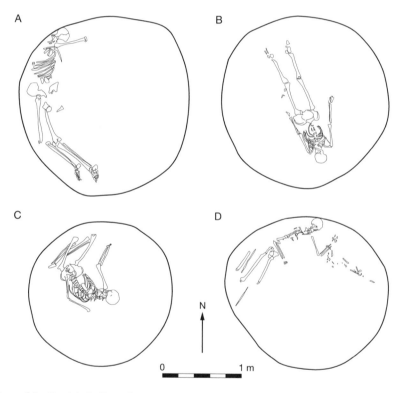

Figure 6.5 Burials in Iron Age grain storage pits at three sites in Northern France. A: Soucy; B: Barbey; C: Varennes-sur-Seine; D: Barbey. Information from Baray *et al.* (1994) and Delattre (2000).

cemeteries were much the same. There is only limited evidence for the superimposition of houses in Iron Age France until the end of the period when some of the settlements adhere to a rigid ground plan. Before that time, the sites of a few buildings overlapped but many others did not. On the other hand, there is little reason to suppose that successive structures were distanced from one another in the way that seems to have happened in Northern Europe. Rather, an intermediate position was adopted and here it was the earthwork enclosures that might be superimposed (Marion and Blancquaert 2000). Whilst the existence of pit burials suggests a connection between death and fertility – the interpretation increasingly favoured by French prehistorians (Delattre 2000b) – there may not have been as strong an emphasis on maintaining the life of the community.

The public and the private

Having considered the interpretation of domestic rituals on either side of the English Channel, we must return to the problem posed by the sequence at Danebury. How were these practices related to the rituals associated with the ceremonial monuments of the Iron Age? Rather than consider the evidence on a large scale, I shall focus on four excavated sites: two in Northern France and two in England. All of these belong to the later part of the Iron Age, and some continued in use into the Roman period.

Acy-Romance and Montmartin

The French sites, Acy-Romance (Lambot and Méniel 2000) and Montmartin (Brunaux and Méniel 1997), were in Belgic Gaul, beyond the region that may have seen the early development of the state. Even so, they were occupied during a period of political change (Haselgrove 1987; Nash 1987; Woolf 1998).

Acy-Romance had been an important ceremonial centre for a long time, and it is where one of the 'big houses' of the Late Bronze Age had been built. In addition to the settlement considered here, there were a number of Iron Age cemeteries. Occupation began in the early second century BC and lasted rather less than two hundred years. The excavated part of the site was laid out along a series of roads and can be divided between a living area and what was really a sanctuary (Figure 6.6). Within the domestic zone these roads were lined by rectangular houses and by smaller structures which are interpreted as barns. There were also four- and six-post settings which seem to have been the sites of raised granaries. The buildings were replaced in the same positions on as many as three occasions and were accompanied by a series of grain storage pits. In this part of the excavated area most of the bones came from these features. They included not only the waste from industrial processes but also a series of human remains. It seems as if parts of a single body could be divided between more than one of these pits.

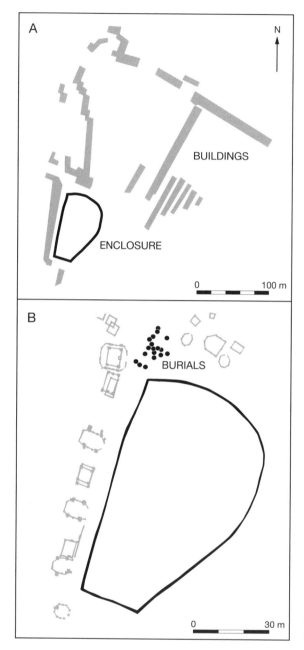

Figure 6.6 The Iron Age sanctuary and associated buildings at Acy-Romance, Northern France, with a detail of the main enclosure and the associated buildings and human burials. Information from Lambot and Méniel (2000).

The focal point of the settlement was a D-shaped enclosure and it was here that an extraordinary quantity of animal bones was found. Some had been deposited in its ditch, whilst the others were in pits located some distance away. These two collections are dominated by different species – cattle and horses within the enclosure and sheep outside it – and different parts of the body are represented in these two collections. The cattle bones are mainly skulls and vertebrae, yet these are just the elements that are absent from the other group. They also contrast with the finds associated with the houses, but it is not clear which are the remains of offerings and which provide evidence of feasts.

Along one side of this enclosure was a row of buildings which are interpreted as shrines or temples. One of them housed a well which the excavators compare with the shafts inside Viereckschanzen. These structures are very similar to the examples recorded at Late Iron Age sanctuaries in the same region of France and yet the small group of artefacts excavated from their post holes includes items that could be found in a domestic assemblage: axeheads, an iron hammer, a sickle and triangular loom weights.

It is the presence of a further group of human remains which makes this part of the site so special. Not only do they differ from the loose bones in the storage pits, they also contrast with the graves in the cemeteries at Acy-Romance. Just outside one limit of the enclosure there was a group of nineteen burials which had been located at the junction of two roads. These were tightly flexed and it seems possible that they were deposited there after the bodies had been dried. They occupied shallow pits quite distinct from the grain silos on the same site and did not share a single orientation. Rather, some of the bodies were aligned with the roads or with the course of the enclosure ditch. Few of them could be identified, but the best preserved skeletons were all of men. They have been interpreted as the results of human sacrifice.

Close to these burials there was a second group of timber buildings, but this time they seem to have been associated with grain storage pits, one of which was cut by a grave containing the extended burial of a man who had suffered a violent death. This remarkable group of features posed some problems of interpretation:

> If they had not been found so near [the burials], the . . . structures would have been interpreted as a domestic unit consisting of the house, a granary . . . two small ancillary buildings and a stock enclosure. [This suggests a] model of exploitation by a family unit, the elements of which are regularly encountered . . . within rural settlements . . . The finds, including the pottery and animal bones, are no different from what one discovers in the storage pits and the less productive ditch deposits within the settlement.
>
> (Lambot and Méniel 2000: 87; my translation)

On the other hand, these structures were particularly well built and, unlike the houses in other parts of the site, they had not been replaced. They also seemed to be grouped with a certain order and were laid out on roughly the same axis as one side of the enclosure. Lambot and Méniel conclude that they may have played a part in the ceremonies conducted at Acy-Romance, but they do not rest much weight on that argument.

Similar problems affect many other features of this site. Human bones were deposited in the storage pits associated with some of the houses, yet at the centre of the settlement there was a group of burials which may have originated as sacrifices. There were formal deposits of animal bones in the ditch of the central enclosure and others in a series of shallow pits, yet the main species that were represented there – cattle, horse and sheep – also provided much of the inhabitants' food. In the same way, the few artefacts associated with the timber shrines were of types that might be found in domestic contexts. Even at a site that had some extraordinary characteristics, it may be wrong to distinguish too rigidly between ritual and domestic activities.

Some of the same issues arise with the excavated site at Montmartin (Brunaux and Méniel 1997). It was located on a promontory between a river and a dry valley and was defined by two spaced earthworks running across open ground (Figure 6.7). The outer enclosure seems to have been a high-status settlement, whilst the inner ditch marked the limit of another sanctuary. These elements coexisted for almost two hundred years, from the early third century until about 100 BC when the site was destroyed by fire. Not all the enclosed area was excavated but large parts of the interior were sampled before the construction of a railway.

The settlement and the sanctuary contained quite different structures from one another. In the outer, domestic enclosure there were the remains of timber houses of a type that is found elsewhere, as well as the post holes of raised granaries and the usual corn storage pits. There were also two shafts which could have been wells. The inner part of the site may have had only one building, a setting of wooden posts which is closely paralleled at other sanctuaries. This is interpreted as a shrine. The perimeter earthworks were of more than one phase, but both seem to have been used over the same length of time. They were substantial features and each seems to have included a timber barrier. The inner ditch was two metres deep, while its counterpart was dug three metres into the bedrock and was broken by a complex entrance.

The excavators argue that the two parts of the site had quite different functions. The outer enclosure was a residential site, possibly belonging to a social elite, whilst the inner part was a kind of sanctuary where public ceremonies took place. The settlement was certainly a rich one and provided evidence of a number of craft activities, including woodworking, leather-working and the production of metal artefacts, especially those of iron. The main concentration of finds came from in and around one of the houses and suggested a high level of consumption. The inner enclosure, on the other hand,

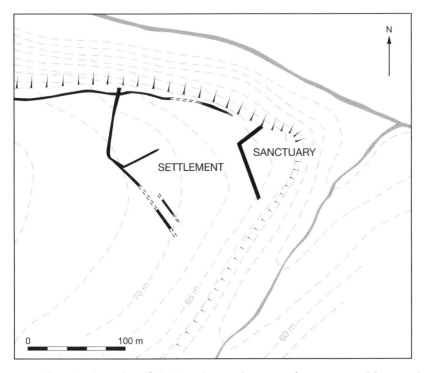

Figure 6.7   Outline plan of the Iron Age settlement and sanctuary at Montmartin, Northern France. Information from Brunaux and Méniel (1997).

was principally a location where offerings were put on display. These consisted mainly of weapons and human skulls, which may have been hung from the perimeter wall before they entered the ditch. They were accompanied by a large collection of animal bones and by a number of brooches. These are the same elements as were found at the nearby sanctuary at Gournay-sur-Aronde where similar practices have been inferred (Brunaux *et al.* 1985). At both sites it seems as if the remains of different species of animals were placed in separate sections of the ditch. For example, around the entrance to the inner enclosure at Montmartin there was a concentration of horse skulls.

In practice that neat separation was not maintained throughout the excavated area and it is clear that the material associated with the settlement overlapped to a significant extent with that deposited in the sanctuary. As we saw at Acy-Romance, it is impossible to make a clear distinction between a domestic assemblage and a series of 'ritual' offerings. The filling of the inner ditch at Montmartin included a number of distinctive deposits, but it also contained the same kinds of material as the principal house. The excavators explain this by its position on the site: the artefacts may have entered the earthwork from both enclosures. But that would not explain why the deposits of human skulls were not confined to the sanctuary. In fact, further examples were associated with the main domestic building, as was a quantity of metal-work, including weapon fragments and a torc. Again there are similarities and contrasts. The filling of the house contained the bones of sheep, goats and dogs, and cattle were relatively uncommon, whilst pig was the main species deposited in the inner ditch. On the other hand, both the ditches included an unusually high proportion of iron artefacts and they share this feature with the main dwelling at Montmartin. This is not to suggest that the excavators' interpre-tation is wrong, but simply to make the point that the distinction between a high-status settlement and a sanctuary may not be sufficiently subtle. Some of these issues are equally relevant to sites in England.

Hayling Island and Thetford

Both these sites are in lowland Britain. Hayling Island is in Wessex, close to the waters of the English Channel, and Thetford is located in East Anglia. Again they belong to a time of rapid political change (Creighton 2000), and in each case the archaeological sequence extends from the Iron Age into the Early Roman period.

In some respects the sequence at Hayling is easier to comprehend, for a Roman temple was built in its final phase (King and Soffe 1998). This has been compared with examples in Northern France, but excavation has shown that such a connection had been present from the outset. The earliest structure dates from the early to middle first century BC and is strikingly reminiscent of some of the sanctuaries in Iron Age Gaul, a connection which is reinforced by the origin of the some of the coins that were deposited at the site. It also recalls the latest of the structures at Danebury with which this chapter began.

The first feature at Hayling consisted of a rectilinear enclosure with its entrance facing east (Figure 6.8). It was defined by two or more palisades running parallel to one another. Within this enclosure, but offset towards that entrance, was a post setting which defined an area approximately eleven and a half metres long and nine metres wide. Again this was entered from the east, and just beyond the opposite wall there was a large pit. This monument has a similar plan to that of a Northern French sanctuary like Gournay-sur-Aronde (Brunaux *et al.* 1985), and in the first century BC it would have stood out from the predominantly circular tradition of domestic architecture in Wessex, although its orientation towards the rising sun would have been familiar. In its original form it looks like a Continental shrine transposed to Southern Britain and compares quite closely with the monuments considered by Venclová.

To judge from the associated coins, the Hayling temple may have gone out of use for a while, but activity certainly resumed early in the first century AD. The perimeter was defined by a ditch which enclosed a slightly smaller area. The inner enclosure was removed, but the pit, which had formed the focus for

EARLIER PHASE

LATER PHASE

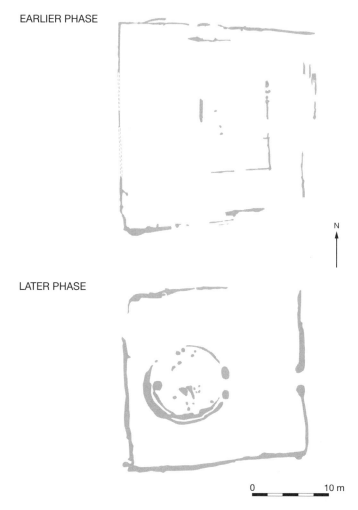

N

0   10 m

Figure 6.8   The evolution of the Iron Age temple on Hayling Island, Southern England. Information from King and Soffe (1998).

a series of offerings, retained its original significance. Now it was enclosed by a circular building that was replaced in stone after the Roman Conquest.

The construction of that timber building represents a new departure, for it has all the attributes of an Iron Age house of specifically British form. It is of about the normal size, the outer wall is accompanied by a drainage trench and it is entered on the east side through a porch. But the associated artefacts are quite different from a domestic assemblage. They include a substantial number of coins, brooches, equipment associated with horse-riding, broken weapons, and animal bones, mainly those of sheep and pig. All these finds would have

183

been in place at a Gallic sanctuary. Other items are more often associated with high-status burials, including traces of chain mail and part of a broken mirror. There are even a few human bones, although there is no sign of a grave.

Some of these objects had been placed in the central pit which seems to have retained its significance through both the Iron Age phases, but the majority were found around the entrance of the main enclosure. Here there was a concentration of finds to the left of the principal axis of the monument. These details are important for they recall some of the conventions that seem to have governed the deposition of cultural material inside Iron Age round houses. As I said in Chapter 2, these finds were generally associated with the doorway, which was normally towards the east, or they were placed in the southern half of the building. It seems as if the conventions that applied to Iron Age settlements extended to this extraordinary site where there is nothing to suggest any phase of domestic activity. The Hayling temple was located on an island close to what may have been a royal capital near Chichester, and this could be another case in which the elements of daily life were ritualised in a special setting. That seems only appropriate during a period when Southern Britain underwent political changes as it was drawn into the Roman world (Creighton 2000).

The evidence from Thetford sheds rather different light on that process (Gregory 1991). In some ways it provides the ideal counterpart to the Hayling temple. Again the basic architectural model is the same – a circular building or buildings at the centre of a square enclosure – but there are important differences between these sites. At Hayling, the circular building replaced a rectangular structure, but this has no counterpart at Thetford. Instead, the major monument was built over the remains of a settlement and for a while some of the activities that had taken place there may have continued outside the main enclosure.

As the excavator acknowledged, it is difficult to establish the sequence at Thetford. The subsoil features extended over a large area so that few of them cut one another, there were not many artefacts from reliable contexts, and it is not clear whether the pottery from the site provides adequate dating evidence. Of the alternatives that he offers in his account, I have chosen to follow the simpler version which divides the history of this complex into three stages. The first may have started as early as the fourth century BC (or as late as the second), whilst the last dates from the later years of the first century AD.

The remains of the earlier settlement are not easy to interpret. Gregory draws attention to the strange mixture of elements during this period. It consisted of a series of separate enclosures, linked by occasional ditches. In that respect it is like many of the Iron Age occupation sites that have been excavated more recently. At Thetford, there are traces of circular buildings, and there is even a small group of pits associated with burnt cereals. Yet all is not what it seems. The grain may have been introduced after it had been processed, and two of the ditched enclosures seem to be associated with graves. Indeed, one of them included a newly built round barrow within its area. The most remarkable of these structures is an oval earthwork, defined on three sides by a ditch which enclosed another burial. This feature is superficially similar to a number of Neolithic monuments but is clearly of Iron Age date (for two similar structures see Bradley 2002a: fig. 5.14). It contained a grave. It seems to have been orientated on the burial mound in one direction and, in the other, it was aligned on an area which was used for metalworking – one of two workshops belonging to this period (Figure 6.9).

In Phase 2, the central area of the site was occupied by a square enclosure defined by two broad ditches with an intermediate fence (Figure 6.10). It had an elaborate entrance to the east and was supplemented by a ditched annexe which may have contained an artificial pool. The principal enclosure was dominated by just one building, an exceptionally elaborate circular structure which was aligned on the gateway to the compound. This was the equivalent to the central structure at Hayling, but it was larger and more massively built.

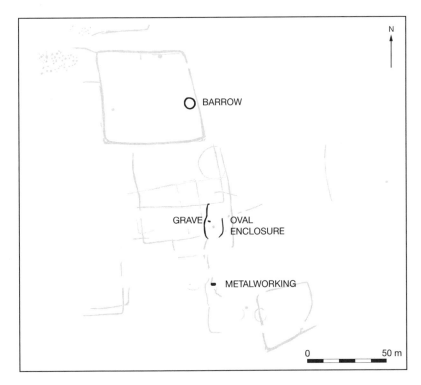

Figure 6.9   Plan of the first Iron Age settlement at Gallows Hill, Thetford, Eastern England, emphasising the possible alignment between an oval enclosure associated with a grave, a metalworking area and a round barrow. Information from Gregory (1991).

185

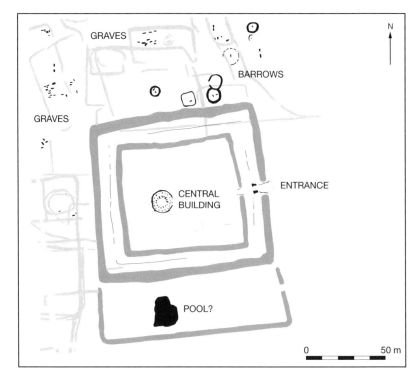

Figure 6.10   Plan of the first sanctuary and associated structures at Gallows Hill, Thetford, emphasising the positions of a series of barrows and graves. Information from Gregory (1991).

This remarkable complex was flanked on two sides by enclosures and burial mounds. Again their positions often overlap and there are traces of several features which resemble the round houses recorded at other sites. They are interspersed with no fewer than six ring ditches; there is also a square enclosure which incorporates the round barrow built during the previous phase. All are associated with graves. Further clusters of burials occur in four of the larger enclosures. One of these included the remains of a circular building and a workshop which was minting coins. Whilst the central area at Thetford must have played a role in public affairs, the area outside it shows the same variety of activities as the features of Phase 1.

Finally, the site was remodelled (Figure 6.11). During this period, it consisted of an enormous rectangular enclosure defined by two ditches and a series of other obstacles. The site was reached by a complex eastern entrance. The new design retained the circular building erected during the previous phase, but now it was flanked by two very similar constructions, with simpler circular buildings placed in front of them. There is a further clue to the

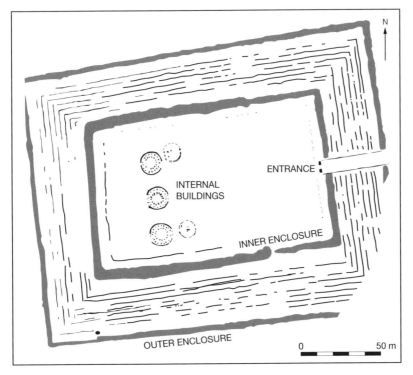

Figure 6.11   Plan of the latest sanctuary at Gallows Hill, Thetford. Information from Gregory (1991).

relationship between the public and private aspects of the site, for during this final phase domestic activity apparently ended. True to Venclová's formulation, the ceremonial centre at Thetford occupied a conspicuous position set apart from the everyday world, but this happened at the end of a lengthy history. As at Hayling, it also occurred during a period of political change.

Summary: settlements, shrines and history

This chapter began with two questions. How far were shrines separate from other aspects of Iron Age life? And did the relationship between public and private rituals change with the political developments of this period?

The first point to make is that there was never a sharp separation between the activities that took place in the settlements and those associated with sanctuaries or similar monuments. They could be found in close juxtaposition, as they were at Acy-Romance, Montmartin or in the earlier phases at Thetford, or they might be distanced from one another. That was always the case at Hayling, and the same relationship developed in the course of the sequence at Danebury and Thetford.

Even when that happened, the public and private worlds were never far apart. The excavators of Acy-Romance experienced some difficulty in distinguishing between domestic buildings and certain of the shrines, and again at Montmartin the contents of the settlement overlapped with those of the sanctuary. That is not to deny that there were some important differences. The deposits found on domestic sites emphasise the importance of the agricultural cycle, whilst those at Montmartin and Hayling include large numbers of broken weapons. Dress ornaments were important too, and it would be wrong to overlook the high proportion of brooches among the finds from sanctuaries. There were also coins.

At the same time, the architecture of the ceremonial monuments might be based on domestic prototypes. We have seen how difficult it was to distinguish between shrines and houses in the excavated parts of Acy-Romance. The Hayling 'temple' had exactly the same structure as an Iron Age dwelling, and the circular buildings inside the great enclosure at Thetford drew on the same source of inspiration, although these were more akin to the 'big houses' discussed in Chapter 2.

In the Iron Age there does not seem to have been the clear distinction between domestic and ceremonial structures that Continental scholars had anticipated, but there are at least some suggestions that these buildings may have moved apart over time. This is most clearly demonstrated by the sequence at Thetford, a site which began as a settlement in which some specialised activities took place and ended as a massive enclosure cut off from the landscape around it. That did not happen everywhere, but when the two domains did become more distinct this seems to have occurred during a period of social change. Three of the sites discussed in detail – Acy-Romance, Montmartin and Hayling – belong to a period of political centralisation that shows the growing influence of the Roman state. The sanctuary at Thetford was built after the conquest of Britain, but it may have provided a symbol of native resistance to foreign rule. Not one of these sites can be treated in isolation.

Coda: South Cadbury

That brings as back to our original starting point at Danebury, for it was here that Cunliffe identified an important sequence, in which the earlier buildings interpreted as shrines were integrated into the occupation of the hill fort, whilst the latest example was used when the enclosure was largely empty.

We have seen how that distinctive sequence emerged out of a long programme of fieldwork. Something similar happened in the case of another Southern English hill fort, South Cadbury, but in this case the chronological relationships were not established until the results of the project were prepared for publication (Barrett *et al.* 2000). Excavation between 1966 and 1973 revealed a small building on the hilltop which was identified as a shrine. It resembled two of the buildings at Danebury and, like them, it was attributed to the main period of occupation on the site. Now it seems as if it belonged, not to the Iron Age, but to an Early Roman phase, when settlement there had ended (ibid.:116 and 323).

In this case the form and setting of the shrine have suggested wider connections. In 1997, Downes noted the points of similarity between this structure and the raised granaries in the Iron Age phases at South Cadbury (Figure 6.12), and the same observation might apply to the earlier of the shrines at Danebury which share the size and orientation of these buildings and are found in the same part of the site. The redating of the Cadbury shrine does not negate this argument. The construction of the shrine could have happened after the hill fort was attacked by the Roman army and that may have given it a special significance for local communities. If it was meant to resemble a granary, this might have been taken as a reference to the earlier history of the monument.

There are other reasons for taking this view, as the highest part of the enclosed area at South Cadbury includes a remarkable juxtaposition of archae-ological features, some of them extending back to the end of the Bronze Age. There is evidence for the accumulation, working and deposition of metalwork

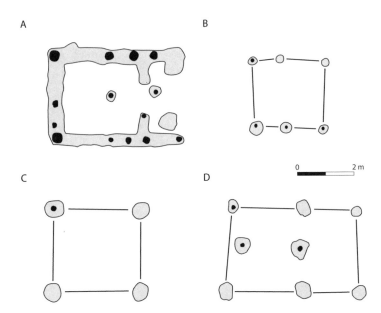

Figure 6.12 Plan of the shrine (top left) and other timber buildings interpreted as possible granaries within the hill fort at South Cadbury, South-West England. Information from Downes (1997) and Barrett *et al.* (2000).

throughout the prehistoric sequence, and the authors of the definitive report comment that this:

> Confirm[s] the quite specific nature of activities on this part of the plateau and remind[s] us that our analytical distinctions between the utility of production and the ritual of consumption may be misplaced.
>
> (Barrett *et al.* 2000: 301)

That view is supported by another characteristic of this complex. The timber shrine was located in the same area as the finds of metalwork, but their distribution was complemented by a series of animal burials. Some of these had been disturbed and it was not possible to work out the length of time over which they had been deposited or to establish whether any of them were contemporary with the shrine itself. But that hardly matters. It seems more important that here many of the processes considered in Chapters 4 to 6 come together at a single site. Again it provides a warning, if warning is needed, of the dangers of making any dogmatic distinction between the archaeological evidence of ritual and the residues of daily life. It also illustrates the vital importance of sequence.

The implications of all these case studies are considered in the final chapter.

7

WHAT REMAINS TO BE SEEN

Some implications of the argument

Blunt instruments

My interest in ritual and domestic life goes back to an experience that happened in 1977. Together with John Barrett, I was excavating a Middle Bronze Age enclosure and cemetery at South Lodge Camp in Southern England (Barrett *et al*. 1991: 144–83). The site was located on a private estate and when our project began we were surprised to discover that our team was not the only one working there, for this was the 'secret' location where a television series about life in the Iron Age was being filmed (Percival 1980). It was a programme that traced the fortunes of a group of people living in a reconstructed prehistoric village. It was represented as a sociological exercise, but it was also an attempt to see how far archaeological interpretations of later prehistory could be put into practice.

In some ways our own project had similar objectives. The excavation was concerned with the origins of enclosed settlements and field systems in prehistoric Wessex. It was also concerned with reinterpreting one of the type sites of the Middle Bronze Age which had first been investigated many years before (Barrett *et al*. 1991: 145–6). The television programme considered how a small enclosed settlement of rather later date might have functioned and the ways in which modern people could adapt to an Iron Age way of life.

The television programme was not particularly successful, but during our excavation we got to know some of the people taking part in the series. They asked us many questions, but one of these has assumed a greater significance in the light of the issues considered here. How were the volunteers to prepare food when the iron sickles with which they had been provided were incapable of harvesting crops? That seemed surprising, as those taking part in the programme had been issued with exact replicas of objects from excavated sites.

Initially, I favoured a practical explanation. The objects which had been copied at such expense entered the archaeological record when they could no longer be used. They had been worn out of shape and that was why the modern copies did not work. Such an argument might account for the poor performance of the sickles, but it did not explain why their Iron Age prototypes had been available in the first place. Those objects could have been repaired, or the metal might have been recycled by the smith. Neither had happened, and these artefacts remained intact. In Chapter 6 I argued that similar processes affected many of the items found in later prehistoric settlements, among them agricultural tools. They had not been discarded casually but seem to have been formal deposits.

Our excavation was identifying anomalies of a similar kind. Although we had commenced the project with the aim of investigating the workings of a Bronze Age settlement and its fields, the site had certain features that we had not expected (Barrett *et al.* 1991: chapter 5) . One of the aims of the first year's work was to establish whether the positions of wooden houses had been missed by the previous investigation, but when we discovered the post holes of one such building they turned out to enclose the burial of a cow, whose body had been cut in half in the manner of Damien Hirst. This was set so shallowly in the ground that it must have been put there when the structure was no longer in use. We found a second round house nearby, and this presented similar problems for it turned out that its position had been marked by a circular mound of cultural material which would have resembled a small barrow (ibid.: 183).

With growing confidence, we could recognise other anomalies in the archaeology of South Lodge Camp. The buildings had been placed within a square enclosure and the previous excavator had found deposits of bronze artefacts in three of the corners of this earthwork (ibid.: fig. 5.13). Our investigation added some evidence of metal production. The main deposits were along one edge of the site towards a small cemetery which contained similar kinds of material. Moreover, when we excavated two of the mounds in that cemetery we discovered that they had been laid out according to the same principles as the domestic buildings. Both of them were circular monuments surrounded by a shallow ditch which was interrupted by an entrance towards the south (Bradley 1998b: 152). Again it seemed impossible to explore the workings of a prehistoric settlement without encountering features that defied a practical explanation. The archaeology of the 1970s and early 1980s was proving to be another blunt instrument.

Just as the television programme 'Living in the Past' attempted to present an image of Iron Age people as farmers who shared the concerns of their modern counterparts, the field archaeologists of the time were most concerned with food production and adaptation. And just as our experiences during the excavation of South Lodge Camp challenged our original expectations, the prevailing assumptions were coming under attack from another direction.

Two archaeologies

The history of archaeology has never been entirely stable. There are some periods which are characterised by a quest for general principles, and others in which there is more emphasis on points of detail (Kristiansen 1996; Sherratt 1997: 1–6). The first kind of research considers extensive geographical areas and long periods of time. In practice, it places a considerable emphasis on population, environment, subsistence and human ecology. This tradition has emphasised the importance of universal processes rather than the local and particular, and, as Edmund Leach (1973) once told an audience of prehistorians, archaeology of this kind is influenced by functionalist anthropology of a sort which has long been out of favour.

On the same occasion Leach predicted a rapprochement with structural anthropology, and this new alliance represents the other tendency in the discipline. It may have developed in ways that Leach could not have foreseen, but often it is concerned with the local and small-scale and places greater emphasis on symbolism, meaning and agency. For some scholars this approach is currently in the ascendant but, for others, a middle ground remains, and that is the view taken in this book.

Renfrew (1994a and b) has observed how the archaeologists of the 1960s and 1970s were reluctant to investigate the roles of ritual and religion: a position that echoes that of Gordon Childe in his studies of European prehistory. Ritual was either rationalised as adaptive or dismissed as epiphenomenal. That view might seem natural to a Marxist like Childe, yet for different reasons the Cambridge school of 'palaeoeconomists' took an equally hard line. Ritual, they said, was not important in the past and not worth studying in the present. Most activities that might be described by this term played a role in human adaptation. As Higgs and Jarman put it, 'the soul leaves no skeleton' (1975: 1).

If there has been a change of emphasis, it has been towards a greater concern with the very areas that were avoided by an earlier generation of archaeologists. To some extent this has resulted from the changes that Leach anticipated. After a prolonged period in which the two fields had drifted apart, there is more common ground between archaeology and anthropology. That is due to a new emphasis on material culture. It can be illustrated by recent research on ancient art, mortuary practices, landscape and architecture. The irony is that all these formed part of a more traditional set of studies fifty years ago. The main difference is not one of subject matter but approach.

Some of these developments reflect a change of fashion, but rather more is involved. One point is particularly important here. There remains a fundamental disagreement over the feasibility of conducting any kind of cognitive archaeology. As we have seen, there is confusion among the people engaged in fieldwork as to the right ways of distinguishing between the residues of daily life and those of ritual activity, and the specialists who study excavated material offer little assistance. Many of them seem to be more concerned with the formation of the archaeological record than they are with its interpretation (Schiffer 1976 and 1996).

To some extent the difficulties result from the influence of textual models. Structuralism developed from linguistics, and many of the major works of Lévi-Strauss are studies of myths that were recorded in writing. The dominance of the text has extended into recent archaeology (Hodder 1989; Tilley 1990 and 1991). By definition, prehistorians have no access to any documents; instead they must come to terms with ancient material culture. It has been tempting to think of this as a kind of text and even to study it using models taken from literary theory. But the process involves certain dangers, for one of the tenets of structural linguistics is the arbitrary relationship between the signifier and the signified. Language can be thought of as a network of relationships; the meaning of any single element must be established by its position in relation to others. There are literary critics who have taken this approach to its logical conclusion by denying the authority of any text. If the late nineteenth century saw the death of God, the late twentieth century claimed the death of the author.

There are difficulties in applying the same approach to material culture. If this is to be read in the same manner as a text, then it follows that its meaning will always elude the investigator. Indeed, it may not be acceptable to suppose that it possessed a single meaning in the first place. At best, this approach is unrewarding; and, at its worst, it seems futile. It is a prospect that some prehistorians have contemplated (Bapty and Yates 1990) but those who continue to practise archaeology seem to have drawn back from the implications of this argument.

How do they justify that change? One solution is suggested by the studies brought together here. Many of the rituals that seem to have taken place in prehistoric Europe employed the material items that were familiar in daily life (Boivin in press). They may have been made in more elaborate styles, and they could have been deployed in a much more specialised manner, but their original connotations would still have been apparent. Of course, they might have taken on additional meanings depending on the contexts in which they were used, but they overlap with the items used in the domestic sphere to such an extent that it seems unlikely that the relationship between them was irrelevant. The connection between signifier and signified was not as arbitrary as it is in speech or written texts. Rather, certain features – artefacts, buildings, visual images and monuments – can be regarded as 'material metaphors' (Tilley 1999) and could have owed their power to the very fact that their external frame of reference was comprehensible. If so, the allusions to the domestic world must surely have been important.

That is not to suggest that their meanings were completely transparent. They must have been changed by the very fact that they were deployed in such a formal manner. Thus great timber circles like those at Durrington Walls or Navan, or great houses like those at Gamla Uppsala and Antran, were not

194

domestic dwellings, and yet the allusion to the buildings in which people lived could still have been understood even though that comparison did not exhaust their significance. In the same way, a wooden implement made to look like a plough had an added importance when it was deposited in a peat bog. It could never have functioned as an agricultural tool, but its frame of reference would be considerably expanded if it were found in the same context as other artefacts. The situation can be even more complex, so that a dagger made of Grand Pressigny flint did not cease to be thought of as a weapon when it was used to harvest crops. Rather, that action might have invested it with a greater importance by bringing together two apparently unrelated themes. The point that matters is that both of them – warfare and food production – can still be identified by archaeology. That is because the procedures of daily life provided such a potent source of metaphors. It was this feature that led to the confusion that I described in Chapter 1.

The overlap between ritual and domesticity is certainly not universal and it is worth considering the limits of this interpretation. One has been suggested by Renfrew who argues that the major investment of meaning in material culture came, not with the emergence of the modern human mind, but at a later stage:

> I have sought to show how strange it is, on the conventional view of the 'human revolution', . . . that the new genotype producing the new phenotype Homo sapiens sapiens did not at once produce a whole range of interesting behaviour patterns . . . Usually when a new species emerges it develops the new behaviour patterns by which we recognise it . . . In retrospect we may regard this new human animal as a very special one . . . But why is it only in the past ten millennia that we see strikingly new behaviour patterns – constructions, innovations, inventions – which are changing the world?
>
> My answer is that the true human revolution came only much later, with the emergence of a way of life which permitted a much greater engagement between the human animal and the world in which we live. Human culture became more substantive, more material. We came to see the world in new ways, and became involved with it in new ways. I suggest that the key to this new embodiment, this new materialization, may have been sedentism.
>
> (2001: 128)

It is a point to which I shall return, but it is apposite to comment that at very few stages in this book have I referred to the ritualisation of domestic life by hunter gatherers. It may be a phenomenon which becomes clearly recognisable in the Neolithic period.

If we can talk of the early stages of this process, what can we say of the circumstances in which it reached its limits? There are two aspects to this question, both of which will be considered in more detail later. There is the possibility that rituals were set apart from settlement sites and took place at special locations during the Late Iron Age. There are also some indications that the rituals that were carried out there placed a decreasing emphasis on the domestic sphere. Both these suggestions are consistent with a broader interpretation that relates the changing character of public rituals to the transformations that were taking place during the late pre-Roman period. One of the crucial elements may have been the emergence of a group of religious specialists who seem to have played an important role in society. Classical writers knew them as Druids, and it interesting that Venclová, who has argued that the sanctuaries of this period occur in isolation, thinks that a stone sculpture from her site at Mšecké Zehrovice depicts one of these people (Venclová 2002). Such arguments are consistent with the idea that public ritual became more directly integrated into the political process in the complex societies of the time.

What remains to be seen?

I have sketched some of the broad outlines, but have still to consider these issues in any detail. There are a number of points which need to be addressed.

Domestication and sedentism

The first is the origin of these practices, for this has important implications for the nature of prehistoric studies. I have already described two opposing tendencies in the discipline and the predicament of those field archaeologists who have to negotiate a path between them. On the one hand, there are accounts of settlement, subsistence and the natural environment of a kind that has continued largely unaltered from the 1960s. On the other, there are those studies, unhelpfully called 'post-processual', which consider material culture as an active element in ancient social life and place more emphasis on its meanings for the people who created it. That approach includes the study of ritual.

Just as these approaches may be opposed in the interpretation of individual sites, they tend to be associated with the investigation of different periods. Thus the archaeology of the Mesolithic is more concerned with subsistence and adaptation, whilst Neolithic scholars have increasingly turned to studies of ideology and belief: so much so, that there are doubts over whether there was a distinctive 'Neolithic' economy. According to Thomas (1988), the Mesolithic–Neolithic transition in Northern and Western Europe has been so hard to discuss because it involves two groups of scholars with different interests. As a result, there is no common basis from which to work.

That is not completely fair. Although many students of the Mesolithic have different concerns from Neolithic scholars, the division between the two groups is too clear-cut. There are Neolithic specialists who are as interested in the subsistence economy as their colleagues who study hunter gatherers, and there have been a number of attempts to write a social archaeology of Mesolithic Europe, although these have been less ambitious than accounts of later periods. The problem is not entirely one of approach. Put simply, it would not be possible to extend some of the methods of Neolithic archaeology to the remains of the preceding period. Why is this?

Renfrew's hypothesis may supply part of the answer. In his view it was only with the development of more stable settlements that social relations were 'materialized' in a lasting form through significant changes in the range and complexity of artefacts. The same argument applies to the built environment in which substantial dwellings and specialised monuments were constructed for the first time. He attributes all these developments to the increasingly intense interactions that resulted from sedentism.

It is an argument that works well in Western Asia where farming developed among settled hunter gatherers (Renfrew 2001), but it does not account for the situation towards the agricultural frontier in Northern and Western Europe which has provided the source of many of the examples considered here. In this case there may have been sedentary hunter gatherers with a restricted material culture, and more mobile farmers who employed a complex range of artefacts and who built monuments. Indeed, the evidence considered in Chapter 4 suggests that during the earlier part of the Neolithic certain practices that had first developed during the Mesolithic period received a greater emphasis than before. In this case the main source of contrast may have been the adoption of domesticates.

In recent publications I have interpreted some of these contrasts in terms of the different world views of hunter gatherers and farmers. Hunter gatherers, I suggested, were *integrated into* the natural world, whilst farmers *acted upon it* (Bradley 1998b: chapter 2; Bradley in press). The adoption of domesticates involved a new notion of property and their successful exploitation developed a novel conception of time. The artefacts of the Mesolithic period often made use of organic raw materials, including bone, antler, teeth and shells, and the treatment afforded to the dead might even suggest that humans and animals were not considered as separate kinds of being; we have seen the same idea expressed by the therianthropes in Palaeolithic and Mesolithic art. Neolithic material culture, on the other hand, involved a greater transformation. The obvious examples include the making of decorated pottery and polished axes. These may well have circulated for a longer time than their predecessors and they were more often deposited in specialised locations. Whereas Mesolithic rituals may have happened at unaltered places in the landscape, during the Neolithic period space was completely transformed by the building of monuments.

Such arguments seem to account for a number of recurrent features in the archaeology of Western, Central and Northern Europe, but they are inevitably weakened by the tendency to treat hunter gatherers and farmers as ideal types, a tradition in Western thought that can be traced back to the Enlightenment (Plucinnik 2001). On the other hand, many of these features are documented in the archaeology of individual areas. South Scandinavia provides an ideal example, for this is a region where the change from mobility to sedentism cannot be explained by the use of domesticates.

At this point it may be helpful to recall the situation described in Chapter 4. This involved a number of elements. There was the contrast between the hunters, foragers and fishers of the Ertebølle period, who were in contact with farming communities further to the south, and the people of the TRB Culture who were the first to make regular use of domesticated plants and animals. For this purpose it is not important whether the local population had changed. What matters is that for a while many of the same places remained in use without any obvious differences in the lengths of time over which they were occupied. Ertebølle and Early TRB settlements show much the same mixture of short- and long-term occupations, and the situation did not change significantly until the Middle Neolithic period when there is more evidence of cereal-growing (Fischer 2002; Malmer 2002).

Despite the continued occupation of certain places, there were important changes in the ways in which artefacts were made and used. Pottery became more common and more elaborately decorated, and ground and polished axes assumed considerable importance. There was a greater variety of material equipment in the Early Neolithic and there are indications that a grow-ing proportion of it was deployed in a specialised manner. This is shown by the settlement deposits considered earlier, and by the distinctive groups of artefacts associated with bogs and early monuments. In those rare instances in which excavation has revealed a continuous sequence it is clear that these changes occurred without any major disruptions in the character of occupation sites. Rather, the most obvious relationship is between the appearance of domesticates and the elaboration of portable equipment.

In Chapter 4 I commented on the different ways in which the term Neolithic had been employed in Scandinavian archaeology. It was applied to farmers in Denmark and Southern Sweden and to sedentary hunter gatherers in Western Norway. The term even extended to the Pitted Ware Culture which also seems to have been characterised by the use of wild resources. Again a direct comparison is revealing.

The remains of domesticated plants and animals are practically absent from the Norwegian sites, and yet these were coastal settlements that seem to have been occupied over significant periods of time. Although there is some spatial patterning among the contents of these places, there is little to indicate a pattern of structured deposition like that found at Skumparberget and Skogsmossen. There is no evidence of a more complex material culture, although the deposition of ground stone axes in natural places had begun during the Mesolithic period. Despite a laudable effort to investigate the social archaeology of this phase, the region lacks any monuments and the main source of information is provided by the exchange of lithic artefacts (Bergsvik 2002).

The developments of the Pitted Ware Culture are particularly interesting here. According to Malmer (2002), they could have happened after a phase in which local communities had made use of domesticates. Now they seem to have returned to an economy that was based on wild resources. It is not clear whether this involved any changes in the lengths of time over which individual sites were occupied, but it is known that some of their settlements were very extensive indeed. Several other developments ran in parallel with this change. Local material culture seems to have been simpler, and less use was made of elaborately decorated pottery. There were fewer changes in the repertoire of stone tools, but there was little evidence for the provision of offerings in watery locations. The building and use of monuments ended altogether. Instead, it seems as if mortuary rituals focused on some of the domestic sites, and these locations may be associated with a small number of placed deposits. In short, the renewal of hunting, gathering and fishing seems to be associated with a simpler material culture and with a reduction in the archaeological manifestations of ritual activity.

Malmer argues that the situation changed during the Battle Axe phase when farming and monument building both resumed. Again there is little to show whether individual settlements were occupied by sedentary communities. What is clear, however, is that the elaboration of material culture ran in parallel with the ownership of crops and animals. It also corresponds to the reuse of existing megaliths and to a new group of votive deposits whose characteristics recall those of the TRB.

The value of considering a regional sequence in this way is that it avoids the danger of treating farmers and hunter gatherers as ideal types. Nonetheless this evidence is consistent with the idea that with the adoption of domesticates material culture was employed in a more structured manner. The pattern seems to cross-cut the distinction between sedentism and a mobile pattern of settlement and is most clearly evidenced in the archaeology of Northern Europe, although similar trends could be suggested in other areas. Perhaps the ritualisation of domestic life increased significantly during the Neolithic period. That should not be taken to imply that other communities lacked rituals of their own: merely that these are not so clearly indicated by their surviving material culture and need not have focused to the same extent on living sites. It is not an absolute contrast, as the evidence of Pitted Ware settlements makes clear, but the practice of making offerings in bogs and pools also originated among late hunter gatherers in Scandinavia and could provide one indication of a different kind of system (Karsten 1994). So could the placing of Mesolithic axeheads under screes or isolated boulders in Western Norway (Lødøen 1998).

To return to my original question, why has there been such an obvious division between Mesolithic and Neolithic studies? It is true that these epitomise separate traditions of research, but the very nature of the archaeological record has required some differences of approach. It may be unjust to accuse Mesolithic specialists of neglecting the issues that captivate Neolithic scholars, for the material available to them is not the same. That need not be the result of taphonomy or poor preservation. In fact it may be a consequence of how people chose to organise their lives.

Degrees of freedom

Now I must consider a further problem. At various points I have discussed the relationship between the rituals that took place within settlements and those that were consigned to other parts of the landscape. In some cases they occurred at specially constructed monuments, but this did not always happen. Thus there were structured deposits within the settlements described in Chapter 4, but very similar material was associated with enclosures and tombs. It was also found in natural features like lakes and bogs. A similar range of possibilities offered itself during later periods. Thus deposits of pottery and animal bones might be associated with Bronze Age settlements, whilst metalwork of the same date could be found some distance away. Chapter 3 summarised the situation in the Southern Netherlands, where different kinds of artefact had been deposited at varying distances from the places where people lived: sickles and pins were found in the domestic arena, spears were located on the edge of the settled land, whilst swords and the more elaborate ornaments were in rivers even further away (Fontijn 2003).

A similar situation arose in the Iron Age and was discussed in Chapter 6. There seems to have been an important distinction between settlements and sanctuaries. Their positions hardly overlapped, but in this case they also contained separate kinds of deposit: human burials, animal remains and domestic artefacts in the occupation sites, and weapons, coins and brooches at the shrines. Two distinct processes are at work here, and it is important to distinguish between them. In one case the contexts where offerings were made were some distance from one another, even though they contained a similar assemblage. In the other, different places were associated with different kinds of material.

It may be helpful to express these distinctions in diagrammatic form. In Figure 7.1 one axis represents what I shall term *physical distance*, and other *conceptual distance*. Thus deposits associated with houses are directly linked with the domestic domain, whereas precisely the same material may be associated with a causewayed enclosure at a considerable remove. In this case they are *physically* far apart. On the other hand, one kind of material might be associated with an Iron Age house and quite another with a shrine. For example, agricultural equipment might be deposited in corn storage pits, whilst swords, spears and shields might be found in a sanctuary. In this case, one group of deposits seems to be connected with food production, whilst the other is associated with warfare. In that sense they are *conceptually* distinct (Figure 7.1).

This is such an obvious point that it is sometimes overlooked. Figure 7.2 emphasises the distinctions between the archaeology of the domestic domain and a number of places considered in earlier chapters. For example, the contents of the Neolithic pool at Skogsmossen are spatially and conceptually close to those in the adjacent settlement. On the other hand, the deposits at the causewayed enclosure of Etton resemble those from occupation sites of the period, but the monument occupies a marginal location. That approach is also helpful in studying later prehistory. The sanctuary at Montmartin was beside a settlement of the same date, but in this case their contents referred to separate concepts. Similarly, the Hayling temple contained a very different assemblage from the habitations of the Late Iron Age but the structure was built in an isolated position.

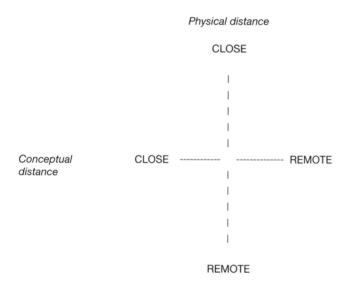

Figure 7.1   A scheme for comparing the similarities and differences between the assemblages from archaeological sites.

This scheme is a very simple one and emphasises the extent to which pre-historic rituals form a continuum extending outwards from the domestic sphere. It may also help to identify certain unwarranted assumptions. One of these is particularly prevalent. It is the notion that, during the Late Neolithic and Early Bronze Age, monuments in a number of regions of Europe clustered in what have become known as 'ritual landscapes'. This is because the very concentration of monumental architecture has encouraged the notion that domestic sites must have been excluded from the same areas. Such a hypothesis

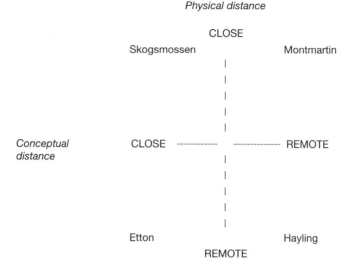

Figure 7.2   The scheme summarised in Figure 7.1 applied to four key sites discussed in the text.

needs to be investigated on the ground, but all too often the idea remains unexamined because of a deep-rooted assumption about the character of ritual itself. Prehistorians have supposed that it must have taken place in areas removed from daily life. That approach is especially unfortunate as it is often difficult to agree on the criteria by which settlements can be identified in the field (Brück 1999c). If we wish to discover the ways in which cultural material was deployed, the evidence must be studied in greater detail.

Such considerations are also important in the Late Iron Age where the distinction between settlements and sanctuaries has assumed a growing importance. The second diagram could be read in the wrong way, for it might suggest that over time rituals moved from the domestic sphere to more special-ised monuments. That would not be true. Monuments of various kinds were built throughout the period from the Neolithic to the Iron Age, but not all of them contained the kinds of assemblage that would be found at occupa-tion sites. From the Late Neolithic or Copper Age (depending on the local terminology) certain groups of cultural material began to stand out from the others, and this was particularly true of the finds from graves and rivers. But all these ran in parallel with the ritualisation of activities in the settlement. The same applies to the evidence from the Iron Age, although here the distinctions between different sites and their associations became more obvious. It is not only that some of the places claimed as sanctuaries were isolated, the rituals that were conducted there involved quite different artefacts from those in the domestic sphere.

I have already suggested that some of these developments may be related to the importance of religious specialists in the politics of the Late Iron Age. It is also true that these distinctions developed at a time when communities across different parts of Europe were exposed to the influence of states in the Mediterranean. In fact it is sometimes claimed that the distinctive forms of the sanctuaries were inspired by Classical prototypes, but such arguments can be taken too far. Not all the monuments that have been claimed as sanctuaries contain a distinctive artefact assemblage. At Acy-Romance and Montmartin the contents of such sites overlap to a certain extent with those of the associated settlements, and in Bohemia and Southern Germany it has been even more difficult to distinguish between the material deposited at Viereckschanzen and the finds from earlier settlements on the same sites. Nor are the buildings that have been interpreted as shrines altogether distinct from the domestic architecture of the Iron Age. Chapter 1 showed how this has led to difficulties in the interpretation of Viereckschanzen, and in Chapter 6 it became apparent how the timber buildings inside the enclosures at Hayling and Thetford seem to have been modelled on the houses in which people lived. It even seems possible that the forms of the small shrines at the hill forts of Danebury and South Cadbury were influenced by the raised granaries which had already been built on those sites.

Perhaps the most striking evidence is actually that of sequence, for a number of the places discussed in earlier chapters share a common property. In each example, an Iron Age or Early Roman shrine had been built over the position of an older settlement. Sometimes the two were used in parallel for a while, but quite often the shrine remained after occupation was over. The evidence takes several forms. The famous Viereckschanze of Mšecké Žehrovice was constructed within an existing settlement which may have been abandoned when the enclosure was built. Venclová observes that the same could have happened elsewhere. At Thetford, the first of the enclosed sanctuaries was in the midst of a domestic landscape and it seems as if daily life had gone on around it. It was only later that the sanctuary was reconstructed and it was then that settlement came to an end. That is rather like the sequence inside the hill fort at Danebury, and something similar may have happened at South Cadbury where animal burials and metalwork had already been deposited in the area in which the shrine was to be built. The sequence varies so much from one site to another that it would probably be wrong to insist on a single interpretation, yet however we view these particular cases they stand for something new.

The importance of the domestic sphere

The last two sections have highlighted some important developments: the first adoption of domesticated plants and animals, and the distancing of Iron Age shrines from the practices of daily life. At the same time, there are certain common elements which run right through this account and these need emphasising here. They may supply some of the reasons why prehistoric rituals so often referred to everyday procedures.

Perhaps these ideas were based on two different features: the symbolic significance of regeneration, and the role of food production in the political economy. Both have been discussed at different points in this account and it is necessary to bring them together now.

The first element is what has been described as the 'agricultural metaphor'. This was discussed in some detail in Chapter 6, but its importance pervades every section of this book. As many writers have observed, the adoption of domesticated plants and animals would have helped to impart a different sense of time from that experienced by mobile hunter gatherers (Meillassoux 1972). Farming is only possible if people look beyond the annual cycles of food production – the birth of new livestock, the growth of crops – and make provision for the longer term. That means that they have to decide how many animals they must retain for breeding when others are consumed. Similarly, they must keep enough seed corn to ensure that there will be sufficient crops in the future. More than that, the very possibility of raising domesticates depends on a long period of care for the land itself. It is difficult to maintain a reliable food supply without a sustained investment.

Prehistorians have also noted that the changing conceptions of time necessitated by agriculture are reflected in other spheres, and, in particular, in attitudes to the dead. In some parts of Europe Mesolithic hunter gatherers did have cemeteries and were generally buried among the settlements of the living (Brinch-Petersen and Meiklejohn 2003). Mortuary monuments were built from an early stage of the Neolithic, and many of these seem to have remained in use for considerable lengths of time. In some cases they were permeable constructions from which relics could be removed as other bones were added, but the most important feature is not the fact that long barrows or megaliths had an extended life span, it is the possibility that their outward forms were modelled on those of domestic buildings (Bradley 1998b: chapter 3). Some were of kinds that were still being used, whilst others were structures of types that had existed in the past.

The connection between mortality and the agricultural cycle was emphasised in different ways in different parts of Europe, but it was pervasive. Thus the artefact assemblages associated with megalithic tombs often referred to the domestic domain, and causewayed enclosures include a combination of human bones and those of farm animals, even during periods when there is some evidence of hunting. In the same way, the artefacts associated with land clearance and food consumption dominate the contents of the votive deposits. The evidence for this is steadily increasing, and it seems possible that in Northern Europe the burning of artefacts, and even that of houses, referred to the ways in which land had been prepared for cultivation. The link with mortuary deposits could hardly be more apparent, for large accumulations of burnt flint are also associated with the tombs.

It might seem as if these ideas would be less important as agriculture became more firmly established, but there is no evidence of this. Early Bronze Age people in Northern Europe expressed many of the same relationships, even if these took a different form. Thus there is important evidence that individual graves might be aligned with plough furrows and that round barrows were deliberately positioned on cultivated land. As I argued in Chapter 1, that relationship is unlikely to be have been fortuitous, especially in those cases where the perimeter of an existing barrow was ploughed immediately before the monument was extended. What applied to arable land applied to houses too, and in the second chapter I described some cases in which a burial mound had been built over the site of a domestic building.

During the Later Bronze Age, the relationship between the dead and the agricultural cycle became, if anything, more direct. Houses, pits, farmyards, ponds and wells all became the focus for structured deposits, and in parts of North-East Europe human bones were a regular component of the settlement assemblage. That is particularly interesting as it was during the same period that model granaries were used to store the relics of the dead. In Southern England something similar may have happened, for here small cemeteries were established just outside the occupied area, whilst isolated cremation burials extend across the interior of many Late Bronze Age settlements (Brück 1995).

That equation between the agricultural cycle and the commemoration of the dead became still more obvious during the Iron Age when one of the dominant symbols was the corn storage pit. I discussed this evidence in detail in Chapter 6. It is not necessary to repeat most of my arguments here, but a few points are important. They concern the differences between the rituals practised on either side of the English Channel. In both areas there was an emphasis on grain silos. These provide an ideal metaphor for death and regeneration and so it is not surprising that when these features went out of use they were filled by special deposits, including human burials.

In England and France there has been a tendency to treat these burials as aberrant, as those of social outcasts or deviant members of society (Wait 1985; Villes 1988), but this may be mistaken. Although it is reasonable to infer that Iron Age communities in France, Belgium, Northern Germany and Southern Britain made a similar equation between the dead and the regeneration of the crop, the pit burials may have had a different significance in Britain than they did in Continental Europe. There are a number of contrasts between these deposits. Those in Britain place as much emphasis on artefacts as they do on burials, whilst the Continental evidence is mainly concerned with human and animal remains. Although there are many exceptions, the bodies found in the storage pits of Southern England favour a common alignment which they share with the houses of the same period. Those on the Continent are much more varied and do not adhere to any norm. The British examples are laid out on the same principle as most of the bodies found in cemeteries, although these groups have very different distributions from one another; pit burials are mostly a feature of Central Southern England, whilst formal cemeteries occur in the South-West and North-East. In Northern France, where Iron Age graves have been studied in more detail, there is no such link between these deposits.

Perhaps a clue is provided by the domestic architecture of the period and the ways in which it was used. In Chapter 6 I discussed the evidence that in the Netherlands and South Scandinavia long houses had been occupied for a limited period before they were replaced in another location. The creation of these buildings was associated with one group of offerings, and its use or abandonment with another. Thus the history of these deposits, which consist of material that was intimately associated with food production, traces the development of the dwelling from its construction to its abandonment. In Britain, on the other hand, Late Bronze Age and Iron Age houses were normally replaced in exactly the same positions; they were superimposed, or their ground plans overlapped. In this case any deposits of cultural material emphasised divisions of space rather than those of time. Moreover these buildings were circular, meaning that they reflected the sky overhead. The sun and moon would have followed the same path around the walls of these buildings, day after day and year after year. Here is an image of continuity to match the placing of the dead in storage pits. These ideas may have been so powerful that in England formal cemeteries were very rare in the region in which such burials occurred.

At the same time, such pits were originally meant to keep food, and this should not be forgotten. The use of agricultural produce played a major part in the political economy, and this may be another factor in accounting for the ritualisation of the domestic sphere. Here the main evidence is of feasting.

A number of these elements have already figured in this section, for many of the accumulations of cultural material in the monuments of the Neolithic probably result from feasts. The most obvious examples are the deposits associated with causewayed enclosures, but they also extend to the domestic sites which can include similar finds. In fact some of the clearest evidence of large-scale food preparation is provided by simpler features. These can be characterised by extensive hearths or by middens containing large collections of discarded animal bones. They have a wide distribution through time and space. Among the places with massive hearths are the coastal aggregation sites of the Pitted Ware tradition (Malmer 2002: 97–126), the henge monuments of Northern Britain (Wainwright 1989), which include considerable examples lined by stone slabs, and the long rows of such features which have been found at Late Bronze Age sites in Scandinavia and the Southern Baltic (Thrane 1974 and 1996).

In the same way, great middens of food remains built up on other sites, and the fact that they were permitted to develop into considerable mounds suggests that they may have been meant for display. The best-known examples are at Southern English sites like Potterne and East Chisenbury (Needham and Spence 1997), but a very similar phenomenon has been identified in the Alps

(Gleirscher 1996; Söder and Zemmer-Plank 2002). Again it has been interpreted in terms of conspicuous consumption. The importance of feasting is equally apparent from another source, for during the Urnfield period cremation burials were often associated with entire ceramic sets which seem to have been made for the service of food and drink (Harding 2000: 331–3). These collections are sometimes called 'ceramic hoards' and the comparison with metal finds is apposite, for during the same period there were formal deposits that include bronze buckets, cauldrons and flesh hooks.

Sometimes the specialised character of food consumption is clear from other sources. In Chapter 1 I described the problems of interpreting the henge monument at Durrington Walls. The deposits on this site were characterised by large accumulations of decorated pottery and animal bones, and the high proportion of pork among the excavated material certainly suggested that it was being consumed at lavish feasts; so did the degree to which inferior joints were wasted. The pigs consumed at Durrington Walls were mostly domes-ticated animals, and yet a re-examination of their remains shows that a number of them had been shot. The tips of flint arrowheads were embedded in their bones, suggesting that they had been killed with some formality and possibly hunted (Albarella and Serjeantson 2002).

In the same way, Chapter 3 drew attention to the significance of the mounds of fire-cracked stones found in the Later Bronze Age of Scandinavia and to their less obvious counterparts in Britain and Ireland. In each case the conventional interpretation of these features is that they represent a by-product of the large-scale cooking of meat, but in both regions they could also be associated with the activities of craft workers, including smiths. The Scandinavian evidence is particularly revealing, for similar deposits are associated not only with settlements but also with the cult houses found near to cemeteries. Some accumulations of burnt stone were associated with metalworking residues, but they could also include food remains and cremated human bone. Perhaps the preparation and service of food provided a series of metaphors in prehistoric society, and it has been suggested that cooking and the treatment of the dead were considered as similar processes (Skoglund 1999). As we have seen, all these different elements – cooking, metalworking, cremations and deposits of bronze artefacts – were found together at Hallunda. They comprise many of the activities considered in this account.

Ritualisation and taphonomy

I began this chapter by commenting on the divisions within modern archaeology. There were two main sources of contention. The first was the distinction between studies based on subsistence, settlement and environment, and those which put a greater emphasis on culture. They overlap with one another in many ways, and both these methods seek to interpret human behaviour in the past. Taken together, they can be compared with a third approach which grows directly from the results of fieldwork. This is the branch of research whose main concern is with the formation of the archaeological record (Schiffer 1976 and 1996). How did deposits come into being, to what extent have their contents been modified, and are there any general principles according to which we can move between these observations and life in prehistoric times? There are many examples of this kind of analysis. Do all animal bones have an equal chance of surviving, or are they differentially preserved? Do certain kinds of pottery fragment more readily than others? Is it possible to tell the difference between deposits which have formed *in situ* and accumulations of cultural material which have been moved from one place to another?

No one would deny the importance of such enquiries, but for the most part they share a common feature: they are concerned with the physical properties of ancient things. They involve a search for reliable general principles that can be used to transform an archaeological assemblage into something approximating to its original state. By allowing for the processes which have intervened between deposition and recovery, they attempt to cleanse the record of bias.

In principle, that ambition should be welcomed by scholars of any persuasion, but in reality much of the analysis has been concerned with traditional practice: the accurate cataloguing and interrogation of artefacts and food remains. Although the study of taphonomy ought to be of general interest, it has had most impact on the investigation of settlement and subsistence. That is probably because its main efforts have gone into redressing the physical alteration to which excavated materials have been subject. Indeed, this task has seemed so demanding that some researchers suppose that it marks the limit of what archaeological interpretation can achieve.

The study of taphonomy is an attempt to restore order, but what kind of order is being sought? If the main objectives are the accurate reconstruction of what people made and ate, then they may be misplaced, for beyond the measurable processes of alteration and decay there were the seemingly chaotic patterns of daily life. Why should the archaeological record retain any obvious patterning when, in principle, it is the aggregate of different actions of many individuals? And yet field archaeologists not only look for clear-cut patterns, surprisingly often they find them.

On one level this may be because prehistoric people followed routines (Giddens 1984: 284–304). Certain activities were conducted in the same sequence from one occasion to another and they happened in particular places. But even that would produce a coarse-grained pattern such as we often encounter at the occupation sites of hunter gatherers. The archaeological record of later periods shows an increasing order. More tasks were undertaken and they required a wider range of artefacts, yet such factors should have obscured any patterning in the excavated deposits. That is not what we find.

I suggest another possibility. Perhaps the archaeological record only retains the amount of order that it does because of the very conventions by which it was formed. These were not only physical but cultural (Hodder 1982: chapter 8). The reason why some deposits can be interpreted today is that they resulted from behaviour that required a certain degree of formality. They achieved this because on particular occasions *those very actions were ritualised*.

If that is true – and the question requires more investigation – it would mean that ritual itself was one of the main processes that formed the archaeological record and helped to imbue it with enough coherence to allow it to be interpreted. That process was fundamental and has an important implication for the ways in which prehistorians carry out their work. They still need to allow for the transformation of archaeological deposits after these had accumulated, but they should not suppose that originally those features were a perfectly neutral document waiting to be read. The very fact that they are not completely disordered may mean that they had undergone a careful selection from the outset. Far from showing that the subsistence economy is the easiest element to study and human culture the most difficult, the balance is reversed. Traditional forms of analysis may only be possible because the material that is studied had been transformed by cultural processes of which we are just becoming aware. Domestic life is not an easy subject to study, nor is ritual activity necessarily out of reach. The doctrinal disputes that have marked the archaeology of the last twenty years seem to have been misplaced.

The granary overflows

I began this book by describing a traditional granary in North-West Spain, and the reader will be aware how many other granaries have featured at different stages in this account. In many ways it is the perfect image with which to conclude.

I used the Galician granary to illustrate one fundamental point. Although it continues to play a role in farming, it is more than an agricultural building. It is a considerable stone monument and a work of architecture in its own right. Its form and decoration make connections with other kinds of buildings, and these are often enhanced by its position in the landscape. Its characteristic decoration suggests connections with the church and its doctrine of death and renewal. Many of the same elements could be recognised among the storehouses of the Incas, and the comparison is all the stronger because their interpretation was not influenced by Christian beliefs.

One of the main points made in the introductory chapter is that the superstructure of the Galician hórreo is much more informative than its ground plan. This was an important lesson for prehistorians who had used this kind of structure as an analogy for the wooden storehouses found in Bronze Age and Iron Age settlements in other parts of Europe. That same lesson was reinforced by my account of agriculture in the Trobriand Islands and the magic that was needed for its successful operation. It was clear from Malinowski's account that variations in the form and siting of raised storehouses were of great social significance. This was reflected in the rituals that accompanied their construction and use.

Later chapters turned to purely archaeological examples drawn from prehistoric Europe, but again they made it clear that granaries were more than agricultural facilities. Two examples were particularly revealing. The rock carvings at Valcamonica have been interpreted as depictions of daily life, and among the most prominent images were a number of drawings of buildings. These are generally interpreted as prehistoric houses and have been used in textbooks to illustrate the domestic architecture of the Bronze Age. But comparison with what is known from excavation suggested another possibility. Perhaps these were really drawings of granaries. In that case they seemed to overshadow any pictures of ordinary dwellings, and on closer examination they proved to possess a number of unusual features. Far from being neutral portrayals of the domestic environment, these buildings seemed to have been rather special. Why else would they have played such a prominent role in rock art?

Another extension of the basic principle of the granary occurred during the same period in Northern Europe, where the characteristic form of these buildings provided the basis for the ceramic models known as house urns. As I explained in Chapter 3, that term was actually a misnomer, for these were surely based on the forms of raised storehouses and a few examples were mounted on stilts like the Galician hórreo. The choice of this prototype might suggest that some of these buildings possessed a special significance, and this was surely confirmed by the contexts in which the vessels were found. They occurred in small numbers in a series of Late Bronze Age cemeteries where they were used to contain the ashes of the dead. Again it was tempting to think in terms of a connection between the death of the human body and the storage and regeneration of the crop.

That same metaphor was at the heart of my study of Iron Age society in Chapter 6, although this was mainly concerned with the ways in which that relationship was expressed through the use of storage pits. Nonetheless the raised granary still had a part to play. Some of the buildings associated with the sanctuary at Acy-Romance possessed a rather similar structure, and this may well have been intended. At the same time, the small shrines that were built inside the hill forts at Danebury and South Cadbury also bore a resemblance to raised storehouses and it may be no coincidence that structures of both kinds had been located in the same parts of these sites. At Danebury, the earliest shrines were contemporary with some of the granaries. At South Cadbury, they were built during a later phase. Although a direct connection was impossible to prove, the coincidence was certainly intriguing.

What is true of the building and use of granaries applies to many other aspects of domestic life. But enough has been said by now to bring this study to an end. Ritual and domestic life went together throughout the prehistoric sequence and it is wrong and – more than that – it is impossible to separate them now.

BIBLIOGRAPHY

Ahlfont, K., Guinard, M., Gustafsson, E., Olsson, C. and Welinder, S. 1995. 'Patterns of Neolithic farming in Sweden', *Tor* 27: 133–84.

Albarella, U. and Serjeantson, D. 2002. 'A passion for pork: meat consumption at the British Late Neolithic site of Durrington Walls', in P. Miracle and N. Milner (eds), *Consuming Passions and Patterns of Consumption*, pp. 33–49. Cambridge: McDonald Institute for Archaeological Research.

Anati, E. 1961. *Camonica Valley*. New York: Knopf.

Anati, E. 1976. *Evolution and Style in Camunian Rock Art*. Capo di Ponte: Edizioni del Centro.

Anati, E. 1984. *Valcamonica Rock Art*. Capo di Ponte: Edizioni del Centro.

Andersen, A.G. 1994. 'Frugtbarhedsofringer i Sydvestfyns ældre jernalder. Private eller kollektive ofringer?', *Kuml* 1993/1994: 199–210.

Andersen, S. 1993. 'Early and Middle Neolithic agriculture in Denmark: pollen spectra from soils in burial mounds of the Funnel Beaker Culture', *Journal of European Archaeology* 1: 153–80.

Anderson, N. 1997. *The Sarup Enclosures, volume 1*. Aarhus: Jutland Archaeological Society.

Anderson, S. 1980. 'Ertebølle art: new finds of decorated Ertebølle artefacts from East Jutland', *Kuml* 4: 6–60.

Andersson, M. 2003. *Skapa plats i landskapet. Tidlig- och mellanneolitiska samhällen utmed två västskånska dalnångar*. Stockholm: Almqvist and Wiksell.

Andersson, M. 2004. 'Domestication and the first Neolithic concept', in M. Andersson, P. Karsten, B. Knarrström and M. Svensson (eds), *Stone Age Scania*, pp. 144–90. Lund: Riksantikvarieämbetet.

Aner, E. and Kersten, K. 1977. *Die Funde der älteren Bronzezeit des nordischen Kreises in Dänemark, Schleswig-Holstein und Niedersachsen, Band 3*. Copenhagen: Verlag Nationalmuseum.

Aner, E. and Kersten, K. 1978. *Die Funde der älteren Bronzezeit des nordischen Kreises in Dänemark, Schleswig-Holstein und Niedersachsen, Band 4*. Copenhagen: Verlag Nationalmuseum.

Apel, J., Hadevik, C. and Sundström, L. 1997. 'Burning down the house. The transformational use of fire and other aspects of an Early Neolithic TRB site in eastern central Sweden', *Tor* 29: 5–47.

Arca, A. 2004. 'The topographic engravings of Alpine rock-art: fields, settlements and agricultural landscapes', in C. Chippindale and G. Nash (eds), *The Figured Landscapes of Rock-Art*, pp. 318–49. Cambridge: Cambridge University Press.

Asingh, P. 1987. 'Diverhøj – the excavation of a complex burial mound and a Neolithic settlement', *Journal of Danish Archaeology* 6: 30–54.

Bailly, M. 2001. 'Stone tool production and use in Bell Beaker domestic sites from eastern France and western Switzerland: from lithic technology towards patterns of social organisation', in F. Nicolis (ed.), *Bell Beakers Today*, pp. 497–506. Trento: Servizio Beni Culturali.

Bánffy, E. 2001. 'Notes on the connection between human and zoomorphic representations in the Neolithic', in P. Biehl, F. Bertemes and H. Miller (eds), *The Archaeology of Cult and Religion*, pp. 53–71. Budapest: Archaeolingua Foundation.

Bapty, I. and Yates, T. (eds) 1990. *Archaeology After Structuralism*. London: Routledge.

Baray, L., Le Goff, I., Thébault, D. and Villeneur, I. 1994 'La nécropole de Soucy/ Mocques Bouteilles', in L. Baray, S. Deffresigne, C. Leroyer and I. Villeneur (eds), *Nécropoles protohistoriques du Séonais*: 84–171. Paris: Éditions des Sciences de l'Homme.

Barber, M., Field, D. and Topping, P. 1999. *The Neolithic Flint Mines of England*. London: English Heritage.

Barfield, L. 1971. *Northern Italy Before Rome*. London: Thames and Hudson.

Barfield, L. and Chippindale, C. 1997. 'Meaning in the later prehistoric rock-engravings of Mont Bégo, Alpes Maritimes, France', *Proceedings of the Prehistoric Society* 63: 103–28.

Barfield, T. (ed.) 1997. *The Dictionary of Anthropology*. Oxford: Blackwell.

Barker, G. and Rasmussen T, 1998. *The Etruscans*. Oxford: Blackwell.

Barnard, A. 2000. *History and Theory in Anthropology*. Cambridge: Cambridge University Press.

Barnard, A. and Spencer, J. (eds) 1996. *Encyclopaedia of Social and Cultural Anthropology*. London: Routledge.

Barnatt, J., Bevan, B. and Edmonds, M. 2002. 'Gardom's Edge: a landscape through time', *Antiquity* 76: 50–6.

Barndon, R. 1996. 'Mental and material aspects of ironworking: a cultural comparative perspective', in G. Pwiti and R. Soper (eds), *Aspects of African Archaeology. Papers from the 10th Congress of the Pan-African Association for Prehistory and Related Studies*, pp. 761–72. Harare: University of Zimbabwe Publications.

Barndon, R. 2004. 'A discussion of magic and medicines in East African iron working: actors and artefacts in technology', *Norwegian Archaeological Review* 37: 21–40.

Barrett, J. 1989. 'Food, gender and metal: questions of social reproduction', in M.L.S. Sørensen and R. Thomas (eds), *The End of the Bronze Age in Europe*, pp. 304–20. Oxford: British Archaeological Reports.

Barrett, J., Bradley, R. and Green, M. 1991. *Landscape, Monuments and Society. The Prehistory of Cranborne Chase*. Cambridge: Cambridge University Press.

Barrett, J., Woodward, A. and Freeman, P. 2000. *Cadbury Castle, Somerset: the Later Prehistoric and Early Historic Archaeology*. London: English Heritage.

Bartolini, G., Buranelli, F., D'Atri, V. and De Santis, A. 1987. *Le urne a capanna rinvenute in Italia*. Rome: Bretschneider.

Becker, C.J. 1971. '"Mosepotter" fra Danmarks jernalder: problemer omkring mosefunde lerkar og deres tolkning', *Arbøger for Nordisk Oldkundighed og Historie* (1971): 5–60.

Behn, F. 1924. *Hausurnen*. Berlin: De Gruyter.

Bell, C. 1992. *Ritual Theory, Ritual Practice*. Oxford: Oxford University Press.

Bergmann, J. 1982. *Ein Gräberfeld der jüngeren Bronze- und älteren Eisenzeit bei Vollmarshausen, Kr. Kassel.* Marburg: Elwert Verlag.

Bergsvik, K.A. 2001. 'Sedentary and mobile hunter-fishers in stone age Western Norway', *Arctic Anthropology* 38: 2–26.

Bergsvik, K.A. 2002. 'Task groups and social inequality in Early Neolithic Western Norway', *Norwegian Archaeological Review* 35: 1–28.

Bird-David, N. 1990. 'The giving environment: another perspective on the economic system of gatherer-hunters', *Current Anthropology* 31: 19–44

Bird-David, N. 1992. 'Beyond "the original affluent society": a culturalist reformulation', *Current Anthropology* 33: 25–4.

Birdwell-Pheasant, D. and Lawrence-Zuñiga, D. (eds) 1999. *House Life. Space and Family in Europe*, Oxford: Berg.

Bittel, K. 1998. *Die keltischen Viereckschanzen*, Stuttgart: Theiss.

Bittel, K., Schiek, S. and Müller, D. 1990. *Die keltischen Viereckschanzen.* Stuttgart: Konrad Theiss.

Blanchet, J.C., Buchsenschutz, O. and Méniel, P. 1983. 'La maison de La Tène moyenne de Verberie (Oise)'. *Revue Archéologique de Picardie* 1: 96–126.

Blanton, R. 1997. *Houses and Households: a Comparative Study.* New York: Plenum.

Bloch, M. 1989. *Ritual, History and Power.* London: Athlone Press.

Bloch, M. and Parry, J. 1982. 'Introduction: death and the regeneration of life', in M. Bloch and J. Parry (eds), *Death and the Regeneration of Life*, pp. 1–44. Cambridge: Cambridge University Press.

Bloch, M. and Parry, J. (eds) 1982. *Death and the Regeneration of Life.* Cambridge: Cambridge University Press.

Boast, R. 1995. 'Fine pots, pure pots, Beaker pots', in I. Kinnes and G. Varndell (eds), *Unbaked Urns of Rudely Shape*, pp. 69–80. Oxford: Oxbow.

Boivin, N. in press. 'Mind over matter? Collapsing the mind-matter dichotomy in material culture studies', in C. Gosden, E. DeMarrais and C. Renfrew (eds), *Rethinking Materiality.* Cambridge: McDonald Institute for Archaeological Research.

Borna-Ahlvist, H. 2002. *Hällristarnas hem.* Stockholm: Riksantikvarieämbetet.

Borna-Ahlvist, H., Lingren-Hertz, L. and Stälbom, U. 1998. *Pryssgården. Från stenålder till medeltid.* Linköping: Riksantikvarieämbetet.

Bostyn, F. and Lanchon, Y. 1992. *Jablines. Une site minière de silex au Néolithique.* Paris: Éditions de la Maison des Sciences de l'Homme.

Boulestin, B. and Gomez de Soto, J. 1998. 'Bronzes des grottes et autres lieux en Angoumois au Bronze moyen', in C. Mordant, M. Pernot and V. Rychner (eds), *L'atelier du bronzier en Europe. Tome 3: Production, circulation et consommation du bronze*, pp. 71–86. Paris: Éditions du comité des travaux historiques et scientifiques.

Boyer, P. 1994. *The Naturalness of Religious Ideas: A Cognitive Theory of Religion.* Berkeley: University of California Press.

Boysen, A. and Andersen, S.W. 1983. 'Trappendal. Barrow and house from the Early Bronze Age', *Journal of Danish Archaeology* 2: 118–26.

Bradley, R. 1998a. *The Passage of Arms.* Second edition. Oxford: Oxbow.

Bradley 1998b. *The Significance of Monuments.* London: Routledge.

Bradley, R. 2000. *An Archaeology of Natural Places.* London: Routledge.

Bradley, R. 2001a. 'Orientations and origins: a symbolic dimension to the long house in Neolithic Europe', *Antiquity* 75: 50–6.

Bradley, R. 2001b. 'Humans, animals and the domestication of visual images', *Cambridge Archaeological Journal* 11: 261–3.

Bradley, R. 2002a. *The Past in Prehistoric Societies*. London: Routledge.

Bradley, R. 2002b. 'Death and the regeneration of life: a new interpretation of house urns in Northern Europe', *Antiquity* 76: 372–7.

Bradley, R. 2002c. 'Access, style and imagery: the audience for prehistoric rock art in Atlantic Spain and Portugal', *Oxford Journal of Archaeology* 21: 231–47.

Bradley, R. in press. 'Domestication, sedentism, property and time: materiality and the beginnings of agriculture in Northern Europe', in C. Gosden, E. DeMarrais and C. Renfrew (eds), *Rethinking Materiality*. Cambridge: McDonald Institute for Archaeological Research.

Bray, W. 1963. 'The Ozieri Culture of Sardinia', *Rivista di Scienze Preistorice* 18: 155–90.

Bretz-Mahler, D. 1971. 'La civilisation de la Téne 1 en Champagne.' Paris: *Gallia supplément* 23.

Briard, J. 1965. *Les dépôts Bretons et l'Age du Bronze Atlantique*. Rennes: Laboratoire d'anthropologie préhistorique de la Faculté des Sciences de Rennes.

Bridgford, S. 1998. 'British Late Bronze Age swords: the metallographic evidence', in C. Mordant, M. Pernot and V. Rychner (eds), *L'atelier du bronzier en Europe, tome 2. Du minerai au métal, du métal à l'objet*, pp. 205–19. Paris: Éditions du comité des travaux historiques et scientifiques.

Brinch-Petersen, E. and Meiklejohn, C. 2003. 'Three cremations and a funeral: aspects of burial practice at Vedbæk', in L. Larsson, K. Kindren, K. Knutson, D. Loeffer and A. Åkerlund (eds), *Mesolithic on the Move*, pp. 485–93. Oxford: Oxbow.

Britnell, W. 1982. 'The excavation of two round barrows at Trelystan, Powys', *Proceedings of the Prehistoric Society* 48: 133–201.

Browall, H. 1986. *Alvastra pålbygnad social och ekonomisk bas*. Stockholm: Stockholm University Theses and Papers in North European Archaeology 15.

Browall, H. 1987. 'The Alvastra pile dwelling: its social and economic basis', in G. Burenhult, A. Carlsson, A. Hyenstrand and T. Sjøvold (eds), *Theoretical Approaches to Artefacts, Settlement and Society*, pp. 95–121. Oxford: British Archaeological Reports.

Brück, J. 1995. 'A place for the dead: the role of human remains in Late Bronze Age Britain', *Proceedings of the Prehistoric Society* 61: 245–77.

Brück, J. 1999a. 'Ritual and rationality: some problems of interpretation in European archaeology', *European Journal of Archaeology* 2: 313–44.

Brück, J. 1999b. 'Houses, life cycles and deposition on Middle Bronze Age settlements in Southern England', *Proceedings of the Prehistoric Society* 65: 145–66.

Brück, J. 1999c. 'What's in a settlement? Domestic practice and residential mobility in Early Bronze Age southern England', in J. Brück and M. Goodman (eds), *Making Places in the Prehistoric World*, pp. 52–75. London: UCL Press.

Brück, J. 2001. 'Body metaphors and technologies of transformation in the English Middle and Late Bronze Age', in J. Brück (ed.), *Bronze Age Landscape. Tradition and Transformation*, pp. 149–60. Oxford: Oxbow.

Brunaux, J.L. 1986. *Les Gaulois: sanctuaires et sites*. Paris: Errance.

Brunaux, J.L. and Méniel, P. 1997. *Le residence aristocratique de Montmartin (Oise)*. Paris: Éditions de la Maison des Sciences de l'Homme.

Brunaux, J.L. , Méniel, P. and Poplin, F. 1985. *Gournay 1. Fouilles sur le sanctuaire et l'oppidum*. Revue archéologique de Picardie, numéro spécial.

Buchsenschutz, O., Olivier, L. and Aillières, A.-M. (eds), 1989. *Les Viereckschanzen et les enceintes quadrilaterales en Europe celtique.* Paris: Errance.

Buckley, D. and Hedges, J. 1987. *The Bronze Age and Saxon Settlements at Springfield Lyons, Essex: Interim Report.* Chelmsford: Essex County Council Archaeology Section.

Budd, P. and Taylor, T. 1995. 'The faerie smith meets the bronze industry: magic versus science in the interpretation of prehistoric metal making', *World Archaeology* 27: 133–43.

Bukowski, Z. 1996. 'Kult- und Opferplätze der Bevölkerung der Lausitzer Kultur im Stromgebiet von Oder und Weichsel', in P. Schauer (ed.), *Archäologische Forschungen zum Kultgeschehen in der jüngeren Bronzezeit und frühen Eisenzeit Alteuropas*, pp. 301–33. Bonn: Rudolf Habelt.

Bukowski, Z. 1999. 'Lusatian Culture cult- and sacrifice-places in the Middle Elbe, Oder and Vistula basins', in C. Orrling (ed.), *Communication in Bronze Age Europe:* 43–56. Stockholm: Statens historiska museum.

Burenhult, G. 1973. *En långdös vid Hindby Mosse, Malmö.* Malmö: Malmö Museum.

Burgess, C. and Gerloff, S. 1981. *The Dirks and Rapiers of Great Britain and Ireland.* Munich: C.H. Beck.

Calado, M. 1997 'Cromlechs alentejanos e arte megalítica', *Brigantium* 10: 289–97.

Cameron, C. and Tomka, S. (eds) 1993. *Abandonment of Settlements and Regions. Ethnoarchaeological and Archaeological Approaches.* Cambridge: Cambridge University Press.

Carlie, A. 2004. *Forntida byggnads kult.* Lund: Riksantikvarieämbetet.

Carsten, J. and Hugh-Jones, S. 1995. 'Introduction', in J. Carsten and S. Hugh-Jones (eds), *About the House: Lévi-Strauss and Beyond*, 1–46. Cambridge: Cambridge University Press.

Carsten, J. and Hugh-Jones, S. (eds) 1995 *About the House: Lévi-Strauss and Beyond*, Cambridge: Cambridge University Press.

Case, H. 1973. 'A ritual site in north-east Ireland', in G. Daniel and P Kjaerum (eds), *Megalithic Graves and Ritual*, pp. 173–96. Aarhus: Jutland Archaeological Society.

Case, H. 1977. 'The Beaker Culture in Britain and Ireland', in R. Mercer (ed.), *Beakers in Britain and Europe*, pp. 71–101. Oxford: British Archaeological Reports.

Cassen, S. 2000. 'Stelae reused in the passage graves of western France', in A. Ritchie (ed.), *Neolithic Orkney in its European Context*, pp. 233–46. Cambridge: McDonald Institute for Archaeological Research.

Chapman, J. 1999. 'Deliberate house burning in the prehistory of Central and Eastern Europe', in A. Gustaffson and H. Karlsson (eds), *Glyfer och arkeologiska rum – en vänbok till Jarl Nordbladh*, pp. 113–26. Gothenburg: Gotarc.

Chapman, J. 2000. *Fragmentation in Archaeology. People, Places and Broken Objects in the Prehistory of South Eastern Europe.* London: Routledge.

Clark, J.D.G. 1952. *Prehistoric Europe The Economic Basis.* London: Methuen.

Clarke, D. 1978. *Analytical Archaeology.* Second edition. London: Methuen.

Clottes, J. 1996. Recent studies on Palaeolithic art', *Cambridge Archaeological Journal* 6, 179–89.

Coffyn, A., Gomez de Soto, J. and Mohen, J.-P. 1981. *L'Apogée du bronze Atlantique. (le dépôt de Venat).* Paris: Picard.

Coles, B., Coles, J. and Schou Jørgensen, M. (eds) 1999. *Bog Bodies, Sacred Sites and Wetland Archaeology.* Exeter: Wetland Archaeology Research Project.

Coles, J. and Minnit, S. 1995. *'Industrious and Fairly Civilized'. The Glastonbury Lake Village.* Taunton: Somerset Levels Project and Somerset County Museum Service.

Colquhoun, I. and Burgess, C. 1988. *The Swords of Britain.* Munich: C.H. Beck.

Connerton, P. 1989. *How Societies Remember.* Cambridge: Cambridge University Press.

Constantin, C. 2003. 'Sur l'ancienneté des signes en forme de cornes et de crosses au Néolithique', *Revue Archéologique de l'Ouest* 20: 99–107.

Cooney, G. 1998. 'Breaking stones, making places: the social landscape of axe production sites', in A. Gibson and D. Simpson (eds), *Prehistoric Ritual and Religion*, pp. 108–18. Stroud: Sutton.

Cosack, E. 2003. 'Zur Interpretation jungbronzezeit- und eisenzeitlicher Hortfunde mit angeschmolzenem Inventar aus dem Ldkr. Hildesheim', *Archäologisches Korrespondenzblatt* 33: 75–85.

Creighton, J. 2000. *Coins and Power in Late Iron Age Britain.* Cambridge: Cambridge University Press.

Cunliffe, B. 1984. *Danebury. An Iron Age Hillfort in Hampshire, volume 1.* London: Council for British Archaeology.

Cunliffe, B. 1991. *Iron Age Communities in Britain.* Third edition. London: Routledge.

Cunliffe, B. 1992. 'Pits, preconceptions and propitiation in the British Iron Age', *Oxford Journal of Archaeology* 11: 69–84.

Cunliffe, B. 2001. *Facing the Ocean.* Oxford: Oxford University Press.

Cunliffe, B. and Poole, C. 1991a. *Danebury. An Iron Age Hillfort in Hampshire, volume 4.* London: Council for British Archaeology.

Cunliffe, B. and Poole, C. 1991b. *Danebury. An Iron Age Hillfort in Hampshire, volume 5.* London: Council for British Archaeology.

Cunnington, M. 1929. *Woodhenge.* Devizes: George Simpson.

Debiak, R., Gaillard, D., Jacques, A. and Rossignol, P. 1998. 'Le devenir des restes humains après la mort en Artois aux IVe et IIIe siècles av. J-C', *Révue archéologique de Picardie* 1/2: 25–57.

DeBoer, W. 1997. 'Ceremonial centres from the Cayapas (Esmereldas, Ecuador) to Chillicothe (Ohio, USA)', *Cambridge Archaeological Journal* 7: 225–53.

De Laet, S. 1982. *Le Belgique d'avant les Romains.* Wetteren: Editions Universa.

Delattre, V. 2000a. 'De la relégation sociale à l'hypothèse des offrandes: l'exemple des dépôts en silos au confluent Seine-Yonne (Seine-et-Marne)', *Revue Archéologique du Centre de la France* 39: 5–30.

Delattre, V. 2000b. 'Les inhumations en silos dans les habitats de l'âge du Fer du Bassin parisien', in S. Marion and G. Blancquaert (eds), *Les Installations agricoles de l'Âge du Fer en France septentrionale*, pp. 299–311. Paris: Éditions Rue d'Ulm.

Delibes De Castro, G., Harran Martínez, J., De Santiago Pardo, J. and Del Val Recio, J. 1995. 'Evidence for social complexity in the Copper Age of the Northern Meseta', in K. Lilios (ed.), *The Origins of Complex Societies in Late Prehistoric Iberia*, pp. 44–63. Ann Arbor: International Monographs in Prehistory.

De Lumley, H. 1995. *Le grandiose et le sacré.* Aix-en-Provence: Édisud.

Demoule, J.P. 1999 *Chronologie et société dans les nécropoles celtiques de la culture Aisne-Marne du VIe au IIIe siècle avant notre ère*, Amiens: Revue Archéologique de Picardie numéro spécial.

Dickens, J. 1996. 'A remote analogy? From central Australian tjurunga to Irish Early Bronze Age axes', *Antiquity* 70: 161–7.

Dietrich, M. 2000. 'Das Holzfigurenpaar und der "Brandplatz" aus dem Aukamper Moor bei Braak, Kreis Ostholstein', *Offa* 57: 145–230.

Dillman, F.-X. 1997. 'Kring de rituella gästabuden i fornskandinavisk religion', in A. Hultgård (ed.), *Uppsalakulten och Adam av Bremen*, pp. 51–73. Nora: Nya Doxa.

Downes, J. 1997. 'The shrine at South Cadbury – belief enshrined?', in A. Gwilt and C. Haselgrove (eds), *Reconstructing Iron Age Societies*, pp. 145–52. Oxford: Oxbow.

Driehaus, J. 1965. '"Fürstengräber" und Eisenerze zwischen Mittelrhein, Mosel und Saar', *Germania* 43: 32–49.

Duczko, W. 1993. *Arkeologi och mijlögeologi i Gamla Uppsala. Studier och rapporter 1.* Uppsala: University of Uppsala Department of Archaeology and Ancient History.

Duczko, W. 1997. *Arkeologi och mijlögeologi i Gamla Uppsala. Studier och rapporter 2.* Uppsala: University of Uppsala Department of Archaeology and Ancient History.

Edwards, N. 1990. *The Archaeology of Early Medieval Ireland.* London: Routledge.

Eogan, G. 1965. *Catalogue of Irish Bronze Swords.* Dublin: Stationery Office.

Fairweather, A. and Ralston, I. 1993. 'The Neolithic timber hall at Balbridie: the building, the dates, the plant macrofossils', *Antiquity* 67: 313–23.

Felder, P., Rademakers, P. and De Grooth, M. 1998. *Excavation of Prehistoric Flint Mines at Rijkholt-St-Geertruid (Limburg, The Netherlands).* Bonn: Habelt.

Fendin, T. 2000. 'Fertility and the repetitive partition: grinding as a social construction', *Lund Archaeological Review* 6: 85–97.

Firth, R. 1929. *Primitive Economics of the New Zealand Maori.* London: Routledge.

Fischer, A. 2002. 'Food for feasting?', in A. Fischer and K. Kristiansen (eds), *The Neolithicisation of Denmark: 150 Years of Debate*, pp. 343–93. Sheffield: J.R. Collis.

Fitzpatrick, A. 1997. 'Everyday life in Iron Age Wessex', in A. Gwilt and C. Haselgrove (eds), *Reconstructing Iron Age Societies*, pp. 73–86. Oxford: Oxbow.

Fontijn, D. 2003. 'Sacrificial landscapes. Cultural biographies of persons, objects and "natural" places in the Bronze Age of the southern Netherlands, c. 2300–600 BC', *Analecta Praehistorica Leidensia* 33/34: 1–392.

Ford, D., Goodwin, J., Boothroyd, N., Abby, R., Cook, B. and Youngs, S. 1998. 'A prehistoric Excalibur and other artefacts of divers dates: a catalogue of selected finds from Staffordshire recovered through metal detecting', *West Midlands Archaeology* 41: 36–48.

Fossati, A. 2002. 'Landscape representations on boulders and menhirs in the Valcamonica-Valtellina area, Alpine Italy', in G. Nash and C. Chippindale (eds), *European Landscapes of Rock Art*, pp. 93–115. London: Routledge.

Fowler, P. 1983. *The Farming of Prehistoric Britain.* Cambridge University Press.

Fox, J. (ed.) 1993. *Inside Austronesian Houses.* Canberra: Australian National University.

Frankowski, E. 1918. *Hrankowski, E. 1918. National Universiérica.* Madrid: Museo nacional de ciencias naturales.

Garrido Pena, R. and Muñoz Lopez-Astilleros, K. 2000. 'Visiones sagradas para los líderes: cerámicos campaniformes con decoración simbôlica en la Península Ibérica', *Complutum* 11: 285–300.

Gebers, W. 1985. 'Jungbronzezeitliche und eisenzeitliche Getreidevorraltshaltung in Rullstorf', in K. Wilhelmi (ed.), *Ausgrabungen in Niedersachsen. Archäologische Denkmalpflege 1979–1984*, pp. 146–50. Stuttgart: Berichte zu Denkmalpflege in Niedersachsen, Beiheft 1.

Gent, H. 1983. 'Centralised storage in later prehistoric Britain', *Proceedings of the Prehistoric Society* 49: 243–67.

217

Gerdsen, H. 1982. 'Das Fragment eines eisernen Hallstattschwertes aus dem Oppidum von Manching', *Germania* 60.2: 560–4.

Gerritsen, F. 1999. 'To build or to abandon. The cultural biography of late prehistoric houses and farmsteads in the southern Netherlands', *Archaeological Dialogues* 6.2: 78–114.

Gerritsen, F. 2000. 'The cultural biography of Iron Age houses and the long-term transformation of settlement patterns in the southern Netherlands', in C. Fabech and J. Ringtved (eds), *Settlement and Landscape*, pp. 139–48. Aarhus: Jutland Archaeological Society.

Gibson, A. 1998. *Stonehenge and Timber Circles*. Stroud: Tempus.

Giddens, A. 1984. *The Constitution of Society*. Cambridge: Polity Press.

Gillings, M. and Pollard, J. 1999. 'Non-portable stone artefacts and contexts of meaning: the tale of Grey Wether (www.museums.ncl.ac.uk/Avebury/stone4.htm)', *World Archaeology* 31: 179–93.

Giot, D., Mallet, N. and Millet, D. 1986. 'Les silex de la région de Grand-Pressigny (Indre-et-Loire). Recherche géologique et analyse pétrographique', *Revue Archéologique du Centre de la France* 25: 21–36.

Gleirscher, P. 1996. 'Brandopferplätze, Depotfunde und Symbolgut im Ostalpenraum während der Spätbronze- und Früheisenzeit', in P. Schauer (ed.), *Archäologische Forschungen zum Kultgeschehen in der jüngeren Bronzezeit und frühen Eisenzeit Alteuropas*, pp. 429–49. Bonn: Rudolf Habelt.

Glob, P.V. 1942. 'Pflüge vom Walle-typus aus Dänemark', *Acta Archaeologica* 13: 258–69.

Glob, P.V. 1951. *Ard och plov i Nordens Oldtid*. Aarhus: Universitetsforlaget i Aarhus.

Glob, P.V. 1969. *The Bog People*. London: Faber and Faber.

Glob, P.V. 1983. *The Mound People*. London: Paladin.

Gomes, R.V., Gomes, M.V. and Dos Santos, F. 1983. 'O Santuário exterior do Escoural Sector NE (Montenor-o-Novo, Évora)', *Zephyrus* 36: 287–307.

Goody, J. 1977. 'Against "ritual": loosely structured thoughts on a loosely defined topic', in S. Moore and B. Meyerhoff (eds), *Secular Ritual*, pp. 25–35. Amsterdam: Van Goricum.

Gransar, F. 2000. 'Le stockage alimentaire sur les établissements ruraux de l'âge du Fer en France septentrionale: complémentarité des structures et tendances évolutifs', in S. Marion and G. Blancquaert (eds), *Les Installations agricoles de l'Âge du Fer en France septentrionale*. Paris: Éditions Rue d'Ulm.

Green, M. 2000. *A Landscape Revealed. 10,000 Years on a Chalkland Farm*. Stroud: Tempus.

Gregory, T. 1991. *Excavation in Thetford 1980–1982. Fison Way*. Norwich: East Anglian Archaeology 53.

Gros, E. *et al.* 1987. *Zürich 'Mozartstrasse', Bände 1 und 2*. Zürich: Kommissionverlag.

Günther, K. 1990. 'Neolithische Bildzeichen an einem ehemaligen Megalithgrab bei Warburg, Kreis Höxter (Westfalen)', *Germania* 68: 39–65.

Haaland, R. 2004. 'Technology, transformation and symbolism: ethnographic perspectives on European iron working', *Norwegian Archaeological Review* 37: 1–19.

Haffner, A. 1976. *Die westliche Hunsrück-Eifelkultur*. Berlin: De Gruyter.

Haggarty, A. 1991. 'Machrie Moor, Arran: recent excavations of two stone circles', *Proceedings of the Society of Antiquaries of Scotland* 58: 51–94.

Hallgren, F., Djerw, U., af Geijerstam, M. and Steineke, M. 1997. 'Skogsmossen, an Early Neolithic settlement and sacrificial fen in the northern borderland of the Funnel-beaker Culture', *Tor* 29: 49–111.

Harding, A. 1995. *Die Schwerter im ehemaligen Jugoslawien*. Stuttgart: Franz Steiner.

Harding, A. 2000. *European Societies in the Bronze Age*. Cambridge: Cambridge University Press.

Haselgrove, C. 1987. 'Culture process on the periphery: Belgic Gaul and Rome during the late Republic and early Empire', in M. Rowlands, M. Larsen and K. Kristiansen (eds), *Centre and Periphery in the Ancient World*, pp. 104–24. Cambridge: Cambridge University Press.

Herbert, E. 1984. *Red Gold of Africa. Copper in Precolonial History and Culture*. Madison: University of Wisconsin Press.

Herbert, E. 1993. *Iron, Gender and Power: Rituals of Transformation in African Societies*. Bloomington: Indiana University Press.

Herschend, F. 1993. 'The origin of the hall in Southern Scandinavia', *Tor* 25: 175–99.

Herschend, F. 2001. *Journey of Civilisation. The Late Iron Age View of the Human World*. Uppsala: Uppsala University Department of Archaeology and Ancient History.

Higgs, E. and Jarman, M. 1975. 'Palaeoeconomy', in E. Higgs and M. Jarman (eds), *Palaeoeconomy*, pp. 1–7. Cambridge: Cambridge University Press.

Hill, J.D. 1995. *Ritual and Rubbish in the Iron Age of Wessex*. Oxford: British Archaeological Reports.

Hill, J.D. 1996. 'Hillforts and the Iron Age of Wessex', in T. Champion and J. Collis (eds), *The Iron Age in Britain: Recent Trends*, pp. 95–116. Sheffield: Sheffield Academic Press, 95–116.

Hingley, R. 1997. 'Iron, ironworking and regeneration: a study of the symbolic meaning of metalworking', in A. Gwilt and C. Haselgrove (eds), *Reconstructing Iron Age Societies*, pp. 9–18. Oxford: Oxbow.

Hodder, I. 1982. *Symbols in Action: Ethnoarchaeological Studies of Material Culture*, Cambridge: Cambridge University Press.

Hodder, I. (ed.) 1987. *The Archaeology of Contextual Meanings*. Cambridge: Cambridge University Press.

Hodder, I. 1989. 'This is not an article about material culture as text', *Journal of Anthropological Archaeology* 8: 25–69.

Högrell, L. 2002. 'Åkern och evigheten', *Tidskrift arkeologi in sydöstra Sverige* 2: 11–24.

Hulthén, B. 1977. *On Ceramic Technology during the Scanian Neolithic and Bronze Age*. Stockholm: Akademilitteratur.

Humphrey, C. and Laidlaw, J. 1994. *The Archetypal Actions of Ritual*. Oxford: Clarendon Press.

Ingold, T. (ed.) 1994. *Companion Encyclopaedia of Anthropology*. London: Routledge.

Jaanusson, H. 1981. *Hallunda*. Stockholm: Statens Historiska Museum.

Janzon, G. 1984. 'A megalithic grave at Alvastra, Östergötland', in G. Burenhult (ed.), *The Archaeology of Carrowmore, Co. Sligo, Ireland*, pp. 361–6. Stockholm: Stockholm University Department of Archaeology.

Jeunesse, C. and Ehretsmann, M. 1988. 'La jeune femme, le cheval et le silo', *Cahiers Alsaciens d'Archéologie et d'Art et d'Histoire* 31: 43–54.

Johnston, R. 2000. 'Dying, becoming and being the field', in J. Harding and R. Johnston (eds), *Northern Pasts*, pp. 57–70. Oxford: British Archaeological Reports.

Jones, A. 1999. 'The excavation of a Later Bronze Age structure at Callestick', *Cornish Archaeology* 37/38: 5–56.

Jorge, S.O. 1998. 'Colónias, fortificações, lugares monumentalizados. Trajectória das concepções sobre um tema do Calcolítico peninsular', in S.O. Jorge and V.O. Jorge (eds), *Arqueologia. Percursos e interrogações*, pp. 69–150. Porto: Associação para o Desenvolvimento da Cooperação em Arqueologia Peninsular.

Jorge, S.O. 1999. 'Castelo Velho de Freixo de Numão, Geschichte der Interpretationversuche', *Madrider Mitteilungen* 40: 80–96.

Jorge, S.O. 2002. 'From "fortified settlement" to "monument": accounting for Castelo Velho de Numão (Portugal)', *Journal of Iberian Archaeology* 4: 75–82.

Kaliff, A. 1997. *Grav och kultplats*. Uppsala: Uppsala University Department of Archaeology and Ancient History.

Kaliff, A. 1999. 'Objekt och tanke', in M. Olausson (ed.), *Spiralens öga. Tjugo artiklar kring aktuell bronsåldersforskning*, pp. 91–114. Stockholm: Riksantikvarieämbetet.

Karlenby, L. 1999. 'Deposition i skärvstenshögar', in M. Olausson (ed.), *Spiralens öga. Tjugo artiklar kring aktuell bronsåldersforskning*, pp. 115–25. Stockholm: Riksantikvarieämbetet.

Karsten, P. 1994. *Att kasta yxan i sjön*. Stockholm: Almqvist & Wiksell.

Kaul, F. 1987. 'Sandagergård. A Late Bronze Age cultic building with rock engravings and menhirs from Northern Zealand, Denmark', *Acta Archaeologica* 56: 31–54.

Kaul, F. 1998. *Ships on Bronzes*. Copenhagen: National Museum.

Kaul, F., Nielsen, F.O. and Nielsen, P.O. 2002. 'Vasagård och Rispebjerg. To indhegnede bopladser fra yngre stenalder på Bornholm', *Nationalmuseets Arbejdsmark* (2002), 119–38.

Keilin, T. and Ottaway, B. 1998. 'Flanged axes of the North Alpine region: an assessment of the possibilities of use wear analysis on metal artefacts', in C. Mordant, M. Pernot and V. Rychner (eds), *L'atelier du bronzier en Europe, tome 2. Du minerai au métal, du métal à l'objet*, pp. 271–86. Paris: Éditions du Comité des Travaux historiques et scientifiques.

Kemenczei, T. 1989. *Die Schwerter in Ungarn 1*. München: C.H. Beck.

Kemenczei, T. 1991. *Die Schwerter in Ungarn 2*. Stuttgart: Franz Steiner.

Kent, S. (ed.) 1990. *Domestic Architecture and the Use of Space*. Cambridge: Cambridge University Press.

Kimmig, W. 1992. *Die 'Wasserburg Buchau', eine spätbronzezeitliche Siedlung: Forschungsgeschichte – Kleinfunde*. Stuttgart: Theiss.

King, A. and Soffe, G. 1998. 'Internal organisation and deposition at the Iron Age temple on Hayling Island', *Proceedings of the Hampshire Field Club and Archaeological Society* 53: 35–47.

Koch, E. 1998. *Neolithic Bog Pots from Zealand, Møn. Lolland and Falster*. Copenhagen: Nordiske Fortidsminder Serie B, 16.

Krämer, W. 1985. *Die Vollgriffschwerter in Österreich und der Schweiz*. München: C.H. Beck.

Kristiansen, K. 1984. 'Ideology and material culture: an archaeological perspective', in M. Spriggs (ed.), *Marxist Perspectives in Archaeology*, pp. 72–100. Cambridge: Cambridge University Press.

Kristiansen, K. 1990. 'Ard marks under barrows: a response to Peter Rowley-Conwy', *Antiquity* 64: 322–7.

Kristiansen, K. 1996. 'Old boundaries and new frontiers: reflections on the identity of archaeology', *Current Swedish Archaeology* 4: 103–22.

Kristiansen, K. 2002. 'The tale of the sword – swords and sword fighters in Bronze Age Europe', *Oxford Journal of Archaeology* 21: 319–32.

Lambot, B. 1989. 'Le Bronze final et le premier age du Fer sur le site d'Acy-Romance (Ardennes)', *Gallia Préhistoire* 31: 209–58.

Lambot, B. and Méniel, P. 2000. 'Le centre communautaire du village gaulois d'Acy-Romance dans son contexte régional', in S. Verger (ed.), *Rites et espaces en pays celte et méditerranéen*, pp. 7–139. Rome: École Française de Rome.

Lang, J. 1984. 'The hogback: a Viking colonial monument', *Anglo-Saxon Studies in Archaeology and History* 3: 85–176.

Laporte, L., Marchand, G. and Quesnel, L. 2004. 'Une structure d'habitat circulaire dans le Néolithique ancien du Centre-Ouest de la France', *Bulletin de la Société préhistorique française* 101: 55–73.

Larsson, L. 1982. 'A causewayed enclosure and a site with Valby pottery at Stävie, Western Sweden', *Meddelanden från Lunds universitets historiska museum* 1981–1982: 65–107.

Larsson, L. 1989. 'Brandopfer. Der frühneolithische Fundplatz Svartskylle im südlichen Schonen, Schweden', *Acta Archaeologica* 59: 143–53.

Larsson, L. 1993. 'Relationer till et röse – några aspekter på Kiviksgraven', in L. Larsson (ed.), *Bronsålderns gravhögar*, pp 135–47. Lund: Lund University Institute of Archaeology.

Larsson, L. 2000a. 'Axes and fire – contacts with the gods', in D. Olausson and H. Vandkilde (eds), *Form, Function and Context. Material Culture Studies in Scandinavian Archaeology*, pp. 93–103. Stockholm: Almqvist & Wiksell.

Larsson, L. 2000b. 'The passage of axes: fire transformation of flint objects in the Neolithic of southern Sweden', *Antiquity* 74: 602–10.

Larsson, M. 2003. 'People and sherds – the Pitted Ware site Åby in Östergötland, Eastern Sweden', in C. Samuelsson and N. Yttberg (eds), *Uniting Sea. Stone Age Societies in the Baltic Region*, pp. 117–31. Uppsala: Uppsala University Department of Archaeology and Ancient History.

Larsson, M. and Olsson, E. 1997. *Regionalt och Interregionalt. Stenåldersundersökningar i Syd- och Mellansverige*. Stockholm: Riksantikvarieämbetet.

Layton, R. 1997. *An Introduction to Theory in Anthropology*. Cambridge: Cambridge University Press.

Leach, E. 1966. 'Introduction', in B. Malinowski, *Coral Gardens and their Magic*, pp. vii–xvii. Bloomington: Indiana University Press.

Leach, E. 1973. 'Concluding address', in C. Renfrew (ed.), *The Explanation of Culture Change*, pp. 761–7. London: Duckworth.

Le Contel, L.M. 1997. *Un calendrier celtique: le calendrier gaulois de Coligny*. Paris: Errance.

Lerche, G. 1995. 'Radiocarbon datings on agricultural implements in "Tools and Tillage": revised calibrations and recent additions', *Tools and Tillage* 7: 172–205.

Le Roux, C.-T. 1984. 'À propos des fouilles de Gavrinis (Morbihan): nouvelles données sur l'art mégalithique Armoricain', *Bulletin de la Société Préhistorique française* 81: 240–5.

Le Roux, C.-T. 1992. 'Cornes de pierre', in C.-T. Le Roux (ed.), *Paysans et Bâtisseurs*, pp. 237–44. *Revue archéologique de l'Ouest*, supplément 5.

Leser, P. 1931. *Entstehung und Verbreitung des Pfluges*. Münster: Aschendorffsche Verlagsbuchhandlung.

Levy, J. 1982. *Social and Religious Organisation in Bronze Age Denmark*. Oxford: British Archaeological Reports.

L'Helgouac'h, J. 1965. *Les sepultures mégalithiques en Armorique*, Rennes: Université de Rennes.

Lindqvist, S. 1923. 'Hednatempelet in Uppsala', *Forvännen* 18: 85–118.

Lindqvist, S. 1929. *Gamla Uppsala fornminnen*. Stockholm: Wahlström & Widstrand.

Lindqvist, S. 1936. *Uppsala högar och Ottarshögen*. Stockholm: Wahlström & Widstrand.

Littmark, T. 2002. *Gamla Uppsala from Ancient to Modern Time*. Gamla Uppsala: Old Uppsala Parish Vestry.

Liversage, D. 1992. *Barkaer: Long Barrows and Settlements*. Copenhagen: Akademisk forlag.

Lødøen, T. 1998. 'Interpreting Mesolithic axe deposits from a region of western Norway', *Archaeologia Baltica* 3: 195–204.

Løken, T. 2001. 'Oppkomsten av den germanske hallen – Hall og sal i eldre jernalder in Rogaland', *Viking* 2001: 49–86.

Lund, J. 2000. 'Forlev Nymølle. En offerplads fra yngre førromersk jernalder', *Kuml* 2000: 143–95.

Lynn, C. 1977. 'Trial excavations at the King's Stables, Tray Townland, County Armagh', *Ulster Journal of Archaeology* 40: 42–62.

Madsen, T. 1979. 'Earthen long barrows and timber structures: aspects of the Early Neolithic mortuary practice in Denmark', *Proceedings of the Prehistoric Society* 45: 301–20.

Madsen, T. 1997. 'Ideology and social structure in the earlier Neolithic of south Scandinavia. A view from the sources', *Analecta Praehistorica Leidensia* 29: 75–81.

Makiewicz, T. 1988. 'Opfer und Opferplätze der vorrömischen Eisenzeit in Polen', *Prähistorische Zeitschrift* 63: 81–112.

Malinowski, B. 1922. *Argonauts of the Western Pacific*. London: Routledge.

Malinowski, B. 1935. *Coral Gardens and their Magic: a Study of the Methods of Tilling the Soil and of Agricultural Rites in the Trobriand Islands*. London: Allen and Unwin.

Malmer, M. 1981. *A Chorological Study of North European Rock Art*. Stockholm: Almqvist & Wiksell.

Malmer, M. 1992. 'Weight systems in the Scandinavian Bronze Age', *Antiquity* 66: 377–88.

Malmer, M. 2002. *The Neolithic of South Sweden. TRB, GRK and STR*. Stockholm: Royal Swedish Academy of Letters, History and Antiquities.

Maraszek, R. 2000. 'Late Bronze Age axe hoards in western and northern Europe', in C. Pare (ed.), *Metals Make the World Go Round. The Supply and Circulation of Metals in Bronze Age Europe*, pp. 209–24. Oxford: Oxbow.

Marion, S. and Blancquaert, G. (eds) 2000. *Les Installations agricoles de l'âge du Fer en France septentrionale*. Paris: Éditions Rue d'Ulm.

Martínez Rodriguez, I. 1975. *El Hórreo Gallego*. Montevideo: Fundación Pedro Barrie de la Maza.

Mazarakis-Ainian, A. 1997. *From Rulers' Dwellings to Temples: Architecture, Religion and Society in Ancient Greece*. Jonsered: Paul Åströms förlag.

McOmish, D., Field, D. and Brown, G. 2002. *The Field Archaeology of the Salisbury Plain Training Area*. Swindon: English Heritage.

Megaw, V. and Megaw, R. 2001. *Celtic Art from its Beginnings to the Book of Kells*. Second edition. London: Thames and Hudson.

Meillassoux, C. 1972. 'From reproduction to production', *Economy and Society* 1: 93–105.

Méniel, P. 1992. *Les sacrifices d'animaux chez les Gaulois*. Paris: Errance.

Méniel, P. 1998. *Le site protohistorique d'Acy-Romance (Ardennes) III. Les animaux et l'histoire d'un village Gaulois*. Compiègne: Société Archéologique Champenoise.

Metge, J. 1976. *The Maoris of New Zealand. Rautahi*. Second edition. London: Routledge and Kegan Paul.

Milcent, P.-Y. 1998. 'Le Petit-Vilatte à Neuvy-sur-Barrageon (Cher): lecture d'un dépôt complexe', in C. Mordant, M. Pernot and V. Rychner (eds), *L'atelier du bronzier en Europe. Production, circulation et consommation du bronze*, pp. 55–70. Paris: Éditions du Comité des Travaux historiques et scientifiques.

Mithen, S. 1998. *The Prehistory of the Mind*. London: Thames and Hudson.

Moseley, M. 2001. *The Incas and their Ancestors*. Second edition. London: Thames and Hudson.

Müller-Karpe, H. 1968. *Handbuch der Vorgeschichte, Band 2*. München: C.H. Beck.

Müller-Wille, M. 1966. 'Eine niederrheinische Siedlung der vorrömischen Eisenzeit bei Weeze-Baal, Kreis Geldern', *Bonner Jahrbücher* 166: 379–432.

Murray, M. 1995. 'Viereckschanzen and feasting: socio-political ritual in Iron Age Central Europe', *Journal of European Archaeology* 3.2: 125–51.

Nash, D. 1987. 'Imperial expansion under the Roman Republic', in M. Rowlands, M. Larsen and K. Kristiansen (eds), *Centre and Periphery in the Ancient World*, pp. 87–103. Cambridge: Cambridge University Press.

Nebelsick, L. 2000. 'Rent asunder: ritual violence in Late Bronze Age hoards', in C. Pare (ed.), *Metals Make the World Go Round. The Supply and Circulation of Metals in Bronze Age Europe*, pp. 160–75. Oxford: Oxbow.

Needham, S. and Ambers, J. 1994. 'Redating Rams Hill and reconsidering Bronze Age enclosures', *Proceedings of the Prehistoric Society* 60: 225–43.

Needham, S. and Spence, T. 1997. 'Refuse and the formation of middens', *Antiquity* 71: 77–90.

Newman, C. 1997 *Tara. An Archaeological Survey*, Dublin: The Discovery Programme.

Newman, C. 1998. 'Reflections on the making of a "royal site" in early Ireland', *World Archaeology* 30: 127–41.

Nielsen, V. 1984. 'Prehistoric field boundaries in Eastern Denmark', *Journal of Danish Archaeology* 3, 135–63.

Nilsson, L. 1995. 'The bones from Hindby votive fen', *Lund Archaeological Review* 1: 65–74.

Nordahl, E. 1996. *Templum quod Ubsola dicitur . . . i arkeologisk belysning*. Uppsala: Uppsala University Department of Archaeology and Ancient History.

Oelmann, F. 1959. 'Pfahlhausurnen', *Germania* 37: 205–23.

Olausson, D. 1986. 'Piledal and Svarte. A comparison between two Late Bronze Age cremation cemeteries in Scania', *Acta Archaeologica* 57: 121–52.

Olausson, M. 1995. *Det inneslutna rummet – om kultiska hägnader, fornborgar och befästa gårdar in Uppland från 1300 f Kr till Kristi födelse*. Stockholm: Riksantikvarieämbetet.

Olausson, M. 1997. 'Arkitektur och social praktik. Diskussion utifrån undersökningkar av en uppländsk vallanläggning från senneolitikum och bronsålder', in A. Åkerlund,

S. Bergh, J. Nordbladh and J. Taffinder (eds), *Till Gunborg. Arkeologiska samtal*, pp. 407–22. Stockholm: Stockholm University Archaeological Reports.

Olsen, O. 1965. 'Hørg, hov og kirke. Historiske og arkeologiske Vikingetidsstudier', *Aarbøger for Nordisk Oldkyndighed og Historie* 1965: 5–307.

Oswald, A. 1997. 'A doorway on the past: practical and mystic concerns in the orientation of roundhouse doorways', in A. Gwilt and C. Haselgrove (eds), *Reconstructing Iron Age Societies*, pp. 87–95. Oxford: Oxbow.

Pare, C. 1999. 'Weights and weighing in Bronze Age Central Europe', in I. Kiliam-Dirlmeier (ed.), *Eliten in der Bronzezeit*, pp. 421–514. Mainz: Römisch-Germanisches Zentralmuseum.

Parker Pearson, M. 1984. 'Economic and ideological change: cyclical growth in the pre-state societies of Jutland', in D. Miller and C. Tilley (eds), *Ideology, Power and Prehistory*, pp. 69–92. Cambridge: Cambridge University Press.

Parker Pearson, M. and Richards, C. (eds) 1994. *Architecture and Order. Approaches to Social Space*. London: Routledge.

Patton, M. 2001. 'Le Pinacle, Jersey: a reassessment of the Neolithic, Chalcolithic and Bronze Age horizons', *Archaeological Journal* 158: 1–61.

Pätzold, J. 1960. 'Rituelles Pflügen beim vorgeschichtlichen Totenkult', *Prähistorische Zeitschrift* 38: 189–239.

Pauli, L. 1984. *The Alps. Archaeology and Early History*. London: Thames and Hudson.

Pautreau, J.-P. 1988. 'La Croix Verte à Antran (Vienne)', in F. Audouze and O. Buchsenschutz (eds), *Architecture des âges des métaux. Fouilles récentes*, pp. 47–53. Paris: Errance.

Pautreau, J.-P. 1994. 'Le grand bâtiment d'Antran (Vienne): une nouvelle attribution chronologique', *Bulletin de la Société préhistorique française* 91: 418–19.

Pedersen, J.A. 1986. 'A new Early Bronze Age house site under a barrow at Hyllerup, Western Zealand', *Journal of Danish Archaeology* 5: 168–76.

Penack, J.J. 1993. *Die eisernen eisenzeitlichen Erntegeräte im freien Germanien*. Oxford: British Archaeological Reports.

Percival, J. 1980. *Living in the Past*. London: BBC.

Perlès, C. 2001. *The Early Neolithic in Greece*. Cambridge: Cambridge University Press.

Petrescu-Dîmbovita, M. 1978. *Die Sicheln in Rumänien*. München: C.H. Beck.

Pittioni, R. 1968. 'Zur Interpretation der Station La Tène', in E. Schmid, L. Berger and P. Bürgin (eds), *Provincialia*, pp. 615–18. Basel: Schwabe.

Plisson, H., Mallet, N., Bocquet, A. and Ramseyer, D. 2002. 'Utilisation et rôle des outils en silex du Grand-Pressigny dans les villages de Charavines et de Portalban (Néolithique final)', *Bulletin de la Société préhistorique française* 99: 793–811.

Pluciennik, M. 2001. 'Archaeology, anthropology and subsistence', *Journal of the Royal Anthropological Institute* 7: 741–58.

Prescott, C. 1996. 'Was there *really* a Neolithic in Norway?', *Antiquity* 70: 77–87.

Price, N. 2002. *The Viking Way*. Uppsala: Uppsala University Department of Archaeology and Ancient History.

Pryor, F. 1998. *Etton. Excavations at a Neolithic Causewayed Enclosure near Maxey, Cambridgeshire 1982–7*. London: English Heritage.

Pryor, F. 2001. *The Flag Fen Basin: Archaeology and Environment of a Fenland Landscape*. London: English Heritage.

Raftery, B. 1984. *La Tène in Ireland. Problems of Origin and Chronology*. Marburg: Veröffentlichung des vorgeschichtlichen Seminars Marburg.

Raftery, B. 1994. *Pagan Celtic Ireland.* London: Thames and Hudson.

Randsborg, K. and Nybo, C. 1984. 'The coffin and the sun: demography and ideology in Scandinavian prehistory', *Acta Archaeologica* 55: 161–84.

Rappaport, R. 1999. *Ritual and Religion in the Making of Humanity.* Cambridge: Cambridge University Press.

Rasmussen, M. 1993. 'Gravhøj og boplatser. En foreløbig undersøgelse af lokalisering og sammenhænge', in L. Larsson (ed.), *Bronsålderns gravhögar*, pp. 171–85. Lund: Lund University Institute of Archaeology.

Reid, A. and MacLean, R. 1995. 'Symbolism and the social context of iron production in Karagwe', *World Archaeology* 27: 144–61.

Renfrew, C. 1994a. 'Towards a cognitive archaeology', in C. Renfrew and E. Zubrow (eds), *The Ancient Mind*, pp. 1–12. Cambridge: Cambridge University Press.

Renfrew, C. 1994b. 'Childe and the study of culture process', in D. Harris (ed.), *The Archaeology of V. Gordon Childe*, pp. 121–33. London: UCL Press.

Renfrew, C. 1995. *The Archaeology of Cult. The Sanctuary at Phylakopi.* Athens: British School at Athens.

Renfrew, C. 2001. 'Symbol before concept: material engagement and the early development of society', in I. Hodder (ed.), *Archaeological Theory Today*, pp. 122–40. Cambridge: Polity Press.

Reynolds, N. 1978. 'Dark Age timber halls and the background to excavation at Balbridie', *Scottish Archaeological Forum* 10: 41–60.

Reynolds, P. 1981. 'Deadstock and livestock', in R. Mercer (ed.), *Farming Practice in British Prehistory*, pp. 97–122. Edinburgh: Edinburgh University Press.

Richards, C. 2004. *Dwelling among the Monuments.* Cambridge: McDonald Institute for Archaeological Research.

Richards, C. and Thomas, J. 1984. 'Ritual activity and structured deposition in later Neolithic Wessex', in R. Bradley and J. Gardiner (eds), *Neolithic Studies*, pp. 189–218. Oxford: British Archaeological Reports.

Ricq-de Bouard, M. 1996. *Pétrographie et sociétés néolithiques en France méditerranéenne.* Paris: CNRS.

Rittershofer, K.-F. 1987. 'Grabraub in der Bronzezeit', *Bericht der Römisch-Germanischen Kommission* 68: 5–23.

Rittershofer, K.-F. (ed.) 1997. *Sonderbestattungen in der Bronzezeit im östlichen Mitteleuropa.* Espelkamp: Verlag Marie Leidorf.

Roberts, B. and Ottaway, B. 2003. 'The use and significance of socketed axes during the late Bronze Age', *European Journal of Archaeology* 6, 119–40.

Rogius, K., Eriksson, N. and Wennberg, T. 2001. 'Buried refuse? Interpreting Early Neolithic pits', *Lund Archaeological Review* 7, 7–17.

Rowley-Conwy, P. 1987. 'The interpretation of ard marks', *Antiquity* 61: 263–6.

Rowley-Conwy, P. 2003. 'No fixed abode? Nomadism in the northwest European Neolithic', in G. Burenhult (ed.), *Stones and Bones*, pp. 115–43. Oxford: British Archaeological Reports.

Roymans, N. and Kortelag, F. 1999. 'Urnfield symbolism, ancestors and the land in the Lower Rhine region', in F. Theuws and N. Roymans (eds), *Land and Ancestors*, pp. 33–61. Amsterdam: Amsterdam University Press.

Ruiz-Gálvez, M. 1995. *Ritos de paso y puntos de paso: La Ría de Huelva en el mundo del Bronce Final Europeo.* Madrid: Servicio de Publicaciones, Universidad Complutense.

Ruiz-Gálvez, M. 2000. 'Weight systems and exchange networks in Bronze Age Europe', in C. Pare (ed.), *Metals Make the World Go Round. The Supply and Circulation of Metals in Bronze Age Europe*, pp. 267–79. Oxford: Oxbow.

Runcis, J. 1999. 'Den mytiska geografin. Reflektioner kring skärvstenshögar, mytologi och landskaprum i Södermanland under bromsålader', in M. Olausson (ed.), *Spiralens öga. Tjugo artiklar kring aktuell bronsåldersforskning*, pp. 127–55. Stockholm: Riksantikvarieämbetet.

Runcis, J. 2002. *Bärnstenensbarnen. Bilder berättelser och betraktelser*. Stockholm: Riksantikvarieämbetet.

Russell, M. 2001. *Rough Quarries, Rocks and Hills. John Pull and the Neolithic Flint Mines of Sussex*. Oxford: Oxbow.

Rychner, V. 1979. *L'âge du Bronze final à Auvernier (lac de Neuchâtel, Suisse): typologie et chronologie des anciennes collections conservées en Suisse*. Lausanne: Bibliothèque vauloise.

Rychner, V. 1987. *Auvernier 1968–75. Le mobilier métallique due Bronze final: formes et techniques*. Lausanne: Bibliothèque vaudoise.

Samson, R. (ed.) 1990. *The Social Archaeology of Houses*. Edinburgh: Edinburgh University Press.

Sanches, M.J. 2001. 'O Crasto de Palheiros (Murça). Do Calcolítico à Idade do Ferro', *Portugalia* 22/22: 5–40.

Saville, A. 2002. 'Lithic artefacts from Neolithic causewayed enclosures: character and meaning', in G. Varndell and P. Topping (eds), *Enclosures in Neolithic Europe*, pp. 91–105. Oxford: Oxbow.

Scarre, C. 2003. 'Diverse inspirations: landscapes, longhouses and Neolithic monument forms of Northern France', in G. Burenhult (ed.), *Stones and Bones*, 39–52. Oxford: British Archaeological Reports.

Schauer, P. 1971. *Die Schwerter in Süddeutschland, Österreich und der Schweiz 1*. München: C.H. Beck.

Schiek, S. 1959. 'Vorbericht über die Ausgrabung des vierten Fürstgrabhügels bei der Heuneburg', *Germania* 37: 117–31.

Schiffer, M. 1976. *Behavioural Archaeology*. New York: Academic Press.

Schiffer, M. 1996. *Formation Processes of the Archaeological Record*. Second edition. Salt Lake City: University of Utah Press.

Schindler, R. 1977. *Die Altburg von Bundenbach: eine befestigte Höhensiedlung des 2./1. Jahrhunderts v. Chr. im Hunsrück*. Mainz: Von Zabern.

Schlicht-Herle, H. 1997. *Pfahlbauten rund um die Alpen*. Stuttgart: Theiss.

Schwab, H. 1989. *Archéologie de la deuxième correction des eaux du Jura, vol. 1. Les Celtes sur la Broye et la Thielle*. Fribourg: Éditions Universitaires.

Schwartz, K. 1962. 'Zum Stand der Ausgrabungen in der spätkeltischen Viereckschanze von Holzhausen', *Jahresbericht der Bayerischen Bodendenkmalpflege* (1962): 22–75.

Schwartz, K. 1975. 'Die Geschichte eines keltischen Temenos im nördlichen Alpenvorland', *Ausgrabungen in Deutschland* 1: 324–58.

Scott, L. and Calder, C. 1952. 'Notes on a chambered cairn and a working gallery on the Beorgs of Ulyea, Northmaven, Shetland'. *Proceedings of the Society of Antiquaries of Scotland* 86: 171–7.

Sherratt, A. 1997. *Economy and Society in Prehistoric Europe*. Edinburgh: Edinburgh University Press.

Sidéra, I. 2000. 'Animaux domestiques, bêtes sauvages et objets en matières animales du Rubané au Michelsberg', *Gallia Préhistoire* 42: 107–94.

Sievers, S. 1991. 'Armes et sanctuaires à Manching', in J.L. Brunaux (ed.), *Les sanctuaires celtiques et leur rapport avec le monde Méditerranéen*, pp. 146–55. Paris: Éditions Errance.

Sillar, B. 1996. 'The dead and the drying: techniques for transforming people and things in the Andes', *Journal of Material Culture* 1: 259–89.

Simone, L. 1992. 'La palafitte des Lagazzi (Piadema, Cremona, Italie)', in C. Mordant and A. Richard (eds), *Habitat et l'occupation du sol à l'âge du bronze en Europe*, pp. 419–26. Paris: Éditions du Comité des Travaux historiques et scientifiques.

Skaarup, J. 1975. *Stengade: ein langeländischer Wohnplatz mit Hausresten aus der frühneolithischen Zeit.* Rudkøbing: Langelands Museum.

Skoglund, P. 1999. 'Diet, cooking and cosmology. Interpreting the evidence from Bronze Age macrofossils', *Current Swedish Archaeology* 7: 149–60.

Smith, A. 2001. *The Differential Use of Constructed Sacred Space in Southern Britain from the Late Iron Age to the 4th Century AD.* Oxford: British Archaeological Reports.

Söder, W. and Zemmer-Plank, L. 2002. *Kult der Vorzeit in den Alpen.* Bozen: Verlagsanstalt Athesia.

Sommerfeld, C. 1994. *Gerätegeld Sichel. Studien zur monetären Struktur bronzezeitlicher Horte im nördlichen Mitteleuropa.* Berlin: Walter de Gruyter.

Stålbom, U. 1997. 'Waste or what? Rubbish pits or ceremonial deposits at the Pryssgården site in the Late Bronze Age', *Lund Archaeological Review* (1997): 21–36.

Stead, I. 1991. *Iron Age Cemeteries in East Yorkshire.* London: English Heritage.

Stepanovic, M. 1997. 'The age of clay. The social dynamics of house destruction', *Journal of Anthropological Archaeology* 16: 334–95.

Stjernqvist, B. 1997. *The Rökillorna Spring: Spring-cults in Scandinavian Prehistory.* Stockholm: Almqvist & Wiksell.

Svensson, M. 2002. 'Palisade enclosures – the second generation of enclosed sites in the Neolithic of Northern Europe', in A. Gibson (ed.), *Within Wooden Walls: Neolithic Palisaded Enclosures in Europe*, pp. 28–58. Oxford: British Archaeological Reports.

Svensson, M. 2004. 'The second Neolithic concept', in M. Andersson, P. Karsten, B. Knarrström and M. Svensson (eds), *Stone Age Scania*, pp. 192–248. Lund: Riksantikvarieämbetet.

Tarlow, S. 1994. 'Scraping the bottom of the barrow: the agricultural metaphor in Neolithic / Bronze Age burial practice', *Journal of Theoretical Archaeology* 3/4, 123–44.

Taylor, J. 1970. 'Lunulae reconsidered', *Proceedings of the Prehistoric Society* 36: 38–81.

Taylor, R. 1994. *Hoards of the Bronze Age in Southern Britain.* Oxford: British Archaeological Reports.

Tegtmeier, U. 1993. *Neolithische und bronzezeitliche Pflugspuren in Norddeutschland und den Niederlanden.* Bonn: Holos.

Tesch, S. 1993. *Houses, Farmsteads and Long-term Change. A regional Study of Prehistoric Settlements in the Köpinge Area in Scania, Southern Sweden.* Uppsala: Uppsala University Department of Archaeology and Ancient History.

Therkorn, L. 1987a. 'The inter-relationships of materials and meanings: some suggestions on housing concerns in Iron Age Noord-Holland', in I. Hodder (ed.), *The Archaeology of Contextual Meanings*, pp. 102–10. Cambridge: Cambridge University Press.

Therkorn, L. 1987b. 'The structures, mechanics and some aspects of inhabited behaviour', in R. Brandt, W. Groenman-van-Waateringe and S. Van der Leeuw (eds), *Assendelver Polders Papers 1*, pp. 177–224. Amsterdam: Cingula 12.

Therkorn, L. and Abbink, A. 1987. 'Some levée sites', in R. Brandt, W. Groenman-van-Waateringe and S. van der Leeuw (eds) *Assendelver Polders Papers 1*, pp. 115–67. Amsterdam: Cingula 12.

Theunisson, L. 1999. *Midden-bronstijdsamlevingen in het zuiden van de Lage Landen*. Leiden: Leiden University Faculty of Archaeology.

Thomas, J. 1988. 'Neolithic explanations revisited: the Mesolithic-Neolithic transition in Britain and south Scandinavia', *Proceedings of the Prehistoric Society* 54: 59–66.

Thrane, H. 1974. 'Hundredvis af energikilder fra yngre broncealder', *Fynske Minder* (1974), 96–114.

Thrane, H. 1989. 'Danish plough-marks from the Neolithic and Bronze Age', *Journal of Danish Archaeology* 8: 111–25.

Thrane, H. 1996. 'Von Kultischem in der Bronzezeit Dänemarks. Votivfunde und Kultplätze?', in P. Schauer (ed.), *Archäologische Forschungen zum Kultgeschehen in der jüngeren Bronzezeit und frühen Eisenzeit Alteuropas*, pp. 235–54. Bonn: Rudolf Habelt.

Tilley, C. (ed.) 1990. *Reading Material Culture: Structuralism, Hermeneutics and Post-structuralism*. London: Routledge.

Tilley, C. 1991. *Material Culture and Text: The Art of Ambiguity*. London: Routledge.

Tilley, C. 1996. *An Ethnography of the Neolithic. Early Prehistoric Societies in Southern Scandinavia*. Cambridge: Cambridge University Press.

Tilley, C. 1999. *Metaphor and Material Culture*. Oxford: Blackwell.

Tinevez, J.-Y. 2002. 'The Late Neolithic settlement of La Hersonnais, Pléchatel in its regional context', in G. Varndell and P. Topping (eds), *Enclosures in Neolithic Europe*, pp. 37–50. Oxford: Oxbow.

Todd, M. 1987. *The Northern Barbarians 100 BC–AD 300*. Oxford: Blackwell.

Torbrügge, W. 1971. 'Vor- und frühgeschichtliche Flussfunde', *Bericht der Römisch-Germanischen Kommission* 51/52: 1–146.

Turner, R. and Scaife, R. (eds) 1995. *Bog Bodies: New Discoveries and New Perspectives*. London: British Museum Press.

Turner, V. 1969. *The Ritual Process*. Chicago: Aldine.

Ullén, I. 1994. 'The power of case studies. Interpretation of a Late Bronze Age settlement in Central Sweden', *Journal of European Archaeology* 2.2: 249–62.

Ullén, I. 1996. 'Food ethics, domestication and togetherness. A close-up study of the relation of horse and dog to man in the Bronze Age settlement of Apalle', *Current Swedish Archaeology* 4: 171–84.

Van der Sanden, W. 1996. *Through Nature to Eternity. The Bog Bodies of Northwest Europe*. Amsterdam: Batavian Lion International.

van Meijl, T. 1993. 'Maori meeting-houses in and over time', in J. Fox (ed.), *Inside Austronesian Houses*, pp. 194–218. Canberra: Australian National University.

Varela, A.C. 2000. 'O fénomeno campiniforme mo Interior do Portugal: o contexto de Fraga da Pena', in V.O. Jorge (ed.), *3 o Congresso de Arqueologia Peninsular*, vol. 4, pp. 269–90. Porto: Associação para o Desenvolvimento de Cooperação em Arqueologia Peninsular.

Veit, U. 1996. *Studien zum Problem der Siedlungsbestattung im europäischen Neolithikum*, Mainz: Waxman.

Venclová, N. 1993. 'Celtic shrines in Central Europe: a sceptical approach', *Oxford Journal of Archaeology* 12: 55–66.

Venclová, N. 1997. 'On enclosures, pots and trees in the forest', *Journal of European Archaeology* 5.1: 131–50.

Venclová, N. 1998. *Mšecké Žehrovice in Bohemia. Archaeological Background to a Celtic Hero*. Sceaux: Kronos B.Y. Editions.

Venclová, N. 2002. 'The Venerable Bede, druidic tonsure and archaeology', *Antiquity* 76: 458–71.

Victor, H. 2002. *Med graven som granne. Om bronsålderns kulthus*. Uppsala: Uppsala University Department of Archaeology and Ancient History.

Villes, A. 1988. 'Une hypothèse: les sépultures de relégation dans les fosses d'habitat protohistoriques en France septentrionale', in H. Duday and C. Masset (eds), *Anthropologie physique et Archéologie*: 167–74. Paris: CNRS.

Vouga, P. 1923. *La Tène: Monographie de la station*. Leipzig: Hiersman.

Wainwright, G. 1975. 'Religion and settlement in Wessex, 3000–1700 bc', in P. Fowler (ed.), *Recent Work in Rural Archaeology*, pp. 57–71. Bradford-on-Avon: Moonraker Press.

Wainwright, G. 1979. *Gussage All Saints. An Iron Age Settlement in Dorset*. London: HMSO.

Wainwright, G. 1989. *The Henge Monuments. Ceremony and Society in Prehistoric Britain*. London: Thames and Hudson.

Wainwright, G. and Longworth, I. 1971. *Durrington Walls: Excavations 1966–1968*. London: Society of Antiquaries.

Wait, G. 1985. *Ritual and Religion in Iron Age Britain*. Oxford: British Archaeological Reports.

Waldhauser, J. 1989. 'État de la recherche sur les enceintes quadrilatérales laténiennes (dites Viereckschanzen) en Bohème', in O. Buchsenschutz, L. Olivier and A.-M. Aillières (eds), *Les Viereckschanzen et les enceintes quadrilatérales en Europe celtique*, pp. 43–55. Paris: Éditions Errance.

Waterbolk, H. 1977. 'Walled enclosures of the Iron Age in the north of the Netherlands', *Palaeohistoria* 19: 97–172.

Waterbolk, H. 1995. 'Patterns of the peasant landscape', *Proceedings of the Prehistoric Society* 61: 1–36.

Waterman, D. 1997. *Excavations at Navan Fort 1961–71*. Belfast: The Stationery Office.

Watson, A. 1995. 'Investigating the distribution of Group VI debitage in the central Lake District', *Proceedings of the Prehistoric Society* 61: 461–2.

Weisberger, G., Slotta, R. and Weiner, J. 1981. *5000 Jahre Feuersteinbau*. Bochum: Deutschen Bergbau-Museum.

Werkgroep Prehistorische Vuurstenmijnbouw 1988. *De Prehistorische Vuurstenmijnen*. Maastricht: Nederlands Geologische Veriniging Afd. Limburg.

Whimster, R. 1981. *Burial Practices in Iron Age Britain*. Oxford: British Archaeological Reports.

Wieland, G.1999. *Keltische Viereckschanzen. Einem Rätsel auf der Spur*. Stuttgart: Konrad Theiss.

Williams, J. and Davidson, A. 1998. 'Survey and excavation at the Graiglwyd axe-factory, Penmaenmawr', *Archaeology in Wales* 38: 3–21.

Williams, M. 2003. 'Growing metaphors: the agricultural cycle as metaphor in the later prehistoric period of Britain and North-Western Europe', *Journal of Social Archaeology* 3: 223–55.

Williams, R. and Zeepfat, R. 1994. *Bancroft. A Late Bronze Age / Iron Age Settlement, Roman Villa and Temple-Mausoleum*. Aylesbury: Buckinghamshire Archaeological Society.

Winghart, S. 2000. 'Mining, processing and distribution of bronze: reflections on the organisation of metal supply between the northern Alps and the Danube region', in C. Pare (ed.), *Metals Make the World Go Round. The Supply and Circulation of Metals in Bronze Age Europe*, pp. 151–9. Oxford: Oxbow.

Woolf, G. 1998. *Becoming Roman: the Origins of Provincial Civilization in Gaul*. Cambridge: Cambridge University Press.

Wyss, R. 1971. 'Siedlungen und Verkehrswege', in W. Drack (Red.), *Ur- und Frühgeschichtliche Archäologie der Schweiz, Band 4*, pp. 103–22. Basel: Verlag Schweizerische Gesellschaft für Ur- und Frühgeschichte, Basel.

York, J. 2002. 'The life cycle of Bronze Age metalwork from the Thames', *Oxford Journal of Archaeology* 21: 77–92.

Zürn, H. and Fischer, F. 1991. *Die keltische Viereckschanze von Tomerdingen*. Stuttgart: Konrad Theiss.

INDEX

Åby 134–5
Acy-Romance 65–7, 73, 177–80, 181, 187, 188, 203, 210
Adam of Bremen 41, 43, 46
allées couvertes 69
Alvastra 134, 140–2
animal models 93, 95
Antran 65–7, 194
Ards 4, 82–4, 85–6
Assendelver Polders 53
Auvernier 149, 152
Avebury 105
axes: axe quarries 104–5; burnt axes 137–8; jadeite axes 102

Backa 86
Bacon, F. 9
Balbridie 65–7
Bancroft 55
Barbey 176
Barkaer 62
Barnhouse 53
Battle Axe Culture 131, 132, 136, 138, 143, 199
Bell Beakers: in graves 108; in settlements 108
Beorgs of Ulyea 104–5
Bigholm 64
bog deposits: agricultural tools 82, 84–6; animals 82, 85, 135–6; ards 82–4, 85–6; human bodies 81–2, 84, 136–7, 172; metalwork 85, 110–11, 136; vehicles 82
Bohuslän 86
Brück, J. 30, 104–5

Bua 134
Bucrania 94–5
burning: of agricultural land 142–4; of artefacts 129–30, 137–8, 141; of houses 52, 57, 60, 129; of monuments 69, 76–7, 138–9
burnt mounds 106–7
Bwaymas 90–2

Callestick 52
Castelo Velho 113–14, 199
Celtic Fields 4–5, 24, 169–70
Chapman, J. 162–3
Chasséen 102
Childe, G. 193
Cissbury 103
Clark, G. 87
Clarke, D. 9, 30–1
clearance cairns 107
closing deposits 52–4
cognitive archaeology 193–4
Coligny Calendar 169
contextual archaeology 84
Cornaux 172
craft production 21–3, 37–8, 102–5, 106, 145–64, 180, 194–200
Crasto de Palheiros 112–13
cult houses 70–1

Dagstorp 125, 133
Danebury 52, 165–7, 188, 189, 203, 210
De Boer, W. 65
deposits: in bogs 81–4, 85–6, 110, 135–8, 140–4, 172, 199; in

monuments 20–1, 108–20, 138–40, 142–4; in settlements 51–5, 109, 110, 131–5, 142–4, 168–73; in water 110, 126, 129–30, 135–8, 142–4, 168, 172, 199
Diverhøj 27
Djupvik 134
Doon Hill 67
domestication 196–200
Dornstadt-Tomerdingen 19
Draget 118–19
Druids 196
Durrington Walls 10–16, 29, 73–4, 194, 207

East Chisenbury 206
El Pedroso 111–4, 119
enclosures: earthwork 114–17; palisaded 139; stone 111–14, 117–19
Ertebølle Culture 94, 123, 142, 143, 198–9
Escoural 94
Etton 105

feasting 12, 19, 106, 206–7
feasting halls 43–4, 65
fertility 6, 8, 16, 168–9, 174–7, 205–7
Flag Fen 149, 172
flint mines 103–4
Fochterloo 79
foundation deposits 51–2, 53–4
Fraga da Pena 112–13, 119
fragmentation of artefacts 151–64
Fräkenrönningen 134
Frankfurt-Lossow 109

Gamla Uppsala 41–3, 46, 65, 78, 194
gardening: aesthetics of gardening in the Trobriand Islands 89; magic associated with gardening in the Trobriand Islands 88–92
Gardoms Edge 53
Glastonbury 52
Glob, P.V. 81–7, 108
Goodland 104
Gournay-sur-Aronde 181, 182

Graig Llwyd 104
granaries 3–9, 16, 50, 90–92, 171, 177, 209–10; ceramic models of granaries 99–100, 209–10; relationship of granaries to shrines 6, 9, 88–90, 203, 209–10
Grand Pressigny 102, 195
grave orientations 26, 59–61, 168–70
Grimes Graves 103
Grooved Ware 12

Hågahögen 71
Häggsta 134
Hallunda 107, 207
Handewitt 25, 60
Harrislee 26
Hayling Island 182–4, 185, 187, 188, 201–2
Hedningahällan 134
henge monuments 10–12, 73–5
Herblay 63
Heuneburg 57–8
hillforts 14–15, 19, 35, 78, 106, 165–8, 169, 188–90, 203, 210
Hindby Mosse 139, 143
Hjørdlunde 83
hoards 143–64, 135–6; classification of hoards 155–60
Hodder, I. 108–9, 209
Holzhausen 17–18, 20, 21
Homer 24, 46–8
houses: houses and conceptions of time 54–7; houses and temples 41–6; houses as prototypes for earthwork monuments 73–80; houses as prototypes for megalithic tombs 62–4, 69–70; houses as prototypes for public buildings 63–70, 73–7; houses beneath barrows 57–62; house deposits 51–4; houses in archaeology 47; houses in social anthropology 47–8; house models 50–1, 99–100; relationship of houses to shrines 182–8; replacement of houses 57–62
hunting 102
Hyllerup 59–60
Hyllie 139

Incas 7–8

Jablines 103–4

Karlsfat 132
Kerlescan 68
Kivik 70
Kverrestad 137

La Haut-Mée 63
Lambay Island 104
La Tène 172
Lausitz Culture 109–10
Leach, E. 88, 193
Lejre 44
Le Petit Vilatte 55–6, 161
Le Pinnacle 104
Les Orchettes 63
Linearbandkeramik Culture 62, 102
Lisleby 87
long-beds 72–3

Machrie Moor 74
Malinowski, B. 37, 88–92, 100
Malmer, M. 132–4, 140–2
Manching 17, 20
material metaphors 194
materialisation 194–200
Maori meeting houses 48–50, 55
Mazarakis-Ainian, A. 44–7
megaliths, decorated 94–5
menhirs, decorated 94–5
metalwork 21–3, 143–64; deposition of
    metalwork 110–11, 143–64;
    fragmentation of metalwork 151–64;
    production of metalwork 21–3,
    37–8, 194–200; use of metalwork as
    raw material 155–60; use wear
    analysis and bronze metalwork
    148–50
Michelsberg Culture 102
Mont Bégo 86, 87, 94, 95–8
Montmartin 177, 180–2, 187, 188,
    201–2, 203
Mšecké Žehrovice 17, 21–3, 28, 29, 35,
    196, 203

Navan Fort 75–7, 78, 194

Nebelsick, L. 161–2
Nerthus 82, 84, 86

Obermachtal 17
Odensala Prästgård 117–19

Pléchâtel-La-Hersonnais 67–70
Pitted Ware 124, 131, 132–3, 134–5,
    138, 141, 142–4, 198–9, 206
Pliny 101
ploughing: depicted in rock art 86–7,
    95–7; in relation to barrows 23–4,
    26, 27–8, 35; in relation to graves
    26; in relation to houses 25
polissoirs 105
Poses 63
Potterne 206
Pryssgården 53–5

qollqas 7–8
querns: decorated 101; in cemeteries
    107; in cult houses 71

Rappendam 82
regeneration 6, 8, 16, 68–9, 174–7,
    205–7
Renfrew, C. 193, 195, 197
Rhee 76
Ría de Huelva 157–60, 161, 162
Rinkeby 106
Rispebjerg 139–40
ritual: definitions 28–30, 39; definitions
    applied to metal hoards 148–51;
    ritual in archaeology 28–9, 39; ritual
    in social anthropology 3–33; ritual
    landscapes 201–2
ritualisation 33–5, 36–9, 119–20,
    163–4, 207–9
River Thames 149–50
rock art 86–7, 93–8, 101, 111, 113
royal sites, in Ireland 75–6
Ryckholt-St-Gertruid 104

Sandergergård 70
sapropelite 21–2
Sarup 114–16
sedentism 196–200
shafts 18, 19, 20, 109

ship burials 44
shrines 15, 18, 19–20, 38, 165–8,
    177–90, 203
sickles 101, 102, 110, 145, 149, 151–3,
    172–4, 191–2
Siretorp 134
Skogsmossen 124–31, 135, 136, 144,
    198, 201, 202
Skumperberget 124–31, 135, 144, 198
Someren-Waterdael 73
Soucy 176
South Cadbury 188–90, 203, 210
South Lodge Camp 191–2
spears 159–60, 162
Springfield Lyons 150
Stengade 62, 70
Stonehenge 12, 74
storage pits 13–14; burials in storage
    pits 7–8, 13–15, 109, 170–2,
    175–7, 180
Svartskille 137
swords 145, 149, 153–5, 162
Szentgáloskér 154

Tacitus 83, 84, 86, 87
taphonomy 207–9
Tara 76, 78
temples: Early Medieval 41–4; Greek
    44–7; Roman 167, 188
Tengeby 86
textual models 194
therianthropes 93
Thermon 45
Thetford 184–8, 203

Ticooly-O'Kelly 101
Tiryns 45
Tofta 133
Trappendal 60–1
TRB Culture 124, 131, 132–3, 138,
    141, 142–4, 198
Trelystan 74
Trobriand Islands 88–92, 100, 209–10

Uiorara de Sus 152, 153

Valcamonica 86, 94, 95–8, 99, 100,
    210
Varennes-sur-Seine 176
Vedic hymns 24
Vebbstrup 83
Venat 156–7, 161
Venclová, N. 20, 21, 28–9, 167–8,
    203
Verberie 65–7
Viereckschanzen 16–23, 25, 35, 78,
    146, 167–8, 179, 203

Warburg 94
Wasserburg 152
Williams, M. 168–70
Woodcutts 74
world views: of farmers 142–4,
    199–200, 204; of hunter gatherers
    142–4, 197–9
Woodhenge 10, 12

Zeijen 78, 79
Zurich Opera House 152